An invaluable guide for both beginners and seasoned practitioners, offering practical insights and comprehensive coverage of business architecture to drive strategic and transformative change.

Heather Hales, *Partner, Transformation Consulting, EY*

The book I've been waiting for on business architecture! Full of practical insights from trusted experts in the field – advising on frameworks, setting up a service approach and providing key perspectives. This will quickly become a valuable resource on my bookshelf.

Claire Caulfield, *Lead Business Analyst, British Library*

Business Architecture documents a wide range of tools and techniques that can be brought to bear in the field. The book is an invaluable resource and is especially useful for business analysts looking to make the step into the field of business architecture.

Craig Jeffries MBA, *Strategy Business Architect, NHS Supply Chain*

A much-needed exploration of the business architect role with a comprehensive guide to everything you will require to perform this function. The authors provide a thought-provoking and compelling argument for the need for business architecture to be a pre-eminent driver of organisational change, ensuring business' capabilities match its strategies, values and the needs of its customers. I highly recommend it to anyone interested in delivering holistic change.

David Beckham, *Principal Consultant, ChuDo Consulting*

A thoughtful and precise guide that gives business architecture clear purpose, rooting it in outcomes and addressing ambiguity with practical frameworks and real-world examples.

David Palzeaird, *Principle Consultant, CBO Projects*

The *Business Architecture* guide is a rich and complete must read for the business architect wanting to provide valuable insights helping businesses and society to face today's complex challenges and threats.

Marwim van Overschot, *Senior Business Analyst, Ilionx and Training Consultant, Le Blanc Academy*

This book is the guide you didn't know you needed – tackling the complexity and importance of business architecture with an abundance of clarity and an engaging style. Whether you're a business architect, or work with one, this book is essential reading; a practical, anchor-point of content that conveys the unique beauty and often untapped value of the profession.

Sam Merrick CBA (Certified Business Architect), *Director, Kanin Consulting*

An insightful guide to mastering business architecture with real examples and pitfalls to avoid. Packed with practical insights on integrating business architecture, analysis and change management. A must-read for transformation leaders.

Sara Mubasshir CEA CBAP, *Head of Change, Experience and Analysis, London Business School*

A comprehensive and practical guide to business architecture, providing actionable techniques for achieving strategic outcome-focused change. An invaluable resource for anyone driving transformative change in their organisation.

Shane Robertson, *Director Digital and Transformation, Stolt Tank Containers*

Business Architecture is a brilliantly insightful guide and resource that combines deep experience with well-researched practical application and approaches. It's an absolute must read for anyone developing a new business architecture.

Paul Taylor, *Business Transformation Consulting Lead, Sopra Steria Next*

In addition to providing clear and comprehensive coverage of business architecture, this book has also succeeded in positioning it in the context of such disciplines as business analysis and service design. This is not surprising, given the breadth and depth of experience of the authors.

Paul Turner FBCS, *Co-author of 'Business Analysis Techniques'*

Combining detailed guidance on the essentials of business architecture, critical thinking on the value business architecture offers and integration alongside service design and business analysis, *Business Architecture* represents an essential addition for practitioners and business leaders alike.

Bruce Prendergast, *CDIO Operational Strategy Lead, HMRC*

This is a book you can pick up and start using straight away, I did. It's suitable for seasoned and aspiring business architects and business analysts wanting a better understanding of business architecture.

Catherine Plumridge, *Lead Business Analyst, Kensington Mortgages*

An essential and comprehensive guide that should interest all change professionals. This book offers clear, actionable insights into business architecture as it bridges theory and practice. Combining real-world examples, practical frameworks and strategic perspectives, it equips both newcomers and experienced professionals with the tools needed to support and drive meaningful, outcome-focused transformation. A must-have resource for anyone seeking to align capabilities, strategies and customer needs to deliver lasting impact.

Ian Glenister, *Director, PCMI Limited*

This book is an invaluable resource to anyone with an interest in business architecture – a clear, well explained introduction to those new to the profession, a handy aide-mémoire to those already working in the area, and interesting and relevant to complimentary professions. Addressing both theory and practice, the explanations and examples make this book an easy read and make business architecture come to life.

Pip Hall, *Business Analyst, Telent*

BUSINESS ARCHITECTURE

BCS, THE CHARTERED INSTITUTE FOR IT

BCS, The Chartered Institute for IT, is committed to making IT good for society. We use the power of our network to bring about positive, tangible change. We champion the global IT profession and the interests of individuals, engaged in that profession, for the benefit of all.

Exchanging IT expertise and knowledge
The Institute fosters links between experts from industry, academia and business to promote new thinking, education and knowledge sharing.

Supporting practitioners
Through continuing professional development and a series of respected IT qualifications, the Institute seeks to promote professional practice tuned to the demands of business. It provides practical support and information services to its members and volunteer communities around the world.

Setting standards and frameworks
The Institute collaborates with government, industry and relevant bodies to establish good working practices, codes of conduct, skills frameworks and common standards. It also offers a range of consultancy services to employers to help them adopt best practice.

Become a member
Over 70,000 people including students, teachers, professionals and practitioners enjoy the benefits of BCS membership. These include access to an international community, invitations to a roster of local and national events, career development tools and a quarterly thought-leadership magazine. Visit www.bcs.org to find out more.

Further information
BCS, The Chartered Institute for IT,
3 Newbridge Square,
Swindon, SN1 1BY, United Kingdom.
T +44 (0) 1793 417 417
(Monday to Friday, 09:00 to 17:00 UK time)
www.bcs.org/contact

shop.bcs.org/
publishing@bcs.uk

bcs.org/qualifications-and-certifications/certifications-for-professionals/

BUSINESS ARCHITECTURE
A comprehensive guide

Jonathan Hunsley, Debra Paul, Victoria Banner,
Michael Greenhalgh and Vicky Rothwell

bcs
The
Chartered
Institute
for IT

The right of Jonathan Hunsley, Debra Paul, Victoria Banner, Michael Greenhalgh and Vicky Rothwell to be identified as authors of this work has been asserted by them in accordance with sections 77 and 78 of the Copyright, Designs and Patents Act 1988.

Published by BCS Learning and Development Ltd, a wholly owned subsidiary of BCS, The Chartered Institute for IT, 3 Newbridge Square, Swindon, SN1 1BY, UK.
www.bcs.org

EU GPSR Authorised Representative: LOGOS EUROPE, 9 rue Nicolas Poussin, 17000, La Rochelle, France. Email: Contact@logoseurope.eu

Paperback ISBN: 978-1-78017-6703
PDF ISBN: 978-1-78017-6710
ePUB ISBN: 978-1-78017-6727

Ebook available

British Cataloguing in Publication Data.
A CIP catalogue record for this book is available at the British Library.

Publisher's acknowledgements
Reviewers: Katie Walsh, Daniel Grist, Catherine Plumridge and Henrietta Blake
Publisher: Ian Borthwick
Commissioning editor: Heather Wood
Production manager: Florence Leroy
Project manager: Sunrise Setting Ltd
Copy-editor: Mary Hobbins
Proofreader: Barbara Eastman
Indexer: David Gaskell
Cover design: Alex Wright
Cover image: shutterstock/Roschetzky Photography
Sales director: Charles Rumball
Typeset by Lapiz Digital Services, Chennai, India

CONTENTS

FIGURES AND TABLES

AUTHORS

Jonathan Hunsley

Jonathan Hunsley is the service development director for Assist Knowledge Development Ltd. Jonathan has worked in a variety of roles across the financial services and consultancy sectors. He specialises in business architecture, business analysis and service design. Jonathan is a Chartered IT Professional, and the lead assessor for the BCS Advanced International Diploma in Business Analysis. He holds an MBA and the Expert Business Analysis Award. He is a regular speaker at international conferences and has contributed to a variety of publications such as *Business Analysis* (Paul and Cadle, 2020) and *Business Analysis Techniques* (Cadle et al., 2021). He is a regular contributor to the BA Brew podcast, co-founded the SD Forum, a networking forum for service designers, and was the chief architect of the A4Q Certified Service Designer award.

Dr Debra Paul

Debra Paul is the CEO of Assist Knowledge Development Ltd. Debra has co-authored several publications, including *Business Analysis* (Paul and Cadle, 2020), *Agile and Business Analysis* (Girvan and Paul, 2024) and *Delivering Business Analysis* (Paul and Lovelock, 2019). She has extensive experience of business analysis and business architecture and is a keen advocate of service science and design thinking. Debra holds an MBA and a doctorate in business administration, and lectures at the University of Reading, where she is a visiting fellow. Debra is a regular speaker at business seminars and IS industry events and has delivered keynote presentations at numerous conferences. She was a founder member of the BA Manager Forum and was the chief architect of the BCS Advanced International Diploma in Business Analysis. She was also one of the founders of the BA Conference Europe.

Victoria Banner

Victoria Banner is a seasoned change professional with over 20 years of experience in business analysis and business architecture. She holds a master's degree in business and strategy, along with several professional certifications, including the Advanced BA Diploma and IIBA® CBAP®. Victoria is an oral examiner, courseware reviewer and contributing expert for BCS. She also serves on the IIBA advisory panel and the IRM BA Conference Europe advisory board. An active member of the business analysis community, Victoria frequently speaks at conferences and industry events. She co-founded the BA4Good movement and resides in Cheshire with her husband and three children.

Michael Greenhalgh

Michael Greenhalgh is the head of business architecture at Places for People and has 25 years' experience working in the global financial services, charity/public body, pharmaceutical, social enterprise and housing sectors. Michael has set up global practices in business architecture, analysis, and improvement, and is an advocate, mentor and contributor to professional communities, conferences and networks across these fields. Michael holds an MBA from the Open University, IIBA CBAP and Lean Six Sigma Black belt.

Vicky Rothwell

Vicky Rothwell is a consulting enterprise architect who has significant experience in the development and implementation of business strategies and subsequent service design and delivery. She has over 25 years' experience in business change and has worked across the public, private and financial sectors. Vicky has previously undertaken the role of oral examiner for BCS qualifications and was among the first to achieve the Expert BA award. She is a strong advocate for business architecture and is keen to promote the profession and the importance of it as an enabler to strategic goal achievement. Vicky has worked to develop business architecture functions in many organisations and has shared her experience by speaking at seminars such as the BA Conference Europe and other industry events. Vicky has appeared on the BA Brew podcast to discuss how the role has developed and has also contributed to other podcast productions to promote women within enterprise architecture.

FOREWORD

Whether or not you are a practising business architect, if you have this book before you then you are in for a treat!

Perhaps you are an early career business architect, hoping for a handbook of sorts – a summary of the fundamentals of the discipline. You need look no further than the excellently researched and presented 'comprehensive guide' that this book most certainly is.

Equally though, any seasoned business architect who wishes to broaden, revisit, explore new angles and understand latest developments is also brilliantly served. In a world where business architecture is evolving apace, with different schools of thought, frameworks and approaches emerging all the time, it can be hard to find that neutral yet wise guide to help you navigate the landscape. This book is just such a guide – one that can equip you with the understanding and confidence to branch out and explore further.

You might be the leader of a business or enterprise architecture team in search of ways to build competency and maturity of the function. This book provides the help you need to establish and grow a team based on an up-to-date and forward-thinking set of approaches. The sections addressing these elements, including history, purpose, skills, maturity evaluation and relationships with adjacent disciplines are disarmingly clear, yet well rounded and complete. They convey the journey that never ends, the evolution that is not a fixed end-state but reflects the very reality of the organisations we work for and that can no longer afford to stand still. So too the reality of business architecture knowledge and skills.

Beyond business architects themselves, those working in a host of other roles at different levels will find this book enlightening on questions such as 'what is business architecture?', 'how can it help me and my organisation?', 'how does business architecture relate to all the other disciplines which seem similar, yet different?'. Buyer beware – you would not be the first to become smitten with business architecture as you come to understand it better!

Business Architecture: A Comprehensive Guide subtly reveals one of the burgeoning truths of our times: that business architecture is on the rise for a very good reason and that organisations are struggling with complexity and ambiguity like never before. A word too here then, on the case studies which bring the experience of practitioners to life with balanced honesty about how there are learnings alongside progress and success. To convey to us all that there is rarely such a thing as the perfect application of theory and models in the real world, is a masterstroke of this book. A great reminder that 'ivory tower' approaches will struggle; value is only realised when an outcome is delivered, not when an architecture diagram has been drawn.

As this book will show though, business architecture is the discipline *par excellence* that can straddle the divides, accelerate decision-making, provide a joined-up view beyond the structures of entities, departments, platform and project teams and all amidst the turbulence of competitive disruption and organisational change. Whether you are a business architect, are working alongside business architects or are a senior leader seeking support to better align the organisation to pursue strategy, objectives and outcomes, there is plenty in this book to enrich your career. Enjoy the journey.

Joanna Goodrick BA Hons, MSc, MBA
Deputy Director of Partnering and Head of Business Architecture at Cambridge University Press & Assessment

Joanna has worked in roles straddling business, strategy and technology for over 20 years, in industries including the United Nations, pharmaceuticals and education. She is a qualified and practising executive coach and mentor. Joanna is a regular speaker and co-chair at Enterprise and Business Architecture conferences.

ACKNOWLEDGEMENTS

This book includes chapter contributions by Victoria Banner, Michael Greenhalgh and Vicky Rothwell. It has been a pleasure to collaborate with them and the book has been enriched due to their wealth of knowledge, experience and ideas.

This book could not have been written without the support of many people. In particular we would like to thank our AssistKD colleagues for the numerous debates and discussions that have helped to clarify our thinking, and their support during the writing and production process.

We would also like to thank the following individuals:

- Ian Borthwick and Heather Wood from the BCS publishing team for their encouragement and support;
- William Ulrich for his business architecture thought leadership and for his assistance in curating the content focused on the BIZBOK®;
- Paul Turner for being instrumental in exploring the field of business architecture and for being an inspiration for us and many other business architects;
- Claire Caulfield, Michael Greenhalgh and Marius Pelser who provided our three case studies;
- Ian Glenister for sharing his wealth of knowledge and experience in the development of the project and change management service frameworks.

Finally, we would like to thank Mary Hunsley and Alan Paul for their continued support and encouragement. Jonathan would also like to add a 'special thanks' to Bertie and Sienna Hunsley for their patience and inspiration.

ABBREVIATIONS

ADM	architecture development method
AI	artificial intelligence
BIZBOK	Business Architecture Guild's Business Architecture Body of Knowledge
BMC	Business Model Canvas
BMM	Business Motivation Model
BPMN	business process model notation
BPR	business process reengineering
BSC	Balanced Scorecard
CALM	capability analysis and leverage model
CATWOE	customer, actor, transformation, worldview (weltanschauung), owner, environment
CCPA	California Consumer Privacy Act
CIPD	Chartered Institute of Personnel and Development
CMMI	Capability Maturity Model Integration
CSF	critical success factor
CX	customer experience
DMAIC	define, measure, analyse, improve, control
DMBOK	DAMA International Data Management Body of Knowledge
EA	enterprise architecture
EPOS	electronic point of sale
GDPR	General Data Protection Regulation
ISO	International Organization for Standardization
IT	information technology
KPI	key performance indicator
OMG	Object Management Group
OSCAR	objectives, scope, constraints, authority, resources
PDSA	plan, do, study, act
PESTLE	political, economic, socio-cultural, technological, legal, environmental
PID	project initiation document
P/IG	power/interest grid

POPIT	people, organisation, process, information and technology
RACI	responsible, accountable, consulted, informed
RAG	red, amber, green
ROI	return on investment
SFIA	Skills Framework for the Information Age
SIPOC	supplier, inputs, process, outputs, customers
SMART	specific, measurable, attainable, relevant and time bound
SUAVE	stable, unique, abstract, valuable, executive
SWOT	strengths, weaknesses, opportunities, threats
TIMWOODS	transportation, inventory, motion, waiting, overproduction, overprocessing, defects, skills
TOGAF	The Open Group Architecture Framework
TOM	Target Operating Model
UML	Unified Modeling Language
UX	user experience
VMOST	vision, mission, objectives, strategy and tactics

PREFACE

The evolution of business architecture as a discipline has been in progress for several years, and during this time many publications have offered business architects relevant and helpful guidance. In writing this book, we wanted to address a gap that we felt existed in the business architecture literature currently available. We believed that a book was needed that offered a pragmatic approach to developing a business architecture and explored how it was applied for business benefit. When considering beneficial business outcomes, we also felt that the service perspective offered an opportunity to enhance business architecture work and relate it to an outcome focus. Our view is that applying this perspective will benefit organisations, business architects, suppliers, customers and other actors within an ecosystem.

The principles, frameworks and techniques used in business architecture have been available for many years, and the power of applying a business architecture viewpoint has evolved during this time. This was brought home to us in the early days of the Covid pandemic as we used our business architecture discipline and perspective to pivot our company. We couldn't have done this in such a timely and effective way without a business architecture perspective. Accordingly, we hold a highly positive view of business architecture techniques and activities and want to support others in conducting this work successfully.

We believe firmly in the service view of organisations and the benefits this can bring, particularly when aligned with other key transformation disciplines such as business architecture and business analysis. The business analysis service framework helped to clarify the value propositions offered by business analysts, so we have applied this approach to explore the role of the business architect. The result is the business architecture service framework, which clarifies the service portfolio offered by business architects and demonstrates the value offered by business architects to their organisations.

The business architecture discipline enables the delivery of change that aligns with and executes organisational strategy in a coherent, directed way. Further, it has the potential to be transformative, improving how organisations innovate and achieve their business aims and objectives. However, this requires business architects to offer a range of services supported by an extensive set of skills. In writing this book, our goal has been to provide comprehensive, practical guidance that helps business architects to develop their skills and understand their role, the services they offer and the benefits they can deliver.

Jonathan Hunsley and Debra Paul
January 2025

1 THE BUSINESS ARCHITECTURE DOMAIN

INTRODUCTION

This chapter introduces the business architecture domain and covers the following topics:

- definition of business architecture;
- origins of business architecture;
- rationale for business architecture;
- principles for using business architecture;
- strategic drivers for using business architecture;
- impediments to the use of business architecture;
- relationship between business architecture and other architecture domains.

DEFINITION OF BUSINESS ARCHITECTURE

Business architecture is focused on building a shared understanding of the organising logic of organisations. The discipline encourages a systemic approach towards making informed and aligned strategic and tactical decisions, through blueprints, which benefit the long-term health of the organisation.

Business architects should be skilled at building and maintaining blueprints (or models) of organisations. Blueprints represent different views of the organisation. They are used to understand and analyse strategic and tactical change and help to provide insight into questions such as:

Why?
- Why is change required?
- Is change aligned to strategy?
- Does the change offer value?

What?	• What is the change?
	• Are the impacts and risks of change understood?
	• Are change dependencies clear?
	• Does the change introduce new or changed concepts (such as capabilities or value streams)?
How?	• How should the change be executed?
	• Have all options and scenarios been considered?
	• Does the change execution strategy improve organisational health over the long term?

Business architects answer the questions '**why?**', '**what?**' and '**how?**' in cascading order of importance. Through analysing these questions, it is possible to discover where there is alignment or misalignment between strategic and tactical decisions. The aim is to inform and enhance the effectiveness and transparency of decisions, but in certain contexts this can lead to business architects being involved in challenging conversations with senior leaders. At no point does business architecture remove decision-making responsibility from the organisation's leadership.

Achieving alignment between the '**why**', '**what**' and '**how**' of strategic and tactical decision-making is the primary concern of business architecture. However, the approach is also concerned with the '**who**', '**where**' and '**when**' of strategic and tactical decision-making.

The Business Architecture Guild has evolved a definition of business architecture since 2008 in their *Business Architecture Body of Knowledge* (BIZBOK Guide). The original definition provided by the Guild in 2008 is:

> A blueprint of the enterprise that provides a common understanding of the organization and is used to align strategic objectives and tactical demands. (Business Architecture Guild, 2024)

Advocates for the original Business Architecture Guild definition argue that it provides insight into both the '**what**' ('blueprints of the enterprise') and '**why**' ('common understanding' and 'used to align strategic objectives and tactical demands') for business architecture. However, it is not focused on '**how**'.

The BIZBOK Guide 2024 also includes the updated 2017 definition:

> Business architecture represents holistic, multidimensional business views of: capabilities, end to-end value delivery, information, and organizational structure; and the relationships among these business views and strategies, products, policies, initiatives, and stakeholders. (Business Architecture Guild, 2024)

Some practitioners prefer the updated definition as it is less abstract than the original, although it has been criticised for its comparative lack of brevity. Its advantage is that it provides detail of the specific views included in a business architecture, referring to the '**what**' ('multidimensional business views') and the '**how**'.

Within TOGAF 9.1, The Open Group used the definition:

A description of the structure and interaction between the business strategy, organization, functions, business processes, and information needs. (The Open Group, 2011)

From TOGAF 9.2 onwards (The Open Group, 2018), The Open Group have aligned their definition to the updated definition of the Business Architecture Guild.

These perspectives on the definitions may seem insignificant at first sight. However, the business architecture discipline needs clarity of communication as it is focused on building shared understanding. When this factor is explored within the emerging nature of the business architecture profession, the subtle move towards '**how**' and arguably away from '**why**' and '**what**' is of potential significance. The potential value, scope and impact of the business architecture profession may be diminished if practitioners focus on '**how**' as opposed to '**why**' and '**what**'.

ORIGINS OF BUSINESS ARCHITECTURE

All organisations throughout history, no matter how large or small, have – or have had – a business architecture.

Some organisations are sufficiently large and complex to employ a formal business architecture approach. Other, typically smaller or less complex, organisations do not employ a formal business architecture approach. In contrast, they rely solely on senior leadership to make informed and aligned strategic and tactical decisions regarding change investments and the evolution of the organisation's capabilities. Within these organisations, it can be argued that the senior leadership are the de facto 'business architects'.

A recognition of the need for business architecture often emerges where organisations are of sufficient scale and complexity to be at risk if they rely solely on the knowledge and skill of senior leadership to make informed and aligned decisions.

There are multiple viewpoints on the key influencing factors and historical events that have led to the emergence of the business architecture discipline. Several factors are discussed in Table 1.1.

The emergence of the information technology (IT) and enterprise architecture (EA) domains has had a significant impact on the evolution of business architecture. The Second World War spurred the advancement of technology, with computers being devised to crack codes such as the Enigma machine. Technology developments were refined and built upon to achieve the position where accounting systems were in use by the late 1960s and personal computers were available by the late 1970s. Gordon Moore (1965) predicted that computer processing speed would double every year. This was proven to be accurate until 1975 when, to account for improvements to transistors and other components, the prediction was revised to state a doubling of speed approximately every 18 months.

Table 1.1 Influencing factors for the emergence of business architecture

Key influencing factor	Description	Perspective on the emergence of business architecture
Emergence of IT architecture domains	Includes the development of architecture domains such as software, application(s), data and infrastructure architecture in the 1980s and 1990s	Business architecture is seen as a logical extension of IT architecture domains. Business architecture provides a means to organise the logic of the business relative to IT architecture(s).
Emergence of the EA domain	Encompasses the business, application(s), data and infrastructure architecture domains EA is heavily influenced by the publications of: • The Zachman Framework • The Open Group Architecture Framework (TOGAF) Both of these publications led to increasing recognition of the need to take a holistic view of the enterprise and its architecture	Business architecture is a core component of the broader EA domain. Without business architecture the EA domain is incomplete.
Emergence of business process reengineering (BPR)	Focused on optimising an organisation's processes in a structured and systematic way BPR gained momentum in the 1990s following the publication of the book *Reengineering the Corporation* (Hammer and Champy, 1993)	Business architecture is seen as a natural extension of the BPR approach as it adds other views (for example, capability, value, motivation, information) to the original process-based work.

Advancement at this pace increasingly meant organisations adopted technology to support the delivery of their business services – automating activities to improve efficiencies and reduce overheads. Companies also began to merge and acquire one another to expand their capabilities, with the most significant of these (certainly in terms of EA) being the merger of three companies: Atlantic Refining, Richfield and Sinclair Oil. Known as the ARCO merger, this was considered the biggest merger of its time and, given the significant architectural challenges the merger presented, P. Duane 'Dewey' Walker from IBM was asked to provide guidance on integrating the companies.

Walker observed the increasing use of technology to improve productivity by performing or supporting the organisations' processes, and he established a tool called Business Systems Planning, which was used for enterprise planning (Hermans, 2015). While at ARCO, Walker formed a working relationship with another ARCO worker: John Zachman. Zachman progressed Walker's work, understanding that, to have structural control over an enterprise, the processes and data should be viewed independently and this is key to enterprise system definition. These independent views provide visibility of the structure of the enterprise, which can then be managed and revised effectively. This considers the enterprise itself as a system with many interconnections (Zachman, 1987). The working partnership between Walker and Zachman created the foundation for the first iteration of the Zachman Framework (see Chapter 3).

Given that the EA profession emerged along with the development and advancement of technology, it is sometimes thought that business architecture has also existed since the early 1990s. However, this view is not universally agreed upon, with many arguing that the role has developed since the early 2000s, more than a decade later.

Some theorists argue that the emergence of the business architecture role has also been influenced by the development of scientific management, championed by F.W. Taylor in 1911. In the early 1900s Henry Ford famously applied this approach to increase the efficiency of production lines within the Ford Motor Company. Other theorists argue that business architecture has been influenced by 'Lean' and the work of the Toyota Motor Company. Lean is an approach focused on systematic enhancement of the work within an organisation. It makes extensive use of principles such as continuous improvement, waste reduction, enhancing value for the customer and enhancing flow and quality.

It can also be argued that the business architecture discipline and role has been heavily influenced by the maturing of the business analysis profession throughout the late 20th and early 21st centuries. Senior business analysts see business architecture as a discipline that provides the opportunity to apply their skills to work holistically, on problems and opportunities relative to the entire organisation. Consequently, business architecture enables business analysts to both progress their careers and be released from the constraint of working within the context of individual change initiatives.

RATIONALE FOR BUSINESS ARCHITECTURE

Through promoting shared understanding of the organisation, business architecture seeks to enable informed strategic and tactical decision-making. Where applied effectively, business architecture is an enabler of strategy. For example, business architecture can provide insight into the complexities, dependencies, risks and impacts of a proposed change prior to it taking place. Through enabling the exploration of different scenarios in advance of decisions, it is possible for an organisation to select a course of action that will enable the achievement of chosen goals or outcomes.

Strategy can be defined as: 'An organisation's long-term plan for success' (Paul and Cadle, 2020). When seeking to execute either an individual change or strategy, the following questions should be considered:

- What is the 'current state'?

- What is the desired 'target state'?
- What is the plan to move between the 'current' and 'target' states?

Each of these questions can be seen as a core building block for understanding the strategic context. Each is shown in Figure 1.1.

Figure 1.1 Core building blocks for understanding the strategic context

Rationale for using business architecture within the context of a single change

One way to understand the rationale for business architecture is to consider the core questions relative to a change to the physical architecture of a building.

Imagine that a homeowner has a strategy to improve his home for the longer term and so is seeking to install a door within a solid wall. This proposed change is shown in Figure 1.2.

Figure 1.2 Example proposed change to a wall

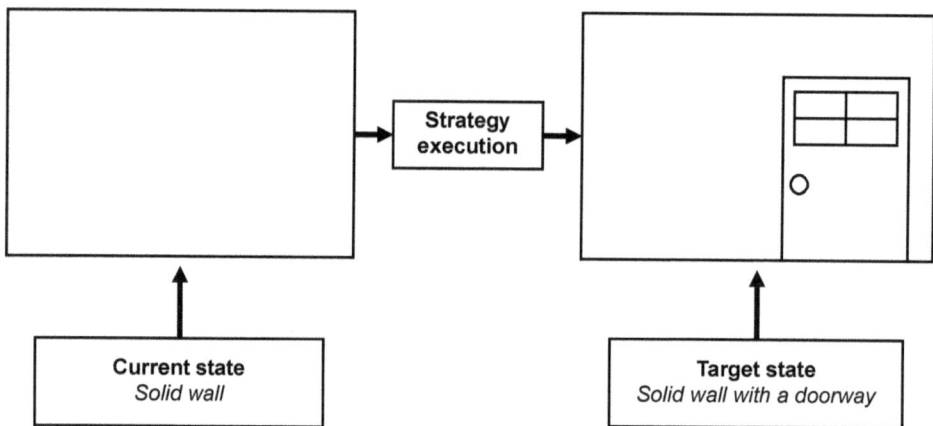

If the change shown in Figure 1.2 is executed without reference to accurate blueprints, the strategy execution is put at risk. For example, the wall may contain gas or water pipes and/or electric cables and could even be critical to the structural integrity of the building.

Cutting through the wall without knowing this information is likely to be dangerous as it could cause the building to collapse or, at the very least, it could cause unnecessary and avoidable delays and expense.

When consulting the blueprints, it is found that the wall is not critical to the building structure. However, it does contain an electric cable and a water pipe. With this information, it is possible to determine with a greater degree of certainty the risk and impact of cutting through the wall to install the doorway. A plan to re-route the electric cable and water pipe can be put in place. In this instance, the blueprints of the wall are enabling a shared understanding and informed decision-making. This reduces the risk of unexpected consequences from making the change and also enables insight into the risks and impacts of the change. Change execution can proceed with a greater degree of certainty than would otherwise be possible. Example blueprints that show the additional information regarding the cabling within the wall are shown in Figure 1.3.

Figure 1.3 Example proposed change to a wall – with reference to blueprints

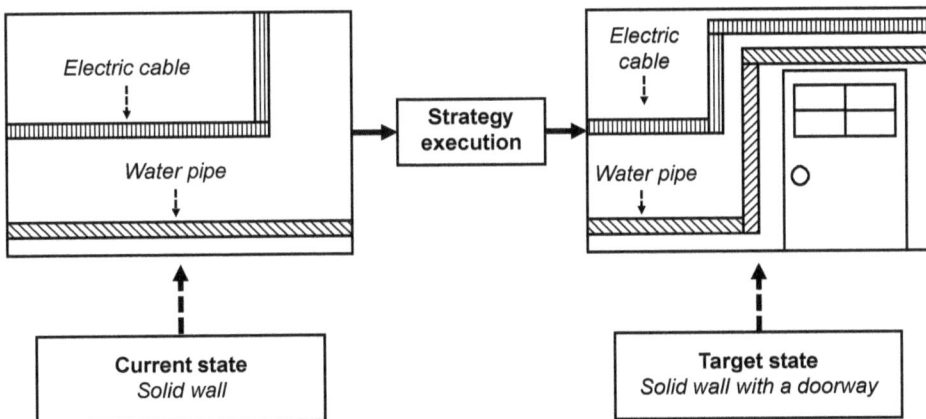

Business architecture is not concerned with change to physical buildings. Instead, it concerns changes to organisations. For example, an organisation may be considering a change of logistics provider in order to reduce costs. This proposal for change is shown in Figure 1.4.

If the decision to change the provider takes place without consideration of the impact on the organisation and its stakeholders, there is a risk that it will lead to unintended consequences. This includes the emergence of unexpected costs, risks and impacts.

For example, the incumbent logistics provider (A) is highly mature and effective in the delivery of its services. Consequently, the customer experience (CX) offered by the

7

Figure 1.4 Example of proposed organisational change – without reference to blueprints

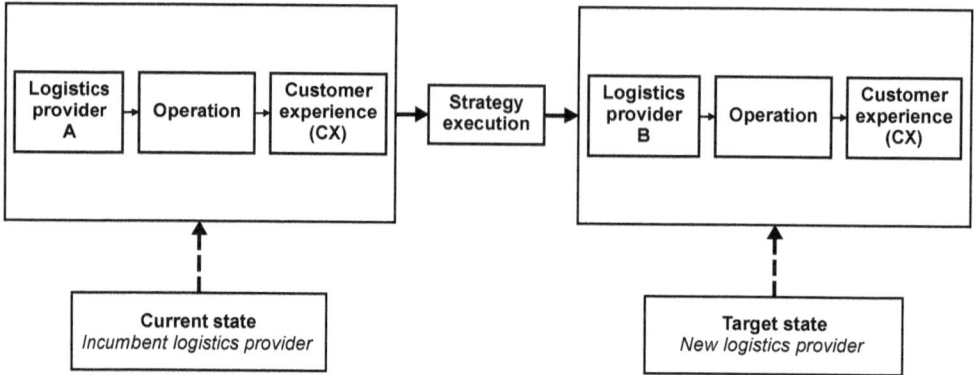

organisation is positive. However, on investigation, it is discovered that the proposed new logistics provider (B) lacks the maturity and capacity required to fulfil the organisation's needs to deliver one of the key services (Service 3) effectively. If the organisation proceeds to change provider, this could lead to the following:

- A need to complete a costly internal change initiative focused on internal processes.
- A need to maintain a relationship with the incumbent supplier.
- A need to accept an inferior overall CX.

The impact of this additional information is shown in Figure 1.5.

Figure 1.5 Example proposed organisational change – with reference to blueprints

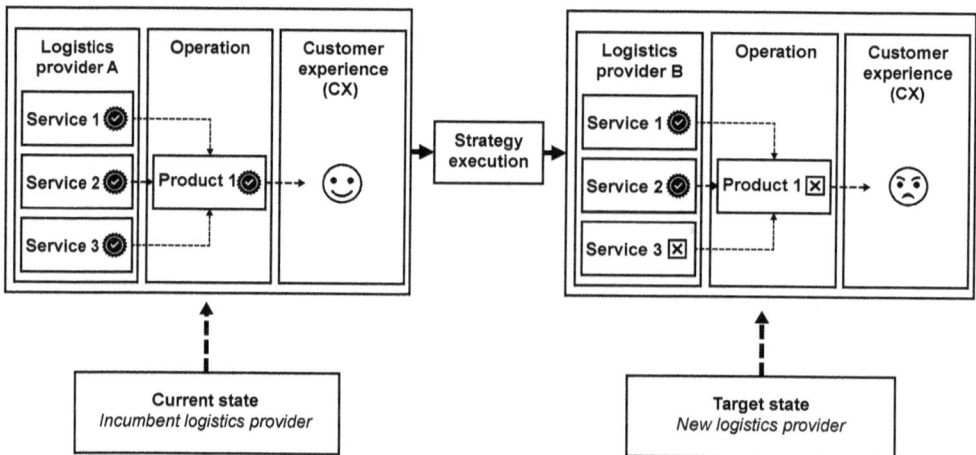

It is possible that, following reference to the blueprints and assessment of the costs, risks and impacts, the organisation's leadership decides to continue with the decision to change logistics provider. Business architecture does not replace or become accountable for business decision-making. However, the business architecture blueprints provide insights into the impacts and risks associated with decisions.

Rationale for using business architecture relative to an organisation's strategy

The impact of business architecture is far greater than a single decision, as it can be used to inform all strategic and tactical change decisions and their subsequent execution.

Figure 1.6 shows a situation where business architecture is used for decision-making. Strategic change decisions drive changes to the business architecture and, in turn, business architecture is used to inform execution. The strategic change execution affects the business architecture blueprints, which are then used as a basis to inform strategy.

Figure 1.6 Using business architecture for decision-making

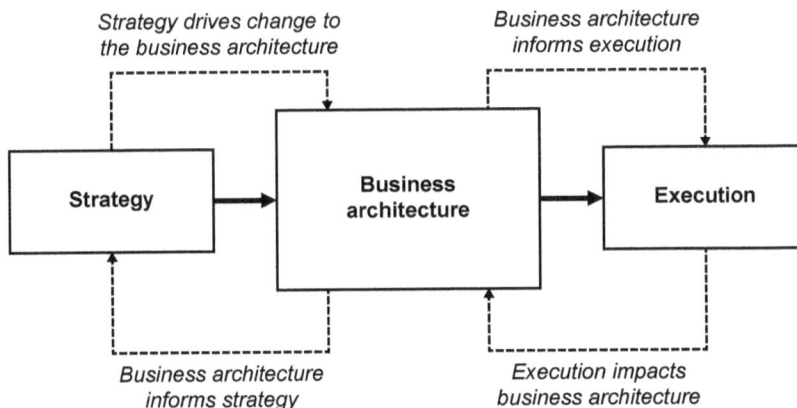

Where the relationship shown in Figure 1.6 exists, organisations are potentially able to benefit from aligned, consistent and considered decision-making. However, the relationships shown in Figure 1.6 often contrast with reality. In many organisations, strategy directly informs execution without consideration of the business architecture. This may be due to several reasons, including:

- lack of maturity within the business architecture domain;
- desire to launch products or services quickly;
- belief that developing and utilising a business architecture is expensive or time-consuming;
- cultural or other organisational issues.

Figure 1.7 shows the situation where execution occurs without consideration of the business architecture.

Figure 1.7 Strategy execution without reference to the business architecture

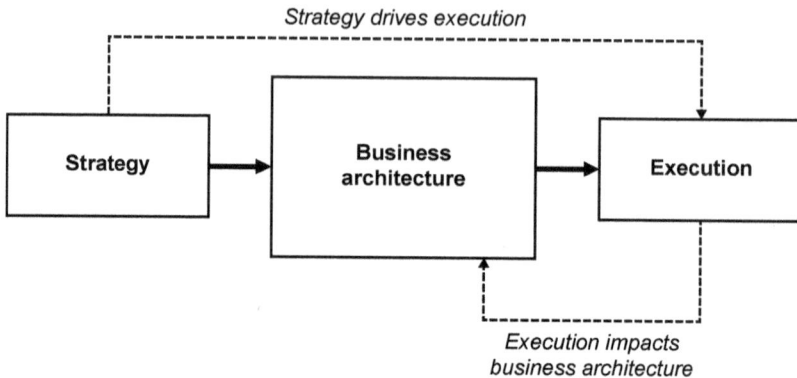

The process shown in Figure 1.7 can lead to several consequences, including misaligned and inconsistent decision-making. While in the short term it may have the advantage of enabling products and services to be launched quickly, over the longer term the approach can prove inconsistent or incoherent and, accordingly, increase complexity and costs. For example, historically an organisation may have executed change initiatives on an independent basis. Over time, this can lead to multiple solutions that duplicate key functionality and information. This approach can affect core back-office solutions, customer-facing websites, apps or solutions supporting key areas such as operations, finance or human resources.

Failing to use a business architecture can increase the difficulty when implementing change. This is particularly the case where multiple variations of business services exist due to each being executed independently. Consequently, each business service has a unique 'how' causing duplication and inconsistency and a proliferation in complexity. In turn, the costs of maintaining the complexity increase and the delivery of change initiatives becomes more difficult. Where an organisation is faced with commercial competitors who are unencumbered by this legacy of multiple service variations, the very survival of the organisation could be put at risk.

PRINCIPLES FOR USING BUSINESS ARCHITECTURE

There is no single 'correct' way to apply business architecture. The approach adopted by individual practitioners differs depending on the organisation's context, architectural principles and standards. For example, using business architecture within the context of a highly regulated organisation that has matured its practices over several years is likely to be vastly different from applying business architecture within a digital start-up that operates in a non-regulated environment. General principles for the application of business architecture are described in Table 1.2.

Table 1.2 Business architecture principles

Business architecture principle	Description
1. Business architecture promotes the long-term health of the organisation.	The approach is focused on promoting decisions that enhance the long-term health of the organisation. It is not a quick fix.
	It highlights where seemingly attractive short-term tactical decisions could compromise the long-term strategic direction of the organisation.
2. Business architecture is holistic.	The approach highlights and encompasses all elements of the organisation and its ecosystem.
3. Business architecture is outcome focused.	The approach seeks to improve outcomes for the organisation and its stakeholders.
4. Business architecture supports value co-creation.	The approach supports collaboration in the identification, development and deployment of strategic and tactical changes that are aimed at creating value with and for stakeholders.
5. Business architecture is context dependent.	The approach varies depending on the context in which it is applied. There is no prescriptive approach for its application.
6. Business architecture is knowledge based.	The approach is based on the acquisition, retention and retrieval of organisational knowledge.
7. Business architecture is iterative.	The approach utilises an iterative approach towards the development of knowledge. Blueprints of the organisation evolve in alignment with strategy and the execution of change.
8. Business architecture is reusable.	The approach develops knowledge that is reusable across all strategic and tactical change.

The Business Architecture Guild suggest in the BIZBOK Guide (2024) that the business architecture is 'not about the deliverables'. Instead, business architects should be focused on improving organisational health as opposed to the creation and maintenance of deliverables.

STRATEGIC DRIVERS FOR USING BUSINESS ARCHITECTURE

The strategic drivers for using business architecture vary between different organisations. Some organisations use the approach by default from their inception. Other organisations are much slower to adopt the business architecture view and, potentially, may never do this. Table 1.3 describes some key strategic drivers for employing the business architecture discipline.

Table 1.3 Strategic drivers for using business architecture

Strategic driver	Description
The need to solve complex business problems	This arises when there a need to solve a complex problem or implement a strategy that has far-reaching implications for the organisation. Examples include: • mergers or acquisitions; • divestment of business units or divisions; • adoption of significant regulatory or compliance driven change; • entrance into the market of a competitor with superior products or services.
The need to better understand change	This arises when there is a realisation that there is a need to better understand the costs, risks and effects of change. The need to understand different change scenarios and options can also be influential. This driver is particularly evident where organisations experience: • growth in the volume and complexity of their change portfolio; • mixed success with the execution of change; • increased supervisory oversight or regulatory scrutiny; • stakeholder frustration regarding the speed, cost or quality of change outcomes.
The need to enhance organisational agility	This arises when there is a realisation that there is a need to increase the speed at which the organisation can both understand and execute change.
The need to increase organisational efficiency	This arises when there is a realisation of the need to increase organisational efficiency. Examples of situations where this driver occurs include: • costs associated with providing products or services are found to be significantly higher than similar organisations or competitors; • external budgets, grants or donations upon which the organisation is reliant are reduced; • loss of market share or key revenue streams, which could be due to a client choosing not to renew a significant contract or to a customer choosing to move to competitors.

There are several other factors that may influence the adoption of a business architecture approach, including:

- a need to provide a foundation from which to determine more detailed business needs;
- a need to provide a foundation from which to drive change to other EA domains;
- a realisation that applying a business architecture view is beneficial to the organisation – increased credibility can result from piloting the use of a business architecture successfully;
- external influences such as engagement with external consultants or experts that advocate for the business architecture discipline.

Some organisations have become disillusioned with agile delivery practices, particularly where they have been adopted without robust strategic oversight and the expected benefits have not been realised. In these instances, business architecture is seen as a complementary approach, helping the organisation to deliver agile change that is aligned with strategic goals and objectives.

IMPEDIMENTS TO THE USE OF BUSINESS ARCHITECTURE

While many organisations benefit from the application of a business architecture, many others resist this because of perceived or real impediments. Table 1.4 describes these impediments and offers some potential remediations.

Table 1.4 Impediments to the use of business architecture (*There is no single perfect strategy that will work in all circumstances to overcome impediments. Attempts to introduce the business architecture discipline into an organisation may end in failure, so individual practitioners should approach impediments with caution.)

Impediment	Description and potential remediations
Lack of shared understanding of the purpose and scope of business architecture	Where there are varied perspectives of what business architecture is, particularly between senior leaders, this can cause confusion. If unresolved, expectations regarding the purpose and value of business architecture services may become misaligned. The risk of uncertainty regarding the scope of business architecture relative to other disciplines, such as EA and business analysis, can also cause negative impact. **Potential remediations* include:** • creation of a clear and concise definition of business architecture that is used consistently across the organisation; • defining the individual services offered by business architects within the organisation – each service should also have a clear and concise value proposition (see Chapter 2); • defining the services of other change disciplines, such as business analysis, may also help to reduce role ambiguity – over the long term this can provide a foundation for shared understanding of the roles and increased collaboration towards outcomes.

(Continued)

Table 1.4 (Continued)

Impediment	Description and potential remediations

Absence of senior leadership support	Where there is an absence of senior leadership support, any attempts to use a business architecture can meet significant resistance.
	
	This is particularly the case where senior leadership actively object to the use of the approach. In some instances, senior leaders can view the holistic and long-term nature of business architecture as a threat to their position, the status quo within the organisation and their personal domains of influence.
	
	Potential remediations* include:
	
	• creation of compelling, evidence-based business cases for the use of a business architecture approach;
	
	• a business case for removing inefficiencies or duplication within organisational siloes that significantly reduces long-term costs; if the senior leader benefits from this cost reduction – by obtaining credit – this can lead to increased support;
	
	• creation of a compelling vision of the future for the organisation focused on enhanced organisational outcomes – this target state may include aspects such as:
	  ▪ significant reduction of costs;
	  ▪ increased ability to:
	    ▪ launch new products and services;
	    ▪ meet regulatory and compliance obligations;
	    ▪ respond to external opportunities and threats.

Significant organisational crisis or instability	Where there is a significant organisational crisis or instability, the use of a business architecture can encounter significant challenges.
	
	In some circumstances, some stakeholders may perceive that there is no time to consider, develop or implement a business architecture.
	
	Instances of crisis or instability include:
	
	• frequent changes to:
	  ▪ senior leadership;
	  ▪ organisational strategy;
	  ▪ operating model or structure;
	• existential threats to the organisation;
	• uncertainty regarding ownership (for example, a threat of a hostile take-over or merger).

(Continued)

Table 1.4 (Continued)

Impediment	Description and potential remediations
	Potential remediations* include:
	• utilising the business architecture knowledge to aid the organisation through the period of instability. This could include using business architecture to:
	■ build shared understanding of the changes to the organisation.
	■ analyse different scenarios.
Cultural or political challenges	Where there are significant cultural or political challenges within the organisation, the use of a business architecture can be met with significant impediments.
	For example, if the organisation has:
	• historically focused exclusively on the achievement of short-term goals;
	• encouraged competition between organisational units for resources – where this is supported by budget allocation and performance measurement processes, opposition to a business architecture can be entrenched;
	• failed to integrate previous mergers or acquisitions – where this is the case, the use of a business architecture can be seen as a significant threat to individual siloes;
	• developed a culture that is non-collaborative.
	Potential remediations* include:
	• utilising political and cultural knowledge of the organisation to position and guide business architecture work;
	• introduction of governance and standards – this can be relative to business architecture or the execution and planning of change within the organisation;
	• development of case studies that highlight the value offered by the business architecture discipline, relative to the achievement of strategic goals and priorities;
	• encouragement of a culture that focuses on outcomes; for example, by asking questions such as 'how will this benefit our customers?' or 'how will this improve outcomes?'

In addition to the impediments cited, there are also several misconceptions regarding the business architecture discipline. These include:

- the belief that business architecture is only relevant for large and complex organisations – this is incorrect as an organisation of any size can benefit from utilising the business architecture view to support and align strategic and tactical decision-making;

- the belief that business architecture is incompatible with agile change delivery practices, which originates from the belief that business architecture is focused on comprehensive documentation and is only useful when associated with waterfall change delivery. This is a false assumption because business architecture is agnostic of change delivery or execution approach. Business architecture is focused on outcomes rather than deliverables and supports the achievement of the desired business outcomes in various, diverse contexts;

- the belief that business architecture creates an impediment to the delivery of rapid change – again, this is a false assumption because business architecture promotes reuse and efficiency and, over time, can increase the speed of change execution significantly.

RELATIONSHIP BETWEEN BUSINESS ARCHITECTURE AND OTHER ARCHITECTURAL DOMAINS

Business architecture and EA are intrinsically linked to each other. Business architecture is both a sub-domain within EA and a driving force for other EA sub-domains. This relationship is shown in Figure 1.8 and described in Table 1.5.

Figure 1.8 EA domains (© Assist Knowledge Development Ltd)

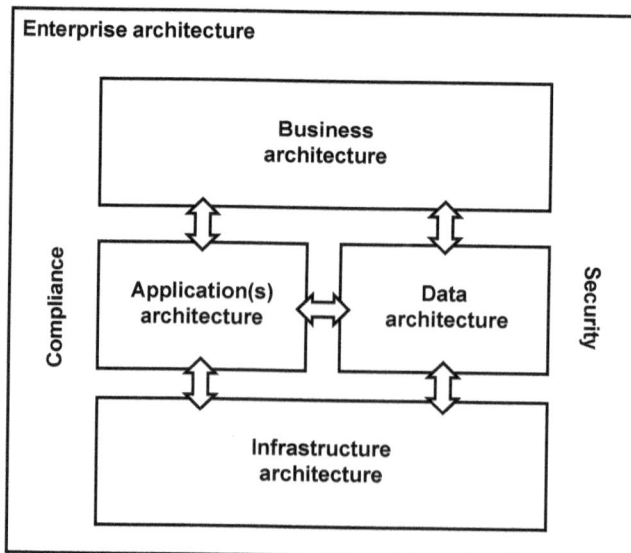

Table 1.5 Description of the six EA domains

EA domain	Description
Business architecture	Business architecture is focused on building shared understanding of the organising logic of organisations. The discipline encourages a systemic approach for making informed and aligned strategic and tactical decisions, through using blueprints that benefit the long-term health of the organisation.
Application(s) architecture	Application(s) architecture is focused on building shared understanding of the organising logic of the portfolio of applications across the enterprise.
	Application(s) should be aligned to and driven by changes to the business architecture.
Data architecture	Data architecture is focused on building shared understanding of the organising logic of data across the enterprise.
	Data architecture should be aligned to and driven by changes to the business architecture.
	Note: Data and applications architecture are linked, as an organisation's data is recorded, processed and reported by the application(s) deployed within the organisation.
Infrastructure architecture	Infrastructure architecture is focused on building shared understanding of the organising logic of infrastructure across the enterprise. This includes hardware, cloud services, operating systems and networks that store the organisation's data and applications.
	Infrastructure architecture should be aligned with data and application(s) architecture.
Compliance architecture	Compliance architecture supports shared understanding of the organising logic required to fulfil an organisation's compliance obligations and encompasses all EA sub-domains.
	This domain includes: • external compliance obligations such as legal and regulatory expectations; • internal compliance obligations such as internal policies and procedures.
	Compliance can be a key driver of change to a business architecture.
Security architecture	Security architecture is focused on the organising logic for protection of enterprise assets from harm, loss or danger. Its scope is across EA sub-domains.
	As with compliance architecture, security can be a key driver for change to business architecture.

17

As discussed previously, business architecture is concerned with asking the questions 'why?', 'what?' and 'how?' In theory, unless there is a valid business 'why?', no change should take place within the application(s), data or infrastructure domains. For these domains, the questions of 'what?' the change is and 'how?' the change should be executed are pertinent (Figure 1.9).

Figure 1.9 EA domains and key business architecture questions (© Assist Knowledge Development Ltd)

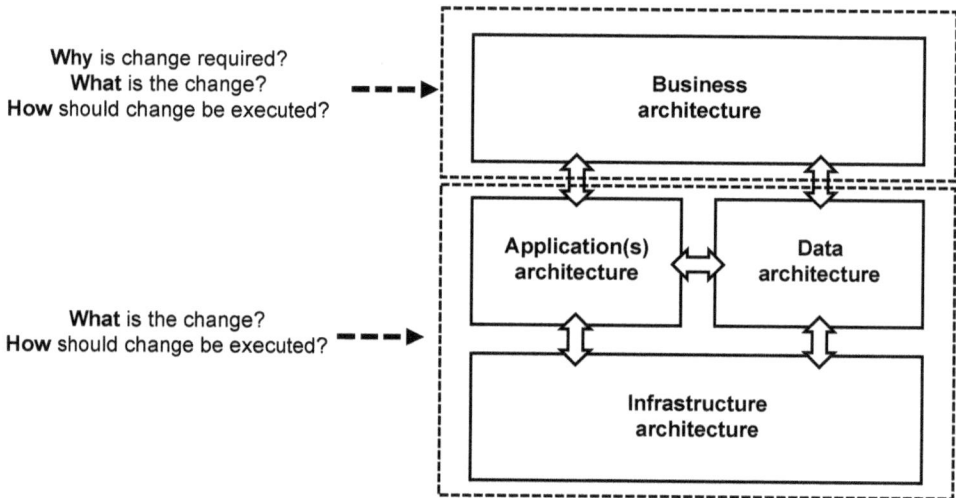

In practice, change can be driven by a desire for change in the application(s), data or infrastructure architecture domains. For example, an executive may take a decision to implement a new technology that impacts the application(s), data or infrastructure domains. While this approach can drive innovation, if it is not aligned with the business architecture and the organisation's strategy it can lead to a variety of issues such as increasing complexity and costs. There is a risk that the new technology duplicates technology already used within the organisation, or introduces additional, unnecessary complexity.

The EA domains and their related artefacts provide a means of understanding, analysing and representing the current and target states relevant to an organisation's strategy execution. This view is shown in Figure 1.10.

Through considering changes across all EA domains, the business architect is better able to support informed strategic and tactical decision-making. The publication *Enterprise Architecture as Strategy* offers the following rationale for EA:

> The enterprise architecture provides a long-term view of a company's processes, systems, and technologies so that individual projects can build capabilities – not just fulfil immediate needs. (Ross et al., 2006)

Figure 1.10 EA and the core building blocks of the strategic context (© Assist Knowledge
Development Ltd)

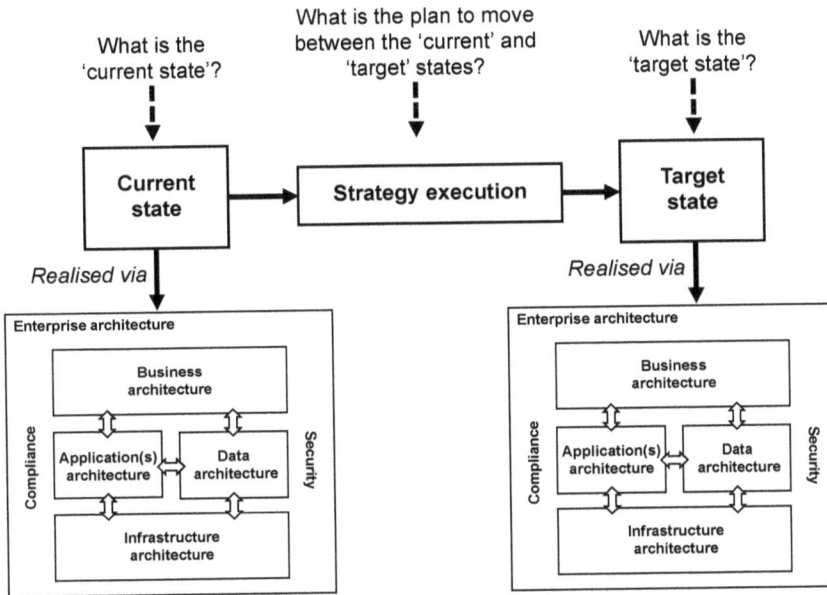

The key element concerns the provision of a 'long-term view', rather than meeting the 'immediate needs'. The paper by Foote and Yoder, 'Big ball of mud' (1997), goes a step further. They argue that an emergent, non-co-ordinated approach to software architecture, focused solely on immediate needs, is a chaotic approach that uses easily available, inexpensive resources. The focus is on the short term, using unskilled labour without considering aspects that require long-term planning, such as infrastructure.

While business architects are not concerned with software architecture, there are parallels that should be considered. Understanding the logic of the organisation through each of the EA domains helps the business architect to apply a systemic approach. This supports and enables informed decision-making that can ensure the long-term health of the organisation. In addition, through understanding the EA domains, the business architect is able to facilitate change that maximises the utilisation of an organisation's resources through the reuse and leverage of the data, applications and infrastructure architectures. This holistic and synergistic approach also underpins the success of change projects and enables the predicted returns on investment.

CONCLUSION

Business architecture has evolved as a key sub-domain within the EA discipline. The business architecture focus is on supporting strategy execution, enabling the organisation's response to change and ensuring organisational health. While there are some perceived barriers to using a business architecture, these can be mitigated and overcome and, ultimately, the adoption of a business architecture approach is beneficial.

2 BUILDING BUSINESS ARCHITECTURE COMPETENCE

INTRODUCTION

This chapter covers the following topics:

- maturity of the business architect role;
- the business architecture service framework;
- the T-shaped professional business architect.

MATURITY OF THE BUSINESS ARCHITECT ROLE

Chapter 1 introduced the business architecture discipline and its history, the principles that underlie this discipline and the drivers for applying a business architecture approach. This chapter focuses on the role of the business architect, the service portfolio offered by business architects and the skillset required of anyone carrying out this role.

You may be considering one of the following:

- becoming a business architect;
- building and refining a business architect skillset;
- wondering how to develop a team of business architects;
- looking to recruit or hire a business architect.

This chapter provides insights into each of these aspects by explaining the following:

- how the business architect role has matured over time;
- the services offered by business architects;
- the skillset of a T-shaped business architect.

The demand for the business architect role did not accelerate at the same velocity as other architectural roles, such as the enterprise and technical architect roles. This may have been because the extensive scope of the enterprise architect role, which addresses the entire spectrum of an organisation, could be perceived to encompass the business architect role. Another explanation is that roles concerned with the data and infrastructure architectures were easier to define clearly and so rose to prominence, which contrasted with the less tangible business architect role.

The abstruse nature of business architecture has proven difficult to clarify from a role perspective. However, as the maturity and understanding of enterprise architecture has developed, the areas of responsibility and artefacts associated with business architecture have gained recognition. This has led to the role becoming more clearly defined and stakeholder awareness of the role increasing. There has also been greater understanding about the need to understand the organisation's ecosystem of stakeholders, partners and customers.

The maturity of the business architect role may be analysed using the structure of the Capability Maturity Model Integration (CMMI). The CMMI was developed by the Software Engineering Institute at Carnegie Mellon University and offers a standard for benchmarking and improving organisational processes.

Figure 2.1 is an adaption of the CMMI model, and defines the stages in the maturity evolution of the business architect role within an organisation. These stages are explained in Table 2.1.

Figure 2.1 Maturity evolution of the business architect role

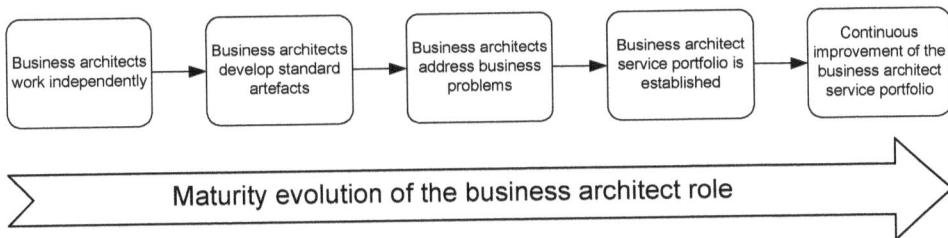

Organisations working to establish a business architecture discipline need to clarify the role they expect their business architects to perform. Without such clarification, there is likely to be role ambiguity and confusion both within the business architecture community and for its stakeholders. Role ambiguity raises the following issues:

- Those performing the role are not clear about their responsibilities, the standards they should apply and the outputs they should deliver. They are also unclear about the business outcomes their work supports and enables. Where business architects are unclear about their role, they may develop models and other artefacts without appreciating the objectives to be achieved.

- Those who are the recipients or 'customers' of the role outputs are unsure what to expect and how to best utilise the skills offered by the role. Where stakeholders are unclear about their expectations of the business architect role, they are also unsure about how to apply any information or guidance provided, and may fail to request a service that the business architect can offer.

A service approach helps to ensure clarity of role definition by defining the portfolio of services offered by a role.

Table 2.1 Maturity stages of the business architect role

Stage	Description
1. Business architects work independently	Business architect is a new role and so lacks clarity of definition and output. Business architects work independently of each other and colleagues in related disciplines, and few standards exist. Business architects respond to requests but are rarely proactive in supporting the organisation.
2. Business architects develop standard artefacts	Synergies across the business architect community emerge leading to the development of standard approaches and artefacts. Business architects respond to requests and offer proactive support to the organisation on occasion.
3. Business architects address business problems	Business architects engage with stakeholders to investigate and advise on problems and opportunities, and are proactive in identifying where they may support the organisation and where opportunities for improvement exist.
4. Business architect service portfolio is established	Business architects adopt a service approach and establish a business architect service framework (see next section) that is tailored to the needs of the organisation. Business architects work proactively to support and enable the execution of the organisation's strategy.
5. Continuous improvement of the business architect service portfolio	Business architects engage with stakeholders to identify opportunities to extend and improve the business architect service portfolio.

BUSINESS ARCHITECTURE SERVICE FRAMEWORK

The business architecture service framework defines a proposed portfolio of business architecture services. It has been developed to enable organisations to define the business architect role clearly and ensure it is in line with the organisation's needs.

The business architecture service framework shown in Figure 2.2 sets out a range of services that may be offered by the business architects working within an organisation. This service framework offers a basis for consistency and role clarity within a community of business architects. The framework is intended to be customised so that it is relevant to a particular organisational context. It offers a basis for discussion with an organisation's stakeholders to clarify what they require and what may be expected from the business architects. Each of the services shown within this framework is described in overview in Table 2.2.

Figure 2.2 The business architecture service framework (© Assist Knowledge Development Ltd)

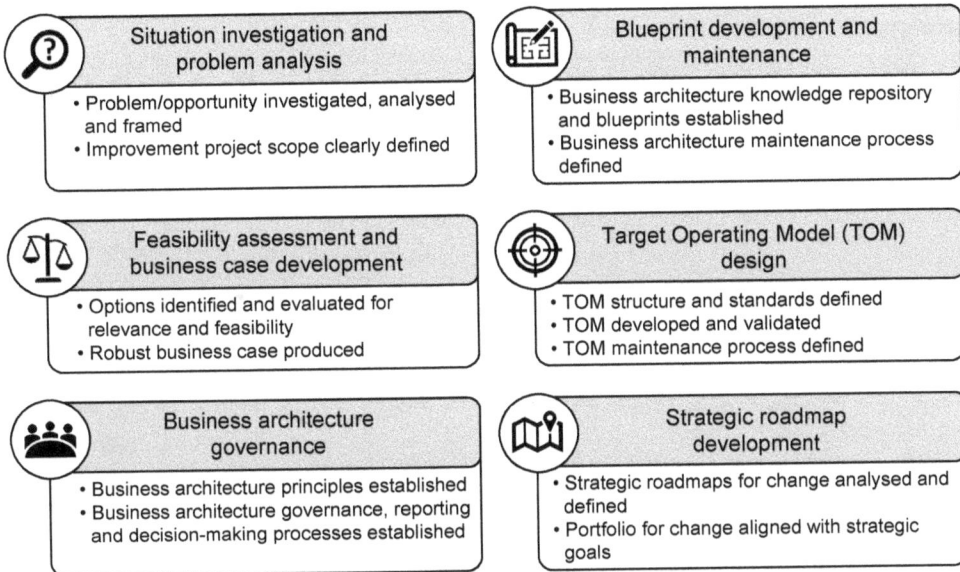

Situation investigation and problem analysis	Blueprint development and maintenance
• Problem/opportunity investigated, analysed and framed • Improvement project scope clearly defined	• Business architecture knowledge repository and blueprints established • Business architecture maintenance process defined
Feasibility assessment and business case development	Target Operating Model (TOM) design
• Options identified and evaluated for relevance and feasibility • Robust business case produced	• TOM structure and standards defined • TOM developed and validated • TOM maintenance process defined
Business architecture governance	Strategic roadmap development
• Business architecture principles established • Business architecture governance, reporting and decision-making processes established	• Strategic roadmaps for change analysed and defined • Portfolio for change aligned with strategic goals

Stakeholder engagement is an auxiliary service.

Table 2.2 Business architecture service descriptions

Business architecture service	Service description
Situation investigation and problem analysis	Investigate business situations that are problematic or offer opportunities for improvement. Identify root causes of problems and distinguish them from the manifest symptoms. Analyse and frame the problem to be addressed. Define the scope of the desired solution.
Feasibility assessment and business case development	Identify and evaluate any proposed solutions from the business, financial and technical perspectives, taking into account the organisational capabilities. Develop a business case that explains the situation and the business needs to be addressed, and explore the options available to the organisation in terms of the financial justification and risk and impact analysis.
Business architecture governance	Define, communicate and maintain the principles that underlie the business architecture. Define how the business architecture will be applied during the organisation's business decision-making process.
Blueprint development and maintenance	Investigate, analyse and document the key business architecture views: motivation; organisational structure; capabilities; value streams; information; people. Define the process for applying and maintaining these views.

(Continued)

Table 2.2 (Continued)

Business architecture service	Service description
Target Operating Model (TOM) design	Investigate, analyse and document the TOM for the enterprise or business area. Define the process for applying and maintaining the TOM.
Strategic roadmap development	Develop the strategic roadmap for change in line with strategic priorities and decisions. Analyse the impact on the business architecture to identify gaps needing to be addressed to meet strategic requirements. Establish and prioritise a portfolio of change programmes and projects.

An auxiliary service – stakeholder engagement – is also offered by business architects. This service is key to the effective provision of all the other business architecture services and is described as: support the delivery of business architect services through stakeholder collaboration, communication and effective stakeholder relationship management. Therefore, the business architecture service framework may be summarised to clarify the business architect role as follows:

The business architect role collaborates with stakeholders to co-create value for organisations through offering the following services:

- situation investigation and problem analysis;
- feasibility assessment and business case development;
- business architecture governance;
- blueprint development and maintenance;
- TOM design;
- strategic roadmap development.

An extensive range of skills is required to offer the services described in Table 2.2. Business architects need to possess the required skills and must be able to apply a range of relevant techniques. Several of the key business architecture techniques are described in Chapters 4 to 8. The value propositions, value streams, activities and techniques of the business architecture service framework are described in further detail in Chapter 9.

THE T-SHAPED PROFESSIONAL BUSINESS ARCHITECT

The concept of T-shaping emerged from research into the nature of 'service' and 'service systems'. A discussion of the different 'shapes' that may be perceived among professional workers concluded:

The 'shape' of a professional is a term we use to understand whether a professional is a deep specialist in one area ('I-shaped'), deep specialist in two areas ('H-shaped'), deep in just one area, but with good knowledge and communication skills across many other areas ('T-shaped'). (Donofrio et al., 2010)

There are many ways of interpreting the concept of a T-shaped professional, but there is a consensus about the need for depth of knowledge and expertise in one area and interpersonal skills that are concerned with various areas.

The T-shaped professional concept may be applied to business architects. A T-shaped professional business architect is required to have broad generic skills that enable effective interactions with the internal and external stakeholders involved in business architecture work. These skills are shown in the horizontal row of the T. The vertical column of the T represents the deep specialist skills required of a business architect; these are the professional skills needed to deliver the business architecture services defined in Figure 2.2. The skills required of a T-shaped business architect are shown in Figure 2.3.

Figure 2.3 The T-shaped business architect

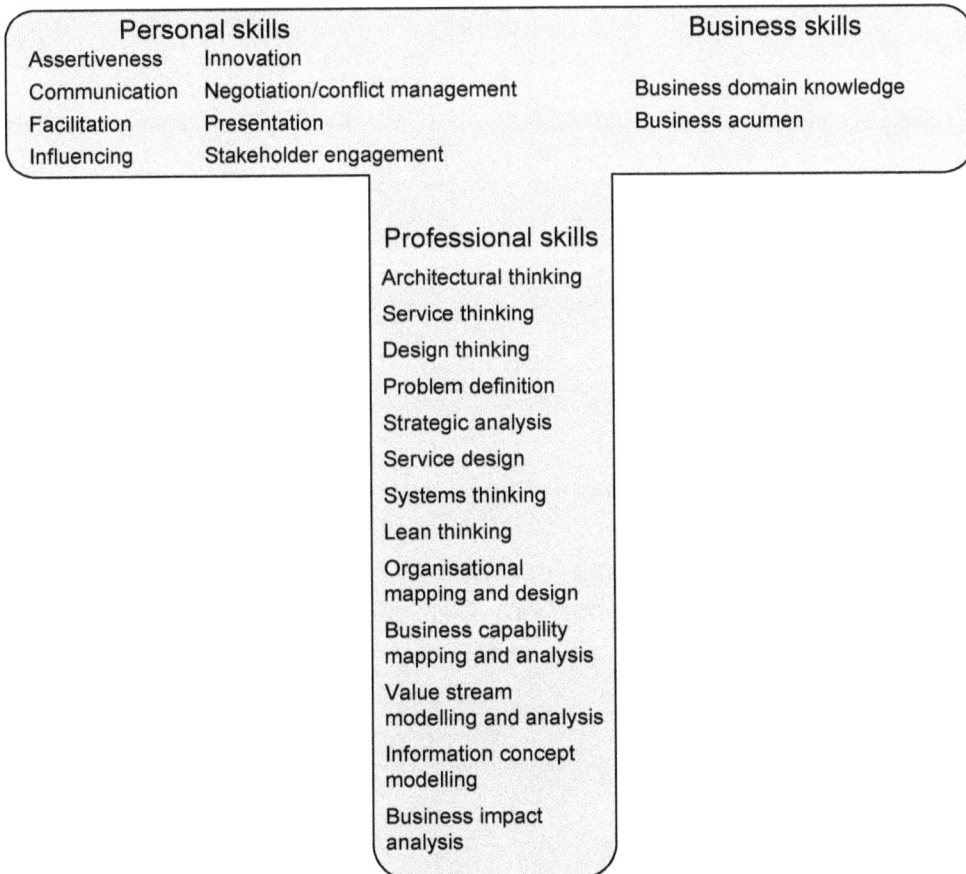

Personal skills		Business skills
Assertiveness	Innovation	
Communication	Negotiation/conflict management	Business domain knowledge
Facilitation	Presentation	Business acumen
Influencing	Stakeholder engagement	

Professional skills

Architectural thinking

Service thinking

Design thinking

Problem definition

Strategic analysis

Service design

Systems thinking

Lean thinking

Organisational mapping and design

Business capability mapping and analysis

Value stream modelling and analysis

Information concept modelling

Business impact analysis

Traits, skills and competences

The business architect needs to have an extensive toolkit of traits, skills and competences to be able to deliver the array of different services defined in Figure 2.2. These terms are defined in Table 2.3.

Table 2.3 Explanations of key terms

Term	Term description
Trait	A trait is a distinguishing characteristic or quality that is inherent in an individual. There are some fundamental traits that a business architect needs to deliver the business architecture services. Traits can be honed and developed, but may be possessed more naturally by some people.
Skill	A skill is an ability that is acquired, typically through learning and experience. Education and employment settings provide the main opportunities to develop skills, but recreational activities can also contribute significantly to a person's skillset. Skills can be tangible (hard) – such as the ability to drive a car – or intangible (soft) – such as emotional intelligence. A business architect needs to be able to draw on a wide range of skills, including using modelling techniques to communicate with colleagues or facilitating a workshop with senior executives to gain agreement on strategic objectives.
Competency	Competency is the level of ability possessed regarding a particular skill. For example, a business architect may possess facilitation skill at a level of competency that enables them to work within straightforward contexts with supportive stakeholders. However, with experience, this competency may be developed to enable a business architect to facilitate in more challenging or complex situations, or where attendees are disengaged or confrontational.

Business architects also need to possess knowledge about several areas if they are to be fully effective in their role. Highly relevant knowledge areas include:

- architecture principles and patterns applied by the organisation;
- legal and regulatory requirements;
- relevant International Organization for Standardization (ISO) standards and their application within the organisational context;
- technological advancements and how they can be applied to meet organisational needs;
- the metrics used within the organisation, what they represent and how they are applied.

These areas may constrain or influence an organisation's VMOST (vision, mission, objectives, strategy and tactics) and, accordingly, may affect the work of the business architect. Producing compliant artefacts will attest to stakeholders that the architect has a wide knowledge of the influencing factors and can be depended upon to define designs, diagrams and views that are business relevant and useful.

The traits

Figure 2.4 shows the key personality traits required of a business architect.

Figure 2.4 Business architecture personality traits

Open-mindedness
Business architects are often involved in situations where major decisions about the direction and strategy of the organisation are made. This places responsibility on business architects to be open-minded and receptive to new ideas. They need to engage with a variety of stakeholders so they can gain and expand their knowledge of the business and help to identify opportunities, risks and threats. Demonstrating receptivity to new ideas also encourages colleagues to contribute freely and to be open-minded.

The development of an open, transparent collaboration where perspectives and ideas are shared enables debate, leading to the creation of innovative solutions that support the organisation's further development. This trait is closely related to adaptability when an approach or a concept that hasn't progressed as anticipated is used as a basis for creativity and the identification of new ideas.

Self-motivation
Business architects need to possess the ability to deal with challenges and have the personal motivation to persist when difficulties arise. They need to focus on the desired outcomes from their work and persist with moving forward towards achieving them. This takes determination, confidence and conviction – all of which are qualities needed to work with the complexity inherent within most organisations and the range of views, beliefs and values that are likely to be encountered from stakeholders.

Emotional intelligence

This trait can sometimes be interpreted as the ability to understand and recognise the feelings and emotions of others. However, emotional intelligence also concerns the ability to identify and manage personal emotions, and to be comfortable with self-reflection.

Business architects are often in situations that raise emotions such as frustration, irritation, self-doubt, anxiety or excitement. Having the ability to recognise such emotions and pause before speaking or acting is key to relationship development and management. Managing these emotions and intuiting the most relevant response also advances professional credibility. For example, attending a workshop with senior executives where a decision regarding a new merger is announced would not be a forum to stand, cheer or even 'whoop' at the news! Recognising the excitement and then harnessing the emotion to progress the required organisational response is a far better use of the positive energy. Business architects that manage their emotional responses and recognise the social cues and feelings of others are able to establish their credibility and gain a position of influence. People tend to collaborate with those who are measured and practical when responding to change drivers.

There are many scenarios where emotional intelligence supports the work of the business architect. Whether supporting executive decisions, guiding tactical managers or working with operational teams, frustration and conflict can often arise. The emotionally intelligent business architect can manage these situations and steer a path forward.

Teamwork

Business architects must be able to work collaboratively with a variety of stakeholders and colleagues. This requires business architects to understand the contribution other roles make to a particular change initiative or project and to engage with them in achieving the desired business outcome. This may also require business architects to possess skills, such as coaching skills, to help others work effectively within teams.

Integrity

Business architects often have access to confidential information and may be aware of activities that could have a wider influence in the external business environment within which the organisation operates. For example, they may be aware of opportunities or proposals for organisational divestment, mergers or acquisitions and may help to develop the future state definition. The business architect often performs a pivotal role in defining a TOM (as identified in the business architecture service framework in Figure 2.2). Therefore, they must demonstrate integrity and respect for the confidentiality of any information with which they have been entrusted.

Resilience

Difficult situations, challenges and setbacks prevail in most organisational contexts, so resilience and perseverance are needed to ensure a positive and practical way forward. Business architects may be challenged about their suggested solutions or receive critical feedback and rejection or ideas. While this can be both disappointing and frustrating, resilience and self-motivation is needed to address the challenges and negative responses, revise any proposals and offer a positive attitude. Truly resilient individuals can turn any such situation into an opportunity for personal learning and growth.

Given that business architects typically work within a team, and are often more senior members of each team, they need to demonstrate resilience and positivity to that they inspire other team members to stay motivated and engaged with achieving desired outcomes.

Cultural sensitivity

Cultural sensitivity is essential for engaging with internal colleagues and external stakeholders. Technology has enabled global communication and engagement, and many organisations have a business presence or work with suppliers and customers in many different countries or continents. Therefore, business architects must understand the organisation's locations, services and processes, and the nature of the roles and actors with whom they must collaborate or engage. This requires cultural awareness and sensitivity if potential issues are to be avoided.

Awareness of cultural differences is essential if architectural design is to support or enable organisational harmony. Recognising the diverse nature of the tapestry of an organisation may constrain the business architecture, but this can be an essential element in grasping the opportunities and realising the competitive advantages that are available to an organisation.

The professional skills

The T-shaped business architect needs a range of professional skills that are specific to the role. A set of key skills is shown in Figure 2.3. These skills are described in Table 2.4.

Table 2.4 The professional skills of a T-shaped business architect

Skill	Skill description
Architectural thinking	This is having the ability to apply an architectural view to an organisation or business area in order to support strategy analysis and execution and business improvement.
Service thinking	This is having the ability to take a service view of an organisation, business area, function or portfolio of products/services. It involves understanding and applying a holistic, customer-centric approach that is collaborative, resource integrating and outcome-focused to co-create value.
Design thinking	This is having the ability to apply design principles, concepts and techniques to discover the business need, define the problem to be addressed, develop and obtain feedback about potential solutions and deploy a product or service into operation.
Problem definition	This is having the ability to investigate the root cause of a problem, analyse different elements that may contribute to the problem and create a clear definition of the problem.
Strategic analysis	This is having the ability to analyse the VMOST for an organisation and the business environment within which the organisation operates in order to identify potential strategic options for achieving organisational growth.

(Continued)

Table 2.4 (Continued)

Skill	Skill description
Service design	This is having the ability to apply service and design thinking to the development or enhancement of a product or service.
Systems thinking	This is having the ability to view each situation as a system that is holistic in nature and comprises a set of interacting components. Systems thinking also views systems as being formed from other systems (in other words, they are systems of systems), with each system gaining additional emergent properties rather than just aggregating the properties of each component system. This is sometimes summarised as 'the whole is greater than the sum of the parts'.
Lean thinking	This is having the ability to apply the principles and practices defined within the Lean approach that focus on removing waste in organisations and aiding continuous improvement.
Organisational mapping and design	This is having the ability to investigate, analyse, document and design the structure, roles and ecosystem for an organisation.
Business capability mapping and analysis	This is having the ability to build a representation of the business capabilities possessed by an organisation and analyse the capabilities to identify gaps, areas needing improvement and possibilities for organisational advantage through capability leverage.
Value stream modelling and analysis	This is having the ability to identify the value items offered by an organisation and to build representations of the value streams, including their activities, that deliver these value items.
Information concept modelling	This is having the ability to identify the key information concepts that are fundamental to an organisation's operations and delivery of products and services.
Business impact analysis	This is having the ability to evaluate the impact of proposed changes on an organisation or business area and determine the required courses of action.

This list is not intended to be definitive for those working or wishing to work as a business architect; however, it provides a core toolkit that may be applied within a variety of contexts. Several of these skills are explored later in this book. Two key skills are strategic analysis and problem definition.

Strategic analysis

Bridging the business gap between where the organisation is today and where the organisation should be requires a business architecture view. The business architect role is foremost in supporting this work, needing to understand the strategic aims of the organisation and having the ability to analyse the capabilities required to achieve these aims. Business architects play a pivotal role in the successful execution of strategy and the corresponding deployment of transformational or incremental change.

Business architects need to be able to take a 'big picture' view, understanding the strategic vision and creating the roadmap that enables the organisation to progress towards the desired outcomes. This requires the ability to interpret and analyse the organisation's VMOST and ensure that an outcome-focus persists. They also need to have the skills to explore, challenge and inform decision makers.

The strategic viewpoint requires business architects to commit to the strategy and ensure that the plan for strategy execution is clear and communicated to all parties. The business architect is there to share the message of the strategy, stick to that strategy and ensure that target state architectural designs are defined and achievable.

There may be occasions where the business architect has concerns about the organisation's ability to achieve the strategy, and they may need to work in partnership with other change professionals, such as enterprise architects, to share concerns and navigate issues. This is where traits, such as resilience, and personal skills, such as influencing and negotiation, are essential.

Problem definition

Problem definition and resolution is a key function of any business architecture service – so is a core professional skill of a business architect. The business architect plays a key role in articulating problems, identifying root causes and framing problems before supporting the identification of options for problem resolution. Figure 2.5 shows the three key qualities, which are a combination of traits, skills and competencies, required of a business architect when defining problems. These qualities are also relevant when undertaking many other business architecture activities.

Figure 2.5 Key qualities for problem definition

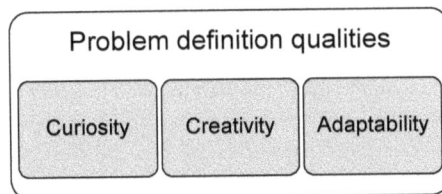

These qualities are defined as follows:

- **Curiosity** to ensure any problems are investigated thoroughly.

- **Creativity** to use divergent and convergent thinking to explore and build shared understanding of the nature of the problem and its impact. Working with others to explore and challenge perspectives of the problem including any patterns, delimiters or beliefs being used to frame the problem and its context.

- **Adaptability** using a variety of techniques to identify and analyse different viewpoints regarding the problem. This should leverage knowledge and understanding of the organisation and its stakeholders.

The personal skills

Business architects require personal skills that enable them to engage and work effectively with the stakeholders within their ecosystem. Key personal skills are shown in Figure 2.3 and described in Table 2.5.

Table 2.5 The personal skills of a T-shaped business architect

Personal skill	Description
Assertiveness	This is the ability to challenge views and present alternatives in a professional, objective manner.
Communication	This is the ability to formulate and deliver messages that are clear and understandable, and to listen actively and understand any messages received.
Facilitation	This is the ability to organise, engage with and lead groups that are brought together in a meeting or workshop to achieve a defined, collective objective.
Influencing	This is the ability to provide constructive advice and ensure it is considered for adoption.
Innovation	This is the ability to view situations, problems and opportunities from different perspectives and formulate novel ways forward using available resources.
Negotiation/ conflict management	This is the ability to navigate situations where alternative views are present and achieve the most positive outcome possible given the constraints and issues that are present.
Presentation	This is the ability to create and deliver information in a polished and engaging manner.
Stakeholder engagement	This is the ability to identify relevant stakeholders within an ecosystem (internal and external), analyse those stakeholders and determine the most relevant approach to work effectively with them. This skill also requires understanding of the need to monitor and revisit the stakeholder landscape on an ongoing basis.

The strategic and business domain of the architecture practice is typically expressed in abstract and conceptual terms, so can be subject to interpretation. Gaining agreement about the available business capabilities, and how they are named or defined, can be challenging as stakeholders often have individual perspectives and priorities. Gaining consensus requires personal skills such as communication and influencing. Conflicts may emerge from such discussions that require negotiation and management. Business architects need to facilitate collaboration where possible, maintaining an objective, constructive approach and applying techniques that ensure different parties can work together.

CONCLUSION

This chapter has highlighted the complexity of the business architect role and the extent of the skillset required to perform the role effectively. The business architect performs a pivotal role within business change and transformation, offering essential guidance and support to their organisation. This requires them to be T-shaped, possessing and developing the key skills and competency levels across the business, personal and professional areas. This is essential if business architects are to attain the required level of professional proficiency and gain credibility within their organisations.

3 BUSINESS ARCHITECTURE FRAMEWORKS

INTRODUCTION

This chapter discusses the following areas:

- enterprise and business architecture frameworks:
  - the Zachman Framework;
  - TOGAF (The Open Group Architecture Framework) Enterprise Architecture Framework;
  - the AssistKD POPIT model (people, organisation, process, information and technology);
  - the Business Architecture Guild's Business Architecture Body of Knowledge (BIZBOK);
- selecting an architecture framework;
- adopting an architecture framework;
- business architecture views;
- business architecture blueprints;
- business architecture tools.

ENTERPRISE AND BUSINESS ARCHITECTURE FRAMEWORKS

An enterprise architecture framework provides a basis for clarity about the activities conducted and the products created by those working within the EA domains. The EA domains encompass business, data, infrastructure and applications architecture, and those working within these domains develop and maintain the artefacts (or 'blueprints') that define different perspectives on the enterprise. These blueprints inform and enable understanding among the organisation's stakeholder community.

Several frameworks that are relevant to the business architecture work are available. Some offer a broad scope that includes business architecture but also extends to cover the entire EA, while others focus solely on business architecture. Organisations need to evaluate the guidance offered by each framework and decide how best to conduct the business architecture work.

Frameworks offer several advantages, including supporting a consistent and repeatable approach to documenting and analysing architecture domains. They help to define the structure, guidelines and language for the practical work that business architects undertake and, when applied effectively, they can help with aligning strategic and tactical decisions against existing or proposed change. They also aid the management of complexity and support practitioner collaboration.

The overall objective when selecting a framework is to ensure that a structure for planning the business architecture activities is in place and decide the blueprints to be developed. It is unlikely that a single industry standard framework meets the requirements of a specific organisational context. Each organisation defines its strategy and objectives, operates using a particular structure and has a unique culture. The framework adopted must align with these characteristics. Different contexts benefit from different business architecture activities and blueprints.

Many frameworks offer comprehensive approaches, but they should not be considered fixed or prescriptive. Instead, they should be used as a basis for establishing guidelines and standards for the business architecture practices that best suit the organisation. This customisation to suit the context increases the likelihood that these practices are accepted, understood and used.

The following frameworks are described in this chapter:

- The Zachman Framework;
- TOGAF;
- The Business Architecture Guild Body of Knowledge;
- The AssistKD POPIT model.

The Zachman Framework

The Zachman Framework provides a taxonomy of the discrete elements that together represent an organisation. This framework provides a basis for recording different key perspectives regarding an organisation and a means from which to analyse the conceptual, logical and physical aspects of an organisation. A summarised version of the framework is shown in Figure 3.1.

Each column in the Zachman Framework addresses a different perspective of the EA and concerns the questions 'what?', 'how?', 'where?', 'when?', 'who?' and, perhaps most important of all, 'why?' These columns are described in Table 3.1.

The rows within the framework look at cascading levels of detail from the executive concept planner perspective through to concept owners, designers, builders, implementers and users. These rows are described in Table 3.2.

Figure 3.1 Summarised Zachman Framework

	What? (data)	How? (function)	Where? (location)	Who? (people)	When? (time)	Why? (motivation)
Business context planner	Inventory identification	Process identification	Distribution identification	Responsibility identification	Timing identification	Motivation identification
Business concept owner	Inventory definition	Process definition	Distribution definition	Responsibility definition	Timing definition	Motivation definition
Business logic designer	Inventory representation	Process representation	Distribution representation	Responsibility representation	Timing representation	Motivation representation
Business physics builder	Inventory specification	Process specification	Distribution specification	Responsibility specification	Timing specification	Motivation specification
Business component implementer	Inventory configuration	Process configuration	Distribution configuration	Responsibility configuration	Timing configuration	Motivation configuration
User	Inventory instantiations	Process instantiations	Distribution instantiations	Responsibility instantiations	Timing instantiations	Motivation instantiations

Table 3.1 Zachman Framework column descriptions

Zachman column	Description
What (data)	This column focuses on investigating and documenting the inventory sets of the organisation.
How (function)	This column focuses on investigating and documenting the process flows of the organisation.
Where (location)	This column focuses on investigating and documenting the distribution networks of the organisation.
When (time)	This column focuses on investigating and documenting the timing cycles of the organisation.
Who (people)	This column focuses on investigating and documenting the responsibility assignments of the organisation.
Why (motivation)	This column focuses on investigating and documenting the motivation intentions of the organisation.

Table 3.2 Zachman Framework row descriptions

Zachman row	Description
Business context planners	This row focuses on the executive perspective of the scope of the organisation. The outputs created for this row tend to be lists covering the key points for each area.
Business concept owners	This row focuses on the business management perspective of the business concepts of the organisation. The outputs created for this row are business definition models.
Business logic designers	This row focuses on the architect's perspective regarding the system logic of the organisation. The outputs created for this row are models that represent various aspects of a system.
Business physics builders	This row focuses on the engineer's perspective of the technology physics of the organisation. The outputs created for this row are technology specification models.
Business component implementers	This row focuses on the technician's perspective of the tool components of the organisation. The outputs created for this row are tool configuration models.
Users	This row focuses on the users' perspective of the enterprise. The outputs created for this row define the implementations or instantiations of the various aspects.

The Zachman Framework offers a basis for considering the scope of business architecture. One view is that business architecture is concerned solely with the business context and business concept rows. Combined with the questions asked within the Zachman columns, these provide a foundation for understanding the business architecture for the enterprise. An alternative view is that, for business architecture to be applied effectively, it must also consider the business logic row for the organisation. Through considering the logic of the organisation, the business architect can increase their visibility and oversight of the logical decisions and outcomes relative to the contextual and conceptual views. This can aid with the development of shared understanding among stakeholders and support their decision-making. Understanding the logical view enables the business architect to co-create value with stakeholders such as business analysts and solution architects, who are likely to be focused on this aspect. Whichever approach is taken, the contextual and conceptual views must be aligned with the logical views if the desired business and stakeholder outcomes are to be achieved.

The TOGAF Enterprise Architecture Framework

The TOGAF framework, developed by The Open Group, offers extensive guidance and includes both an architecture development method (ADM) cycle and a reference enterprise metamodel. The ADM provides a process-based view of how to create and manage the EA and the related architectures for specific domains. The enterprise metamodel provides a means from which to categorise knowledge of the elements within the organisation. Due to the inclusion of a method for developing an EA, the scope of the TOGAF framework is considered to offer greater depth of guidance than that provided by the Zachman.

The ADM includes the architecture domains that comprise the EA, including business, information systems and technology architectures. It supports the alignment of these architecture domains to the EA and to each other.

The ADM deploys an iterative approach to documenting the EA and the other architecture domains. This is reflected in the diagram of the ADM shown in Figure 3.2. The phases of the ADM are described in Table 3.3.

The ADM can be tailored to the requirements of a specific enterprise context and may be blended with other frameworks. For example, some of the work to develop the architectural blueprints may apply guidance from the Zachman classifications.

The Open Group also provide the ArchiMate® standard notation for EA models. This is a standard approach, adopted by many organisations, to represent, describe, analyse and visualise architectural concepts and the relationships between them.

The assumption that the ADM phases are completed in order and all the blueprints will be necessary or useful may not be realistic in practice. For example, the preliminary and vision phases may be carried out as a joint phase, given that they are both concerned with defining the context; the business, information systems and technology architecture phases may take place and evolve in parallel depending on factors such as the scale and complexity of the enterprise.

Figure 3.2 The TOGAF ADM

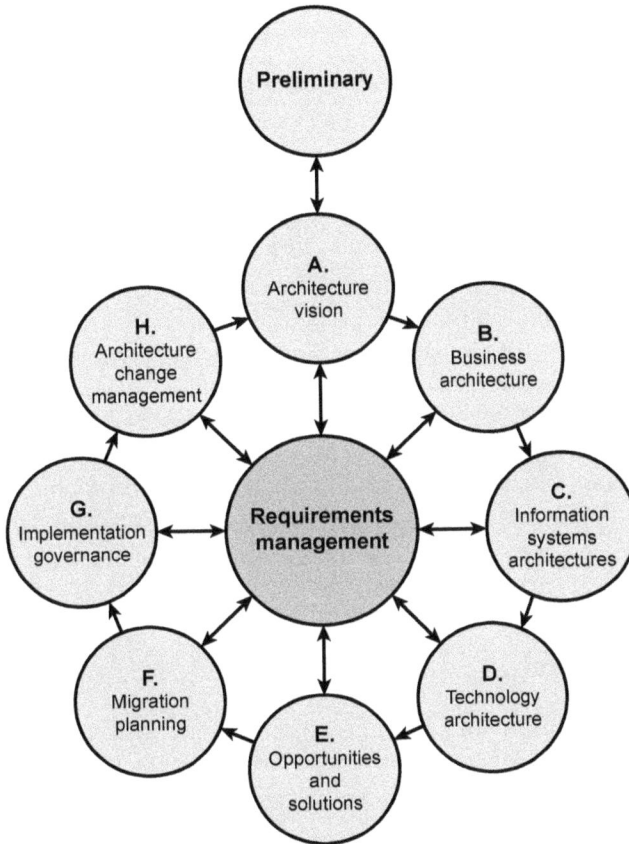

Table 3.3 Phases of the TOGAF ADM (TOGAF is a registered trademark of The Open Group.)

Phase	Description
Preliminary	This phase establishes the scope, approach and principles by which decisions are to be made about the development and management of EA. It is the phase where the governance approach to EA development is agreed.
A – Vision	This phase concerns the definition of the scope and goal of an EA development and the related 'architecture vision'.
B – Business architecture	This phase concerns the development of the business architecture blueprints in line with the EA vision, scope and principles.
C – Information systems architectures	This phase concerns the development of the information systems architecture. This includes the applications architecture and the data architecture.

(Continued)

Table 3.3 (Continued)

Phase	Description
D – Technology architecture	This phase concerns the development of the technology architecture for the enterprise.
E – Opportunities and solutions	This phase concerns the analysis of the opportunities and solutions offered by the EA and the other architecture domains.
F – Migration planning	This phase is concerned with planning the migration to the EA. Considerations include the selection of a migration strategy and identification of the roles required for the successful migration.
G – Implementation governance	This phase is concerned with the governance of the architecture implementation. This is where the approach to governance (agreed within the preliminary phase) is applied.
H – Architecture change management	This phase concerns ensuring the architecture changes evolve with the changing needs of the organisation.
Requirements management	This central phase ensures that the business requirements are elicited, understood, recorded and managed. The business requirements drive all the other phases of the ADM.

AssistKD POPIT model

The AssistKD POPIT model shown in Figure 3.3 provides a means from which to consider and analyse a holistic business system. The model can be used for a variety of purposes including:

- business situation investigation and analysis;
- TOM definition and analysis;
- gap analysis (through comparison of the current and target states);
- scope definition;
- option identification and analysis;
- impact and risk analysis.

The POPIT model dimensions are described in Table 3.4.

Any change to any of the individual elements of POPIT could potentially impact on another element. For example, if a new strategy (part of the organisation element) is introduced, there may be an effect on any or all of the people, process, information and technology elements; if the technology architecture in an organisation is changed, the value streams and processes supported by this technology are likely to require change.

POPIT promotes a holistic view, so reduces any tendency to focus on just one aspect of an enterprise or business architecture. This contrasts with TOGAF, which is often associated with technology architecture due to its information technology origins.

Figure 3.3 The AssistKD POPIT model

Table 3.4 Description of the POPIT model dimensions

POPIT element	Description
People	This element considers the people element of a business system. This concerns the knowledge, skills and motivation of those working within the organisation.
Organisation	This element considers the organisational element of a business system. This includes the strategy, structure, roles and responsibilities, and culture of the organisation plus the partners and suppliers within the wider ecosystem.
Process	This element considers the process element of a business system. This includes the clarity, efficiency and effectiveness of the value streams and processes in achieving the business outcomes.
Information	This element considers the information element of a business system. This includes the capture, storage and usage of information and data. The security of information assets is also considered.
Technology	This element considers the technology element of a business system. This includes the technical infrastructure, software applications and any equipment used within the organisation.

The Business Architecture Guild's Business Architecture Body of Knowledge (BIZBOK)

The following is presented with permission from the Business Architecture Guild.

The Business Architecture Guild's *A Guide to the Business Architecture Body of Knowledge* (BIZBOK Guide) includes a framework that represents the domains of business

41

architecture (see Figure 3.4). The BIZBOK also provides example reference models for various industries.

Figure 3.4 The BIZBOK representation of domains represented by business architecture (Source: Business Architecture Guild, BIZBOK Guide, Part 1: Introduction)

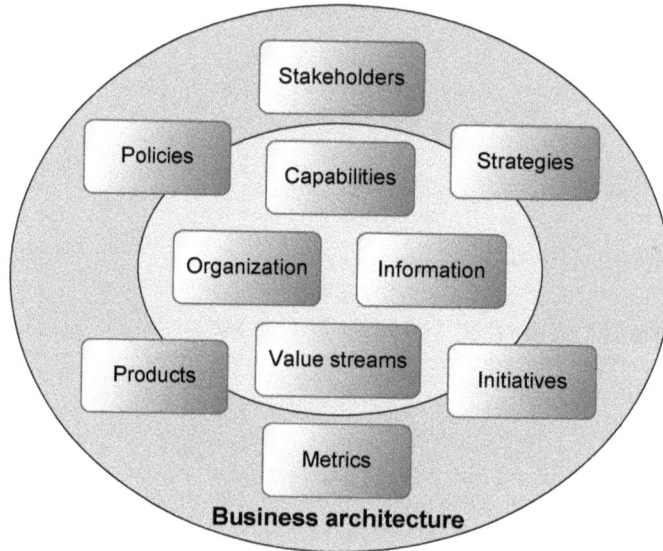

The BIZBOK describes how business architecture domains interact with related architectural disciplines. This includes provision of guidance for business architects that supports the alignment of their work with that of enterprise architects using TOGAF and ArchiMate. This guidance has been developed through collaboration between the Business Architecture Guild and The Open Group.

The BIZBOK identifies the following domains as core to business architecture:

- capabilities;
- organisation;
- information;
- value streams.

These core business architecture domains are described in Table 3.5.

The BIZBOK also identifies the following extended business architecture domains:

- stakeholders;
- strategies;

- initiatives;
- metrics;
- products;
- policies.

These are described in Table 3.6.

Table 3.5 Core business architecture domains defined by the Business Architecture Guild (Source: Business Architecture Guild, A Guide to the Business Architecture Body of Knowledge)

Domain	Description
Capabilities	These are abilities or capacities that an organisation may possess or exchange to achieve a specific purpose or outcome.
	BIZBOK reference: Homann, 2006.
Organisation	These are social units of people who are systematically structured and managed to meet a need or to pursue collective goals on a continuing basis.
Information	This is data that has been verified to be accurate and timely, is specific and organised for a purpose, is presented within a context that gives it meaning and relevance and that can lead to an increase in understanding and decrease in uncertainty.
Value streams	These are end-to-end collections of activities that create a result for a customer, who may be the ultimate customer or an internal end user of the value stream.
	BIZBOK reference: Martin, 1995.

Table 3.6 Additional business architecture domains defined by the Business Architecture Guild (Source: Business Architecture Guild, A Guide to the Business Architecture Body of Knowledge)

Domain	Description
Stakeholders	These are internal or external individuals or organisations with a vested interest in achieving value through a particular outcome.
Strategies	These are patterns or plans that integrate an organisation's major goals, policies and actions into a cohesive whole.
	BIZBOK reference: Quinn, 1980.
Initiatives	These are courses of action that are being executed or selected for execution.

(Continued)

Table 3.6 (Continued)

Domain	Description
Metrics	These are standards of measurement by which efficiency, performance, progress or quality of a plan, process or product can be assessed.
Products	Products can be goods or services, and are distinguished by tangibility: goods are tangible and services are intangible. From the customer perspective, the product is the overall customer experience provided by a combination of goods and services to satisfy the customer needs.
	BIZBOK reference: Geracie and Eppinger, 2013.
Policies	These are courses or principles of action adoption by a government, party, business or individual.

Understanding business architecture domains is only part of the business architecture story. Leveraging them requires a foundational framework, as shown in Figure 3.5.

Figure 3.5 The Business Architecture Guild's Business Architecture Framework
(Source: Business Architecture Guild, BIZBOK Guide, Part 1: Introduction)

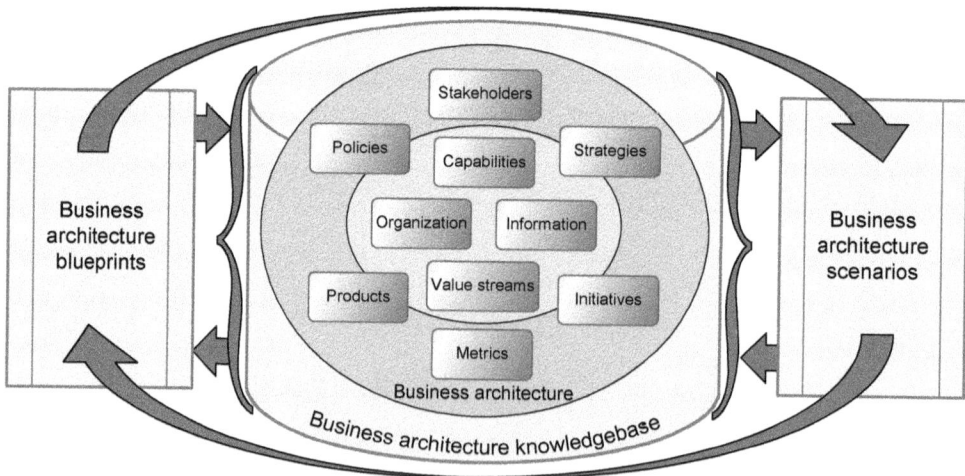

The Business Architecture Guild's Business Architecture Framework shown in Figure 3.5 does not impose restrictions on a practice. Rather, the framework provides a foundation that organisations can build upon to leverage business architecture to meet real-world challenges. The three main framework components are the business architecture knowledgebase, where business architecture and related business and IT domains reside, scenario library, with context specific usage guidelines, and the business architecture blueprints, offering canned and ad hoc perspectives useful in one or another business scenarios. The knowledgebase is structured to align to the Business Architecture Guild's metamodel.

SELECTING AN ARCHITECTURE FRAMEWORK

The frameworks described in this chapter offer a starting point when selecting or customising an architecture framework. They provide a basis for discussion and help to ensure coverage of the different views within a business architecture.

Table 3.7 provides a summary of the advantages and disadvantages of the frameworks discussed in this chapter.

Table 3.7 Advantages and disadvantages of the architecture frameworks

Framework	Advantages	Disadvantages
The Zachman Framework	• It provides a comprehensive means to classify knowledge of the organisation. • It enables insight into different perspectives of the organisation. • It breaks down the individual elements of the organisation into 'primitive' components – together these constitute the whole organisation. • It has stood the test of time. It can provide a foundation for communication and collaboration among enterprise and business architects.	• It does not provide a method or specify an approach to the EA work. • Due to its comprehensive nature, some stakeholders and business architecture practitioners can find the framework challenging to learn and apply. • Some practitioners perceive it as being overly theoretical.
TOGAF	• It is an open standard that is free to use. • It can be adapted to suit the needs of an organisation. • It is subject to continuous improvement/evolution. • It aligns with other Open Group standards such as ArchiMate.	• It may be necessary to modify and extend the ADM to meet organisation needs. • The creation and maintenance of the blueprints for each ADM phase is heavily dependent on active participation of key stakeholders.

(Continued)

Table 3.7 (Continued)

Framework	Advantages	Disadvantages
The AssistKD POPIT model	• It provides a holistic view of the business system. • It provides a standard language for the identification, analysis and discussion of elements of the business system. • It can be learned and applied quickly within a variety of contexts. • It provides a useful perspective to consider relative to the opportunity and impact of change.	• It offers an overview definition of the five POPIT elements, so requires further definition when used to create business architecture blueprints.
BIZBOK	• It provides a detailed and comprehensive view of business architecture blueprints. • It provides example industry reference models. • It is subject to continuous improvement/evolution. • It provides a standard language and suite of blueprints.	• It has been criticised for offering a prescriptive view of how to apply business architecture. • Due to its comprehensive nature, some stakeholders and business architects can find the framework challenging to learn and apply.

The framework adopted by an organisation should support the achievement of business outcomes and the acquisition, retention and retrieval of knowledge about the architecture of the organisation. An adapted framework that is relevant to the organisation context may be more practical than complete adoption of a specific framework across the organisation. A balanced, adaptable framework that has been blended from relevant elements of the available frameworks is typically the best approach.

ADOPTING AN ARCHITECTURE FRAMEWORK

Ensuring alignment to an architecture framework can improve communication, collaboration and resource integration within an organisation's internal and external ecosystems. For example, if the organisation aligns with a framework that is recognised and used by external partners and suppliers, this can ensure standard blueprints are used to communicate with the different parties. The use of a recognised framework may also enhance the credibility of the business architecture work, as it reassures stakeholders that good practice has been adopted.

There needs to be careful consideration of the context, in particular the organisation's culture, strategy and resources where the framework will be used, when preparing to adopt an architecture framework. Considerations for adopting a framework are discussed in Table 3.8.

Table 3.8 Considerations for adopting architecture frameworks

Consideration	Description
Why	• Why is a framework being adopted or adapted for use within the organisation? • Does the application of a framework aid the organisation to achieve strategic goals and objectives? • What stakeholder concerns or issues might the application of a framework address?
What	• What are the organisation's requirements for a framework? • Will the organisation adapt a single framework or apply multiple frameworks? • What aspects of the available framework(s) will be adopted? • What impediments are likely to be encountered when using the framework?
How	• How will a framework be adapted for use within the organisation? • How will the application of a framework affect existing processes? • Is the application of the framework within the organisation practical? • How will any impediments or resistance to the framework be overcome? • Does the organisation's culture align or misalign with the proposed use of a framework? • Does the language used within the framework align with the language of the organisation? • How will the application of a framework fit relative to other architectural domains and change disciplines? • How will lessons be learned and the application of the framework improved for the future?
Who	• Will stakeholders support the application of a framework? • Are business architecture practitioners within the organisation sufficiently skilled and competent in the use of a selected framework? • Are sufficient resources available to enable the adoption and continued use of framework? • Are the cultural conditions within the organisation likely to enable or inhibit the use of any chosen framework? • Do the individuals implementing the chosen framework have sufficient leadership support?

(Continued)

Table 3.8 (Continued)

Consideration	Description
When	• When will the framework be adopted? • Will the framework be applied solely to new strategic and tactical decisions and change initiatives? • Will there be retrospective application of the framework on previous strategic and tactical decisions?
Where	• Where in the organisation will the framework be applied? • Will the framework apply across the entire organisation or will it be restricted to a specific geographical location or division?

It may be necessary to start applying a framework on a relatively contained basis. This can help to build competence and confidence in the use of the framework. A targeted approach can yield valuable lessons and insights that support the wider implementation of a framework.

BUSINESS ARCHITECTURE VIEWS

Business architecture views provide information about an organisation that is meaningful for a stakeholder or group of stakeholders.

ISO/IEC/IEEE 42010:2022 defines a view as:

> A view presents a specific set of architectural information to a standard dictated by the template of the viewpoint.

A view is a representation of a specific perspective for an organisation and offers key stakeholders, such as business executives, a means of understanding that perspective. Views are conceptual or abstract representations. They are not models of the physical, real-world business system. Each view of an organisation is represented using one or more business architecture blueprints.

A collection of views enables a holistic perspective and provides visibility of the underlying architecture of an organisation. Combining and linking views, and the associated blueprints, aids with building shared understanding among stakeholders and supports strategic and tactical decision-making. They also provide clarity regarding complex business situations.

The key business architecture views are identified in Table 3.9.

Relevant business architecture blueprints are developed and made available to the key stakeholders. They are cross-referenced to each other to ensure consistency and completeness. This work highlights where there are any gaps in organisational competency (see Chapter 8) and where opportunities for product or service development

Table 3.9 Key business architecture views

View	Definition
Motivation view	This focuses on the strategic drivers, or 'why?', for the organisation. It considers key organisational drivers including senior stakeholder perspectives, strategic decision-making and external environmental factors. The core purpose and values of the organisation are also considered. See Chapter 4 for further information.
Organisation view	This focuses on 'how?' the organisation is organised. It considers aspects such as the structure of the organisation, its internal and external ecosystem and culture. See Chapter 4 for further information.
Capability view	This focuses on 'what?' the organisation can do. It considers the ability an organisation possesses to perform specific areas of work. See Chapter 5 for further information.
Value/service view	This focuses on 'what?' the organisation does to offer services to customers. It considers the activities conducted to deliver products and services, the service value propositions, customer experiences and value networks. See Chapter 6 for further information.
Information view	This focuses on 'what?' information and data is important to the organisation. See Chapter 7 for further information.
People view	This focuses on the organisational competency. It considers the skills of the people within an organisation. See Chapter 8 for further information.

exist (see Chapter 6). Once created, the business architecture blueprints must be maintained so that they provide up-to-date views on the organisation.

When considering a change in strategic direction, the relevant views are used to assess the impact of the proposed change in the light of the organisation's business capabilities and value streams. Similarly, should an organisation be considering a merger or acquisition, the relevant blueprints may be used to identify differences and duplication between the respective organisations and their business architectures.

BUSINESS ARCHITECTURE BLUEPRINTS

The business architecture 'blueprints' represent the different views of an organisation. The blueprints are used to promote clarity and shared understanding. They support business stakeholders with various activities including decision-making, impact analysis and risk assessment. Stakeholders using these blueprints include senior executives, managers, change managers and business analysts.

The view presented by a single blueprint is limited to a particular perspective, so is sufficient to cover the scope of an entire business architecture. As George Box famously stated (Box, 1979): 'All models are wrong, but some are useful.'

Across several key frameworks, a standard set of core business architecture blueprints has emerged. Each captures organisational knowledge and is produced and maintained as a business architecture output. The key blueprints are defined in Table 3.10.

Table 3.10 Key business architecture blueprints

Blueprint	Description
VMOST definition	This defines the vision, mission, objectives, strategy and tactics either for the organisation as a whole or for an area of the organisation such as a department, function or team.
	See Chapter 4 for further information.
Internal and external ecosystem diagram	This represents the entities, and the associations between those entities, within an organisation's internal or external ecosystem.
	See Chapter 4 for further information.
Organisational chart	This represents the arrangement and structure of the departments, functions and teams within an organisation.
	See Chapter 4 for further information.
Business model	This represents the way in which the organisation is designed to deliver products and/or services.
	See Chapter 4 for further information.
Value network diagram	This represents the tangible and intangible value exchanges between entities or service systems within an ecosystem, organisation or department.
	See Chapter 6 for further information.

(Continued)

Table 3.10 (Continued)

Blueprint	Description
Value chain model	This represents the primary and support activities within an organisation that are involved in the delivery of its products and services. See Chapter 6 for further information.
Value stream diagram	This shows the key activities undertaken to deliver a product or service to a customer. See Chapter 6 for further information.
Business capability model	This shows all the areas of work that an organisation has the ability to perform. See Chapter 5 for further information.
Business information model	This shows the key information concepts, and the associations between them, for an organisation. See Chapter 7 for further information.

Aligning blueprints with principles

The work conducted by business architects should be aligned with the business architecture principles discussed in Chapter 1. The application of a framework, including the creation of blueprints that represent the business architecture views, should also adhere to these principles.

Table 3.11 explains how the core principles should relate to the selected business architecture framework and the blueprints developed to represent the different business architecture views.

BUSINESS ARCHITECTURE TOOLS

Business architecture tools support the creation, retention, management and retrieval of business architecture blueprints. They provide a highly scalable support mechanism that helps to reduce effort in the development and maintenance of architecture blueprints. Business architecture blueprints may contain sensitive information, and support tools offer essential security features that control access and ensure that this is only granted where appropriate.

Tools help business architects to be more accurate and efficient when creating and updating business architecture blueprints, offering functionality that enables model development and cross-referencing of related blueprints. This can be vital when evaluating proposed changes. For example, a tool may identify all value streams and processes potentially impacted by a change to a business capability. Similarly, impact

Table 3.11 Application of business architecture principles to the business architecture framework and blueprints

Business architecture principle	Implication for blueprints or frameworks
1. Business architecture promotes the long-term health of the organisation.	The adoption of a framework is a strategic decision that has the potential to enhance the health of the organisation over the long term. The blueprints developed help to clarify the business architecture and so provide a basis for communication with stakeholders. They also enable impact and risk analysis when evaluating proposed changes.
2. Business architecture is holistic.	The adoption of a framework, and the creation of the specified blueprints, should provide a holistic view of the organisation.
3. Business architecture is outcome focused.	The adoption of a framework, and the creation of the specified blueprints, should enable and support the organisation to achieve business outcomes.
4. Business architecture supports value co-creation.	The adoption of a framework, and the creation of the specified blueprints, should clarify the value propositions offered by the organisation, the value stream activities required to deliver the products and services and the capabilities required to co-create value.
5. Business architecture is context dependent.	The adoption of a framework should be evaluated with regard to the organisational context and the business environment within which it operates.
6. Business architecture is knowledge based.	The adoption of a framework, and the creation of the associated blueprints, should support the acquisition, retention and retrieval of organisational knowledge.
7. Business architecture evolves iteratively.	The adoption of a framework, and the creation of the associated blueprints, should provide a basis for the iterative development and enhancement of the business architecture.
8. Business architecture blueprints support change evaluation.	The adoption of a framework, and the creation of the associated blueprints, enables and supports the evaluation of change proposals and initiatives.

and risk assessments may be completed more quickly where tools are used to analyse and report the impacts of proposed changes on multiple connected blueprints.

Tools can also increase the quality and speed of stakeholder communication through their ability to transform information quickly into a view that is meaningful for a particular stakeholder. Some tools may be customised to store information and deliver reports that address key stakeholder concerns.

The quality of the insights provided by a tool is dependent upon the information recorded within the tool. In line with any support tools or software applications, if insufficient time has been invested in entering information into a tool, inaccurate insights are likely to result. However, a carefully selected tool that has been implemented with care can generate patterns and insights that would otherwise have been missed. These insights can have a positive impact on decision-making and reduce costs.

Some tools align with standard frameworks and associated notations, which can ensure consistency regarding the architecture activities and blueprints across the organisation. Such alignment can also foster clear understanding for those familiar with a particular standard, and can be helpful when building competency on how to use a framework.

CONCLUSION

Architectural frameworks provide guidance on the activities and blueprints to be created by practitioners within the different architecture domains. Some, such as the Zachman Framework, encompass the entire enterprise while others, such as the BIZBOK, focus specifically on one domain. Some, such as the AssistKD POPIT model, provide a taxonomy of concerns while others, such as TOGAF, provide a direction of travel that links the different activities and blueprints. Given these differences, organisations often apply a blended approach, selecting the frameworks and elements that are most relevant to the specific context.

Adoption and adaptation of one or more of the available business or enterprise architecture frameworks can speed up the organisation of business architecture knowledge and application of the business architecture discipline.

4 MOTIVATION AND ORGANISATIONAL VIEW OF BUSINESS ARCHITECTURE

INTRODUCTION

This chapter introduces the motivation and organisational views of business architecture. It covers the following topics:

- rationale for business motivation analysis;
- core purpose and core values;
- techniques for business motivation analysis;
- knowledge management and organisational memory;
- business model analysis;
- organisation structures;
- ecosystem analysis;
- organisational culture.

RATIONALE FOR BUSINESS MOTIVATION ANALYSIS

Chapter 1 explained that business architecture aims to improve the long-term health of an organisation. One way that it seeks to achieve this objective is through ensuring alignment and shared understanding of the organisation's responses to the questions:

- Why does this organisation exist?
- What does the organisation do?
- How does the organisation carry out its work?

Simon Sinek advocates that organisations should 'start with why'. He contends that this helps to increase alignment and engagement from both employees and external stakeholders such as customers (Sinek, 2009).

If stakeholders have different views on the 'why?' for the organisation, this is likely to cause inconsistency in the answers to 'what?' and 'how?' As a consequence, there is a greater risk of non-aligned strategic and tactical decision-making.

If non-aligned decision-making persists, there are likely to be several negative consequences, including:

- Increased disagreement on strategic goals and priorities. This may cause either open or hidden conflict between stakeholders. For example, senior stakeholders may disagree on decisions regarding the allocation of the organisation's resources and possess differing views on the organisation's strategic direction. Such disagreements can undermine collaboration among employees and have a negative impact on trust.

- Reduced transparency in decision-making. In order to reduce the potential for conflict, stakeholders may stop sharing information and discussing individual decisions. In the short term, this can help to reduce disagreements as stakeholders are not able to question the basis for the decisions. However, over the longer term, there is increased potential for misaligned decision-making, a reduction in collaboration towards achieving shared goals and an increase in organisational complexity.

- Decreased motivation for employees working on seemingly non-aligned work. Where employees do not understand the 'why?' for their work, including how this aligns with the overall strategic direction of the organisation, individuals may be demotivated and fail to achieve the organisational, and their personal, objectives.

- Diminished alignment between the organisation's products and services. This is likely to cause duplication of either entire products or services or individual elements. Over time this can result in a negative impact on customer experience and increase long-term costs.

If, in contrast, an organisation has stakeholders with aligned views on the 'why?' for the organisation, consistent and aligned decision-making is likely to result.

If aligned decision-making persists over an extended period of time there will be several positive consequences, including:

- Increased collaboration towards strategic priorities: this is likely to cause synergy in the allocation and application of the organisation's resources.

- Strengthened transparency in decision-making: this is necessary to achieve alignment to strategic goals and priorities. Over the longer term, this can lead to increased employee empowerment and additional aligned decisions. There is the potential that, as a result, an upward spiral of improvement develops. This could help to reduce organisational complexity and enhance customer experiences when engaging with the organisation.

- Increased motivation for individuals working on aligned change initiatives: individuals have a greater understanding of the context, and typically have an increased sense of purpose and find their work to be more rewarding, if they understand the 'why?' for the organisation and appreciate how this relates to its strategic direction.

- Increased alignment between the organisation's products and services: this is likely to positively affect the consistency of customer experience and reduce cost overheads.

CORE PURPOSE AND CORE VALUES

Business architects seeking to understand the motivation of an organisation should also consider the influence of the organisation's core values and core purpose on strategic and tactical decision-making. Collins and Porras state that 'Companies that enjoy enduring success have core values and a core purpose that remain fixed while their business strategies and practices endlessly adapt to a changing world' (Collins and Porras, 2000). These two concepts are defined within Table 4.1.

Table 4.1 Core purpose and core values (Source: Adapted from Collins and Porras, 2000)

Concept	Definition
Core purpose	The organisation's fundamental reason for being.
Core values	The handful of principles that guide how a company acts and operates. Core values may or may not be written down.

The core purpose and core values of an organisation typically originate from the original founders or its current or former senior leadership team. Accordingly, they are a form of corporate tacit knowledge, are often undocumented and may even be unrecognised. An iterative process of investigation, discussion and reflection with senior leaders may be required to clarify an organisation's core purpose and values.

For example, if the core purpose of a department store is to provide unique, high-quality products and services, and a decision is required regarding investment into a capability, product or service, the approach taken to this decision may be very different from that taken for an organisation where the core purpose is to establish a profitable business in order to sell to an investor.

Where business architects are unaware of, or misunderstand, their organisation's core purpose and core values, their ability to collaborate effectively with stakeholders and influence decision-making may be diminished.

TECHNIQUES FOR BUSINESS MOTIVATION ANALYSIS

Business motivation analysis is concerned with investigating and understanding the core purpose of an organisation and the rationale for the strategic and tactical decisions made. A variety of techniques can be used to conduct business motivation analysis, including:

- VMOST (vision, mission, objectives, strategy and tactics) analysis;
- Object Management Group (OMG) Business Motivation Model (BMM);
- stakeholder perspective analysis.

VMOST analysis

VMOST analysis can be used independently or in combination with stakeholder perspective analysis. The elements of VMOST analysis are described in Table 4.2 and an example VMOST analysis for a department store is shown in Table 4.3.

Table 4.2 VMOST analysis (Source: Adapted from Paul and Cadle, 2020)

VMOST element	Description
Vision	This defines the aspirational target state for the organisation without regard to how this will be achieved. The state should be realised through the accomplishment of the 'mission'.
Mission	This defines what the organisation does or will do to support the achievement of the 'vision' for the organisation.
Objectives	This defines specific objectives or outcomes. These are used to guide and measure progress towards the accomplishment of the 'mission' and ultimate achievement of the 'vision'.
Strategy	This describes the organisation's long-term approach and plan for achieving the 'objectives'.
Tactics	This describes the specific and detailed means by which the strategy will be executed. The tactics are adapted when feedback is received.

Table 4.3 VMOST example

VMOST element	Description
Vision	To be the shopping destination of choice for the discerning shopper.
Mission	To provide access to an exclusive range of products and services while delivering outstanding customer experience in-store and online.
Objectives	• To increase operating profit by 8% per annum. • To increase year on year sales volumes by 10%. • To achieve a 98% customer satisfaction rating in the annual customer satisfaction survey.
Strategy	• To ensure operating costs are controlled and enable competitive pricing. • To offer a value proposition based on unique product choice, timely product availability and excellent customer experience.
Tactics	• To work proactively with partners, suppliers and employees to ensure process efficiency. • To collaborate with innovative and well-regarded partners and suppliers to continually improve the product portfolio. • To implement performance rewards based on the achievement of customer satisfaction objectives.

VMOST supports analysis and discussion of the organisation's plans for success. This analysis can be conducted against the entire organisation, an individual team or department or a product or service offering. Example questions for each of the VMOST elements are shown in Table 4.4.

Table 4.4 VMOST analysis example questions (Source: Adapted from Paul and Cadle, 2020)

VMOST element	Example analysis and discussion questions
Vision	• What is the vision for the organisation? • Are the stakeholders' views regarding the vision aligned?
Mission	• What should the organisation do to achieve the vision? • Are the stakeholders' views regarding the required action aligned?
Objectives	• Are the objectives aligned to the 'vision' and 'mission'? • Are objectives SMART (specific, measurable, attainable, relevant and time bound)? • Will achieving the objectives indicate accomplishment of the mission in line with the stated vision for the organisation? • Are the objectives balanced? For example, so they address the four elements of the Balanced Scorecard (BSC). These elements are Financial, Internal Business Process, Learning and Growth or Innovation and Customer (Kaplan and Norton, 1996).
Strategy	• What strategic options are available to achieve the vision, mission and objectives? • What are the advantages and disadvantages of the strategic options?
Tactics	• What tactical options must be deployed to achieve the strategy? • What are the advantages and disadvantages of different tactics?

VMOST can also be used to analyse the alignment of individual products and services, departments, capabilities or change initiatives and the overall organisational VMOST. This is represented in Figure 4.1.

When analysing the VMOST applied at the more granular levels shown within Figure 4.1, the business architect may find that there is alignment with the organisation's VMOST; however, the business architect may find misalignment between the organisational VMOST and that for an individual product, service, department, capability or change initiative. Recognising this misalignment will help to identify where change is needed.

Where there are aligned views on VMOST across the organisation, there is the potential for significant strategic advantage, as all stakeholders are aiming to achieve the same business outcomes and agree on the way to do this.

Figure 4.1 Levels of VMOST analysis

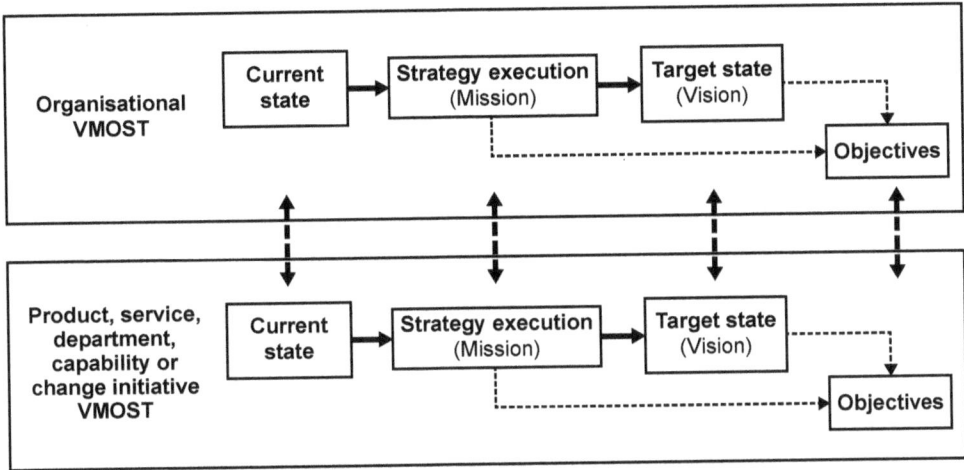

Object Management Group Business Motivation Model

Figure 4.2 shows the OMG BMM version 1.3, which provides a framework for analysing business motivation.

Figure 4.2 OMG BMM overview (Reproduced with permission; adapted from Business Motivation Model Standard 1.3 (p. 22) http://omg.org/)

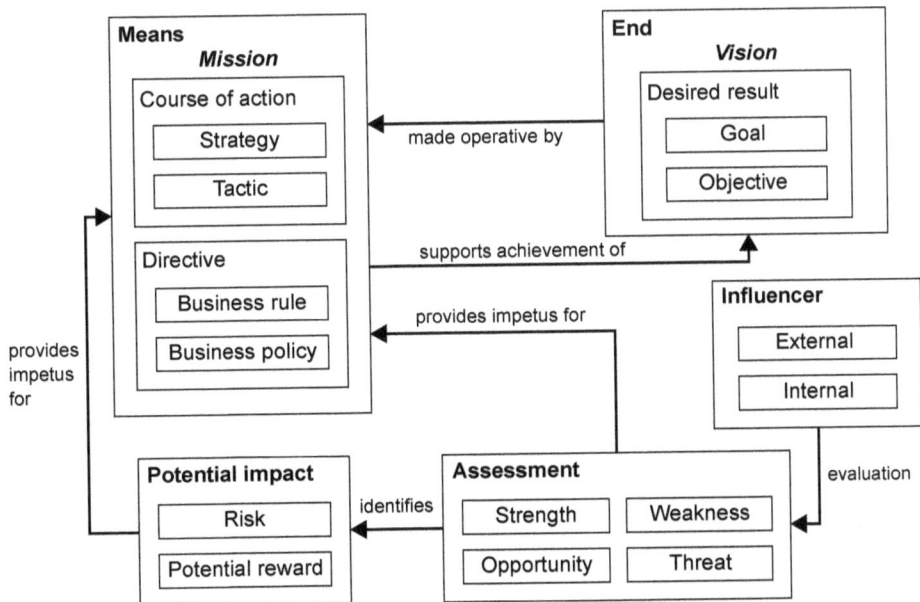

The BMM extends VMOST analysis to include additional aspects such as possible internal and external influences on the organisation and an evaluation of their potential impact. The BMM elements are described in Table 4.5.

Table 4.5 BMM elements

Element	Definition
Vision	A vision describes the future state of the enterprise, without regard to how it is achieved.
Desired result	A 'desired result' is an 'end' that is a state or target that the enterprise intends to maintain or sustain. It is supported by 'courses of action' and includes two lower-level concepts ('goals' and 'objectives').
Goal	A goal is a longer-term qualitative and general (non-specific) statement of a desired outcome. This provides greater detail than in comparison to the vision and in effect amplifies it.
	A goal is narrow in focus and should be quantified by objectives. It is a concept that is often equated to a 'critical success factor'.
Objective	An objective is a statement of an attainable, time-targeted, specific and measurable outcome that the organisation seeks in order to meet its specified goals.
	It will ideally meet the criteria outlined by the acronym SMART. The concept may be correlated with 'key performance indicators'.
Mission	A mission is a definition of what the organisation does or will do as the means of achieving the 'vision'.
Course of action	A course of action is an approach or plan for changing an aspect of the organisation (such as a product, service, capability or department) that is targeted towards the achievement of 'desired results'. It includes the two lower-level concepts of 'strategy' and 'tactic'.
Strategy	A strategy is the organisation's long-term plan for successful achievement of the 'objectives', and the corresponding delivery of the 'mission' and the ultimate 'vision'.
Tactic	Tactics are the specific and detailed means by which the strategy will be executed. The tactics are often adapted when feedback regarding the success of the strategy is received.
Directive	A 'directive' indicates how courses of action should or should not be carried out. They govern courses of action. This element includes the two lower-level concepts of 'business rule' and 'business policy'.

(Continued)

Table 4.5 (Continued)

Element	Definition
Business rule	A business rule is the structured, enforceable, discrete and atomic statement focused on a specific aspect of governance or guidance that limits or constrains how things are done (courses of action).
Business policy	A business policy is the broad statement of governance or guidance whose purpose is to control and shape the organisation's strategy and tactics. Business policies provide a basis for the development of business rules.
Influencer	Influencers are the internal and external forces that influence or impact an enterprise. • **Internal** influencers originate from within an enterprise. • **External** influencers originate outside the organisational boundary.
Assessment	An assessment is the evaluation of an organisation's ability to carry out its mission (means) and support the achievement of its vision (ends). Assessments identify the organisation's strengths and weaknesses, and the opportunities and threats the organisation is facing or may face in the future. • **Strength:** an area of capability possessed by the organisation. • **Weakness:** an area where the organisation lacks capability. • **Opportunity:** an influence from the external business environment that offers the potential for the organisation to gain a positive outcome. • **Threat:** an influence from the external business environment that offers the potential for the organisation to be subject to a negative outcome.
Potential impact	The evaluation identifies the impact or potential impact of an influencer on the organisation's ends and means. • **Risks:** the possible negative impacts that may cause difficulty or loss for the organisation. • **Rewards:** the possible positive impacts that may arise for the organisation.

Stakeholder perspective analysis

Business architects need to identify relevant stakeholders and analyse their views in order to help facilitate and influence their strategic and tactical decisions. Paul and Cadle (2020) explain that stakeholder perspectives on a situation should be analysed in order to understand their attitudes, values and beliefs and identify the most appropriate stakeholder engagement approaches.

Checkland's Soft Systems Methodology (Checkland, 1999) includes the CATWOE technique, which is used to analyse stakeholder perspective. Each of the CATWOE elements are described in Table 4.6.

Table 4.6 CATWOE elements (Source: Adapted from Paul and Cadle, 2020)

Element	Description
(C) Customer	The beneficiaries, victims or recipients of business system outputs.
(A) Actor	The actors that carry out transformation activities.
(T) Transformation	The core business activity of the business system that converts the inputs into the outputs.
(W) Worldview	The worldview of a stakeholder that encapsulates the stakeholder's beliefs about the business system, including why it exists, the priorities and the values.
(O) Owner	The person or group who ultimately controls the business system. They are able to instigate business system changes or even close the business system.
(E) Environment	The external and internal organisational factors that constrain the business system.

CATWOE analysis can provide insight into a stakeholder's view of an organisation and the motivation that underlies the organisation's strategic position. Table 4.7 contains two example CATWOE analyses for a department store.

Table 4.7 describes two different perspectives held by stakeholders within the department store example. These perspectives may be reflected in their approaches to change and the decisions they make. For example, the operations director has a relatively short-term perspective, so may not support business change initiatives that require significant upfront investment and are projected to lead to tangible benefits in three to five years' time. This change proposal may even be opposed by the director because it is perceived to be a threat to their personal objective regarding retirement. In contrast, the customer experience director may be more inclined to take a longer-term view and decide to support this investment opportunity.

In some situations, stakeholders may have different perspectives leading to different views on how the vision for the organisation may be achieved. For example, the vision shown in Table 4.3 states 'To be the shopping destination of choice for the discerning shopper', but this may be viewed as:

- a department store where the products sold are expensive and have a scarcity value;
- a department store where the products sold are sourced from socially responsible manufacturers;
- a department store where the products sold are from current, popular brands.

Table 4.7 CATWOE analysis example

	Operations director	Customer experience director
C	New and established customers that want access to purchase the store's products and services.	
A	Personable and professional sales staff; cost-conscious purchasing staff; warehousing and logistics staff.	
T	Sell exclusive products via a streamlined and cost-efficient sales operation.	Sell exclusive products via a high-quality, personalised customer sales experience.
W	Streamlined, cost-effective sales processes will meet customer requirements and will lead to increased profits and share price. This will provide financial security when I sell my shares and retire in two years' time.	Discerning customers want to feel valued and, as a result, will purchase more products. Enhancing the customer experience will increase the loyalty of our customers and enhance the organisation's brand and reputation over the longer term.
O	George H. Blundell, CEO and majority shareholder.	
E	Fierce competition in the retail sector; increased availability of innovative technologies; pressure to enhance the sustainability of retail operations; desire of customers for exclusive products; sufficient disposable income available to purchase exclusive products.	

Similarly, when considering the goal of achieving growth for the department store, there could be several alternative shareholder perspectives that affect both the target state vision and how this state may be achieved. Figure 4.3 identifies three different business development strategies that may be applied to achieve the target state and defined growth objective. These three strategies are described, with proposed tactics, in Table 4.8.

Figure 4.3 Target state strategic options

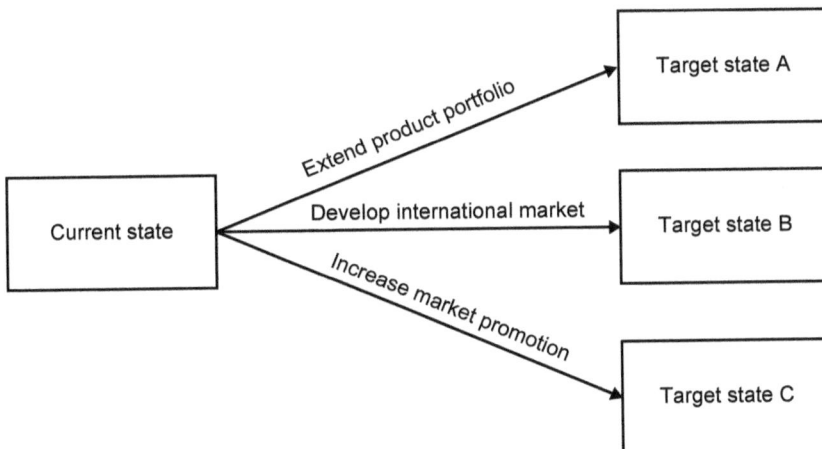

Table 4.8 Strategic perspectives on achieving the vision (target state)

Strategy	Perspective
Product development	The best way to achieve growth for the department store is to extend the product portfolio. This could be achieved by acquiring a competitor that offers complementary additional products.
Market development	The best way to achieve growth for the department store is to enter an international market. This would extend the territory covered by the organisation and could be achieved by establishing a physical presence in an overseas market.
Market penetration	The best way to achieve growth for the department store is to increase/enhance promotion within the current market. This would provide a basis for increasing the customer base and, as a result, increase the volume of in-store and online sales.

The examples shown in Table 4.8 highlight different perspectives regarding the department store and the visions for the future. It is usually beneficial to explore individual perspectives to highlight and resolve differences in stakeholder views. If embarking on a transformation programme, having stakeholders with contrasting perspectives on the desired destination would be a major impediment to a successful outcome. Therefore, understanding these different perspectives, and the impact they may have on any business transformation, provides insights into how to manage the different views and the key areas of disagreement or conflict.

If a business architect is able to identify and understand the perspectives and motivations of stakeholders that are involved in or could influence decisions, they can use this information to tailor how they engage with those stakeholders and help to facilitate coherent strategic and tactical decisions.

KNOWLEDGE MANAGEMENT AND ORGANISATIONAL MEMORY

All organisations acquire, develop, retain, share and deploy knowledge about a range of aspects such as the business environment, the operational business processes and practices and the cultural values and beliefs. This knowledge may be recorded formally so that it may be accessed and applied, or it may be held much more informally and may be difficult to uncover. Table 4.9 identifies four knowledge categories and examples of where they may be found.

Table 4.9 Tacit and explicit knowledge definitions (Source: Adapted from Paul and Cadle, 2020)

Level	Tacit	Explicit
Individual	Skills, values, taken-for-granted knowledge, intuitiveness	Task definitions, job descriptions, targets, volumes and frequencies
Corporate	Norms, culture, networks, organisation history, back-story	Procedures, style guides, processes, knowledge sharing repositories, manuals, company reports

Organisational memory encompasses the repository of data, information and knowledge created that develops across the time span of an organisation. Organisational memory may be defined formally as explicit knowledge or may be more subtle, the taken-for-granted tacit knowledge that is often held by individuals.

The concept of organisational memory is defined by Walsh and Ungson as 'Stored information from an organisation's history that can be brought to bear on present decisions' (Walsh and Ungson, 1991). Walsh and Ungson define three stages in the organisational memory development process. These stages are described in Table 4.10.

Table 4.10 Organisational memory process (Source: Adapted from Walsh and Ungson, 1991)

Stage	Description
Acquire	Information is acquired about the organisation; for example, regarding its business decisions, policies, rules, processes and products.
	Information is not centrally stored and is split across different knowledge repositories. These repositories may include individuals who gain information from their work experiences and interactions.
Retain	Over time, the following information areas are retained: • Individuals: the knowledge, skills and experiences and recollections of individual employees. • Culture: the working practices, values, behaviours, traditions, perspectives and beliefs of individuals within the organisation. • Transformations: the processes or systems for transformation that the organisation employs. These reflect past experiences and decisions and are repositories for embedded knowledge. • Structures: the formal and informal structures that link individuals to other individuals and the wider environment. • External archives: the memory of the organisation held by others in its external ecosystem; for example, former employees, customers, suppliers, partners and regulators.
Retrieve	Retained knowledge is retrieved, which may be either automatic or controlled. 'Automatic' refers to the intuitive and effortless process of accessing organisational memory, usually as part of an established sequence of action or habit. 'Controlled' refers to the deliberate action to access stored knowledge.

An organisation's business architecture is a source of information and organisational memory. As a consequence, business architecture blueprints and other knowledge repositories must be maintained to ensure that they provide accurate information. A business architecture can quickly become out of date, and offer diminished potential value, if it is not maintained and its currency assured.

The information held within a business architecture should be available to all appropriate stakeholders within the organisation's ecosystem. Where this is not the case, decision-making may be flawed and the potential value offered by the business architecture may not be realised.

BUSINESS MODEL ANALYSIS

A 'business model' describes the core logic of the way the organisation is designed and arranged to deliver its value proposition within the context of its ecosystem. An organisation's business model provides a means through which to develop, analyse and execute the organisation's strategy.

There are many different views on the specific components or elements that should be included within a business model. Osterwalder and Pigneur (2010) provide a generic business model template known as the Business Model Canvas (BMC). The structure and content of the BMC is shown in Figure 4.4.

Figure 4.4 Structure and components of the BMC

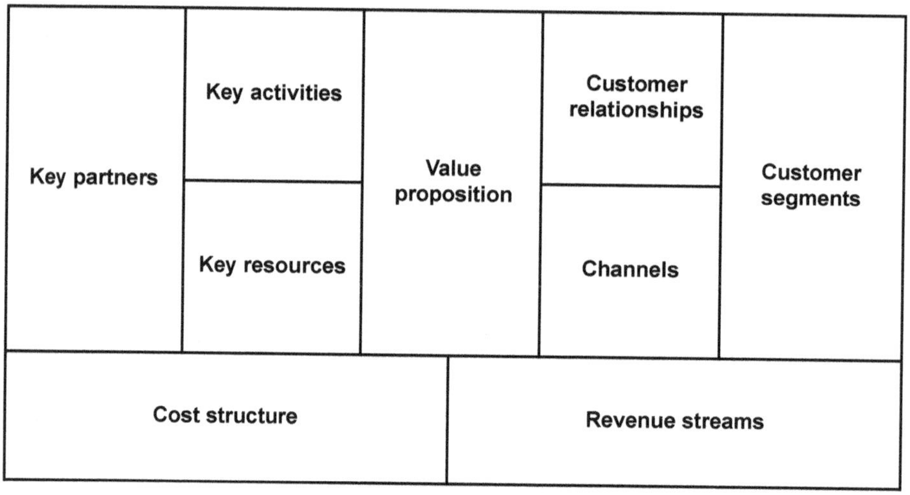

Key partners	Key activities	Value proposition	Customer relationships	Customer segments
	Key resources		Channels	
Cost structure			Revenue streams	

The BMC provides a basis for investigating and representing the organisation's business model. Questions relevant to each of the elements are described in Table 4.11, and an example BMC for a department store is shown in Figure 4.5.

It can be useful to consider techniques such as stakeholder perspective analysis, VMOST and BMM in combination with business model development and analysis; for example, different stakeholder perspectives would provide additional insights when considered during the analysis of the business model.

Table 4.11 The elements of the BMC

BMC element	Questions addressed
Customer segments	• Who are the organisation's important customers? • What are the wants and needs of customers? • What problems and opportunities do customers experience?
Value proposition	• What value does the organisation offer? • Which customer wants and needs do the products or services support or satisfy? • Which customer problems or opportunities does the value proposition solve? • What are the qualities offered by the products or services (for example, price, availability, choice, quality, functions supported)? • What is the organisation's brand or image?
Channels	• How does the organisation interact and communicate with customers? • Is there variance in customer experience across different channels? • Which channels work best? • What additional channels do customers expect?
Customer relationships	• What relationship does the organisation have with each customer segment? • How might customer experience be enhanced?
Revenue streams	• What are the organisation's revenue streams? • How profitable are each of these revenue streams? • How much does each revenue stream contribute? • Do the prices of the organisation's products and services require adjustment?
Key resources	• What key resources are required to support the organisation's value proposition?
Key activities	• What key activities support the organisation's value proposition?
Key partners	• Who are the organisation's key partners and suppliers? • Which key resources or key activities do key partners support?
Cost structure	• What are the costs of the key activities, key partners and key resources? • Is the cost model sustainable?

Figure 4.5 Example BMC for a department store

Key partners	Key activities	Value proposition	Customer relationships	Customer segments
Product suppliers Technology suppliers Landlords Advertising and marketing agencies Recruitment agencies	Supplier management Product purchasing Infrastructure management Sales and customer service	Excellent customer experience offered High-quality products Competitive prices Trusted brand	Longstanding customer loyalty High expectations	High disposable income shoppers Conscientious shoppers who require good, reliable quality products
	Key resources Key supplier relationships E-commerce website Distribution network Brand		**Channels** Town centre stores Website Airport stores	

Cost structure	Revenue streams
Property rental costs Staff salaries Back office/technology costs Marketing/advertising costs	Product purchases (online and in-store) Personalised shopping services Franchise income Additional services (such as wedding lists)

The BMC may be used to document and analyse both the current and target states. It can also be used to support:

- option identification and appraisal;
- business impact analysis;
- risk identification and assessment.

For each target state option shown in Figure 4.3, the business model shown in Figure 4.4 can be discussed and analysed. For example, the effect of pursuing a strategy of developing international markets could significantly impact a variety of the elements of the business model.

ORGANISATION STRUCTURES

The formal structure defined for an organisation clarifies the management and work responsibilities, plus the lines of communication. An organisation chart is used to represent the structure applied within an organisation. There are two key structures: hierarchical and matrix.

Hierarchical structure

A hierarchical structure is based upon a pyramid structure. It incorporates a number of hierarchical levels and clearly depicts the communication lines and chain of management within the organisation. An example hierarchical organisation chart structure is shown in Figure 4.6.

Figure 4.6 Hierarchical organisation chart structure

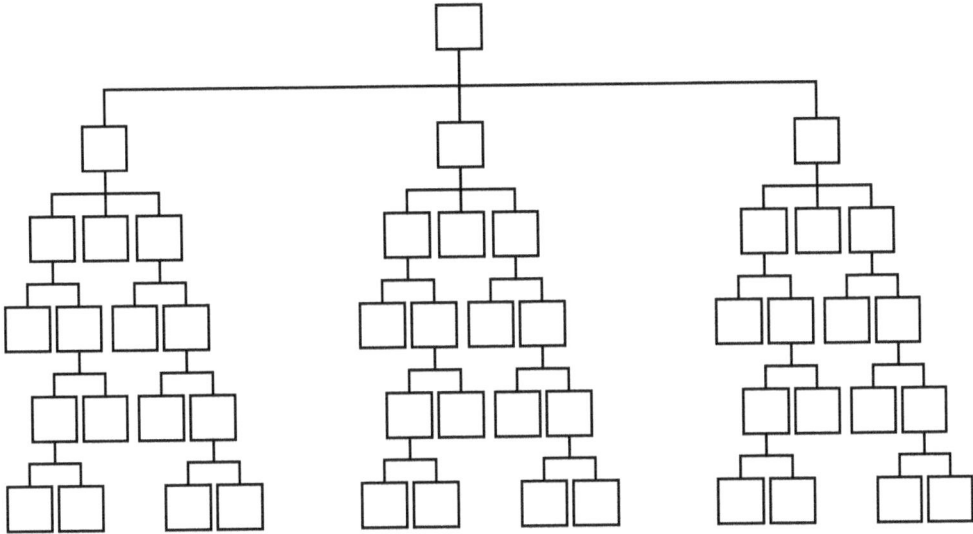

Figure 4.6 shows a hierarchical structure with several layers, which is often called a 'tall' structure. Many organisations minimise the number of layers and apply a 'flat' hierarchy. Where this is the case, managers typically have many more staff reporting to them and have to change their managerial approach from instructional to coaching/empowering. Figure 4.7 shows a flat organisation structure chart. Table 4.12 summarises the advantages and disadvantages of tall and flat hierarchical structures.

Figure 4.7 Flat organisation chart structure

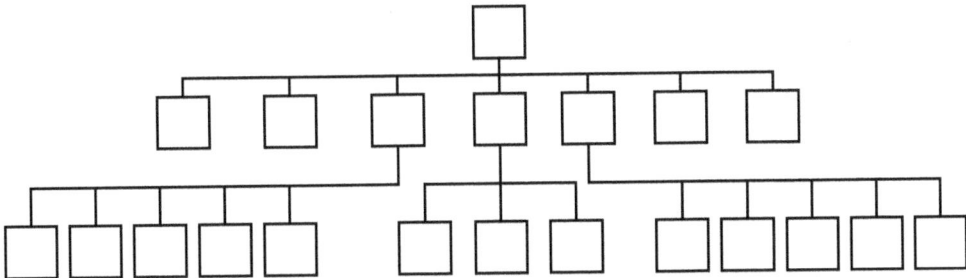

Matrix structure

Hierarchies can work as silos whether a tall or flat structure is in place. This can result in managers focusing on their own area of responsibility and working towards

Table 4.12 Advantages and disadvantages of 'tall' and 'flat' structures

Structure	Advantages	Disadvantages
Tall organisation structure	• small number of staff reporting to each manager, allowing greater personal engagement; • risk exposure is limited as managers tend to be involved in key decisions.	• speed of decision-making can be slow; • reduced autonomy and empowerment; • innovation can be stifled due to the need to obtain approval from multiple layers of leadership and management.
Flat organisation structure	• increased speed of decision-making; • increased autonomy and empowerment.	• managers have responsibility for a large number of staff, so may appear remote; • increased risk exposure. For example, an employee may make a decision that is not aligned with the manager's viewpoint.

achieving their personal or domain objectives. The consequence of which can be that organisational objectives are not addressed and collaboration between departments or teams may be limited.

The disadvantages of hierarchical structures are often addressed using a structure that combines a hierarchy with a service or outcome-based structure. This arrangement is known as a matrix structure. An example matrix structure is shown in Figure 4.8.

Figure 4.8 Example matrix structure

	Information systems	Business transformation	Procurement	Finance	Marketing
Project A	Software engineer	Business analyst	Purchasing officer		Marketing manager
Project B	Software engineer	Business analyst		Management accountant	
Project C		Business analyst	Purchasing officer	Management accountant	Marketing manager

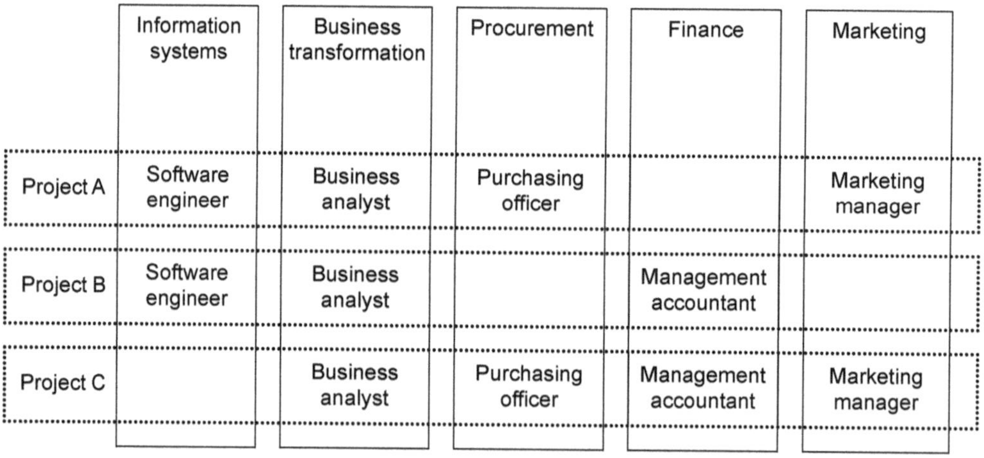

The structure in Figure 4.8 identifies five departments where individuals are employed in particular roles. This figure also shows three projects, each of which requires a team drawn from across the organisation's departments. Some individuals may work within more than one team. For example, the purchasing officer may be one individual who has been assigned to both Project A and Project C.

Inevitably, a matrix structure results in an individual having a fixed reporting line, typically to a senior manager within the employing department, and an additional reporting line to a senior member of the project or service team. The purchasing officer shown in Figure 4.8 reports to the head of procurement and has an additional 'dotted' reporting line to the project manager for Project A and the project manager for Project C. Unfortunately, this can mean that there is a lack of clarity regarding work priorities, which could lead to limited productivity, confusion and conflict. Where two senior managers have conflicting views on priorities, the individual employees may not know where to focus their work efforts.

ECOSYSTEM ANALYSIS

In addition to understanding an organisation's structure, it is also useful to understand an organisation's internal and external service ecosystem.

A service ecosystem is defined as:

> Relatively self-contained self-adjusting systems of resource-integrating actors connected by shared institutional arrangements and mutual value creation through service exchange. (Vargo and Lusch, 2016)

Every organisation operates via an internal ecosystem that carries out the organisation's work. Each organisation also operates within an external ecosystem. Business architects should understand the internal and external ecosystems that enable the operation of their organisations. The interacting entities within an ecosystem are known as service systems or actors. Table 4.13 defines internal and external service ecosystems.

Ecosystem diagrams

An ecosystem diagram shows all the organisations (or business functions) that are collaborating with a central service system to carry out areas of its work. Figure 4.9 shows an external ecosystem for the department store example.

A similar approach to that shown in Figure 4.9 may be used to represent an internal ecosystem. An example internal service ecosystem for a department store is shown in Figure 4.10.

The organisation's capabilities and value streams are dependent upon each service system performing their work in line with expected performance requirements. These are usually defined within supplier contracts that set out the terms of engagement between the central organisation and the service systems within its external ecosystem. Each line on the ecosystem diagram represents a business relationship. Ensuring this relationship works effectively in line with the organisation's values and expectations

Table 4.13 External and internal service ecosystems

Term	Definition
Internal service ecosystem	This is the network of service systems that are internal to the organisation. Internal ecosystems encompass standard business functions (the 'service systems') that may be grouped using the two activity categories identified in Porter's value chain (Porter, 1998) (see Chapter 6): • primary business service systems: sales, marketing, operations, logistics, customer service; • support business service systems: human resources, legal and compliance, procurement, digital transformation, finance. The service systems collaborate to deliver the organisation's products and services, and interact with the organisation's external service systems, where relevant.
External service ecosystem	This is the network of service systems that are separate legal entities from the organisation. External service systems interact and work with the organisation to deliver products and services, typically through a contractual arrangement. External ecosystems reflect that organisations work with other organisations, each of which provides a particular service required by the context of the ecosystem. The types of organisation that may be identified within an ecosystem are: • suppliers of resources such as staffing, finance, components, products, raw materials; • regulators such as those required by law or governing a particular industry; • reseller or partner organisations who act as intermediaries for product or service provision; • customer organisations where there is a business-to-business relationship; • outsourcing organisations that are external suppliers procured to provide business function services such as software development or marketing.

Figure 4.9 External service ecosystem for a department store

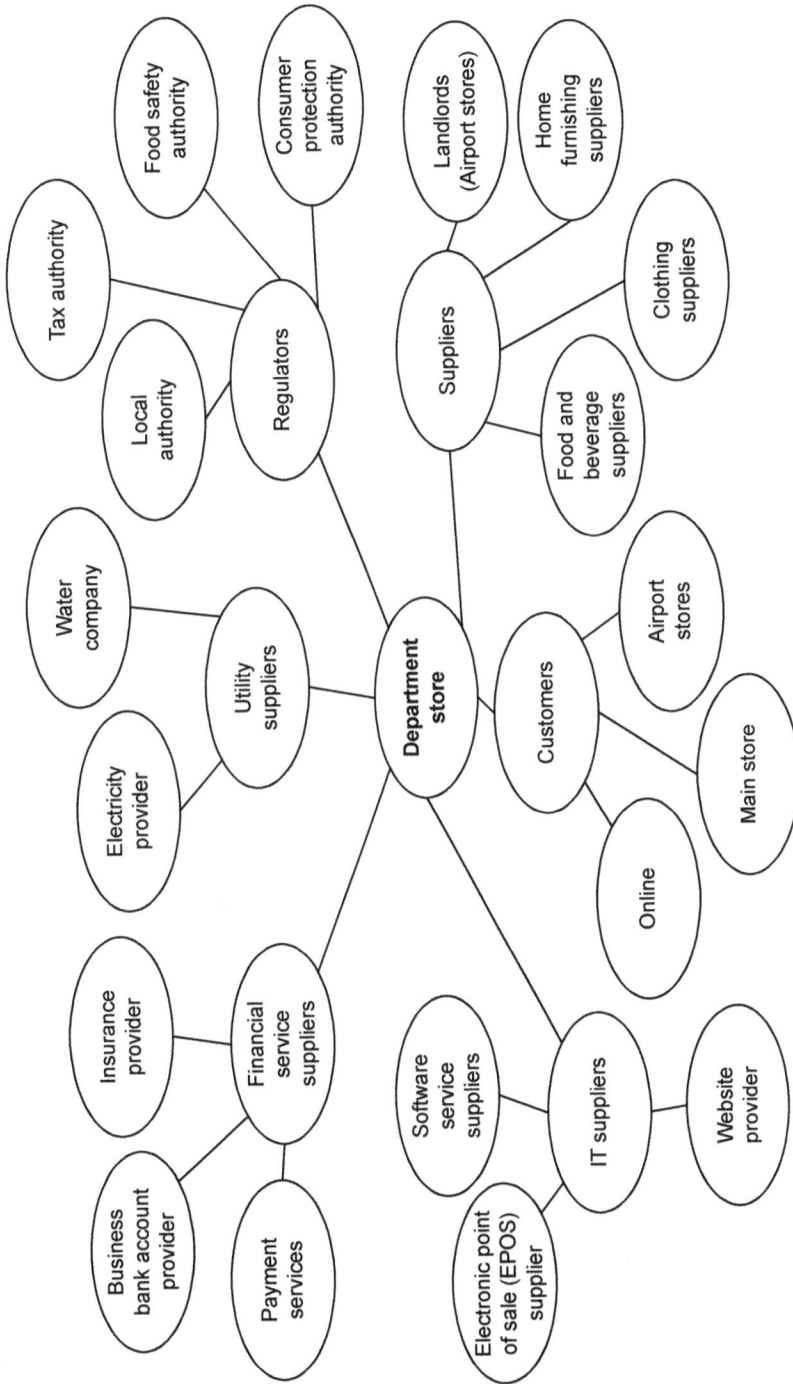

Figure 4.10 Internal service ecosystem for a department store

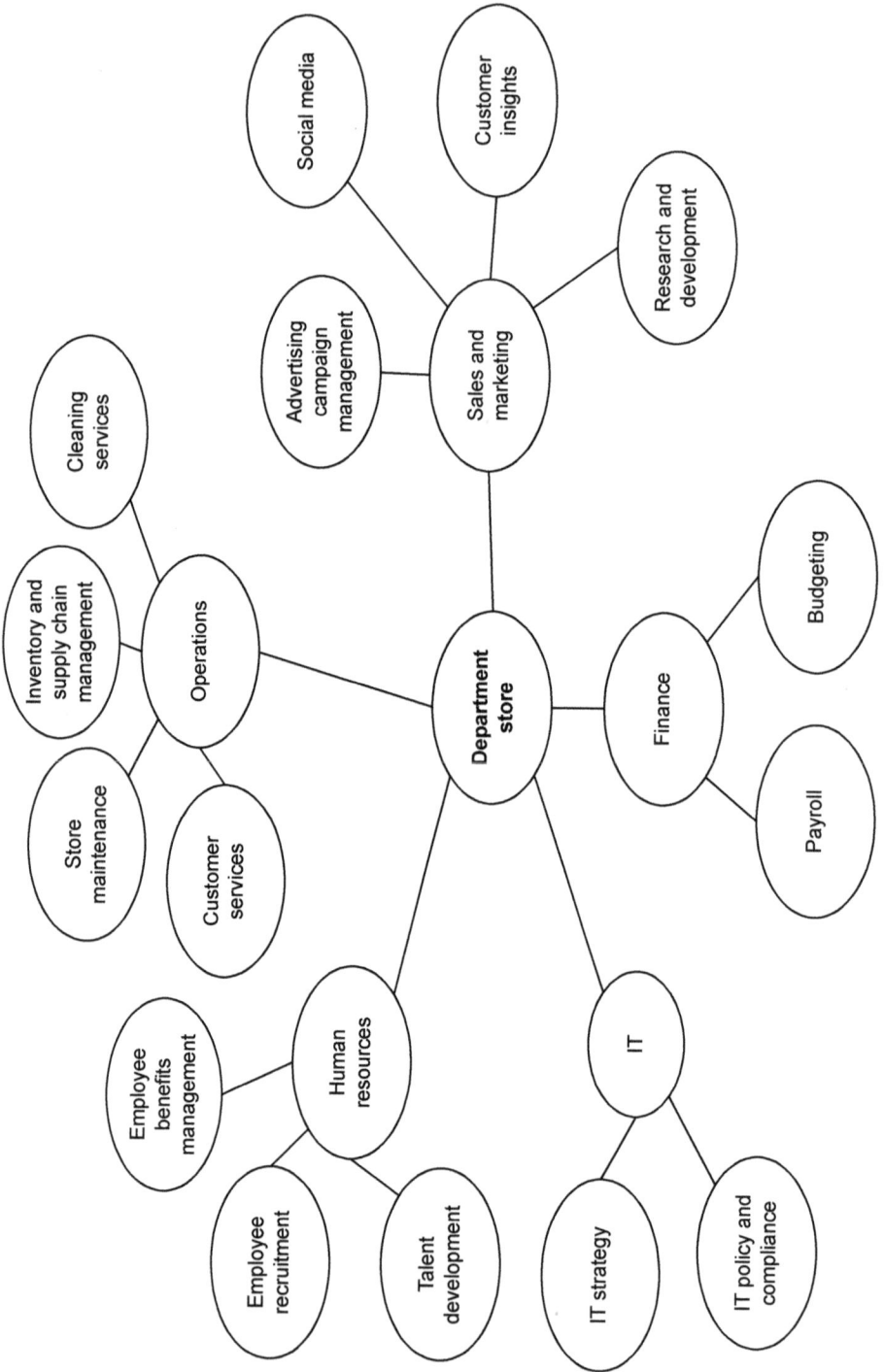

is essential if the organisation is to fulfil its customer value propositions and operate within the relevant legal and regulatory frameworks.

When analysing an ecosystem, business architects should focus their attention on the relationships between the service systems and the central service system of the organisation. These relationships have the potential to impede or diminish the ability of the organisation to deliver its products and services and co-create value with customers. The relationships may be areas of weakness that need to be addressed if customers are to be retained.

Relationship management is typically a business capability identified within an organisation's capability map (see Chapter 5). Understanding where there are problematic relationships helps to identify the need for business transformation. This may result in change projects being established to address problems within the ecosystem. Work may be needed to ensure each service system provides the required level of service and that this level of service is clearly defined. It is also likely that any contractual relationships are reviewed and updated where necessary. In extreme situations, where a service system is not offering the required level of service, this may involve installing an alternative supplier organisation.

The internal and external service ecosystem diagrams are blueprints that represent the environmental context for an organisation, so can support the development of shared understanding and improve strategic and tactical decision-making. Service ecosystem diagrams can be used independently or in combination with other techniques such as business motivation and business model analysis, or value network analysis (see Chapter 6). When considering strategic or tactical change, service ecosystem analysis can help with option identification and appraisal, scope definition, business impact analysis and risk identification and assessment.

ORGANISATIONAL CULTURE

The culture of an organisation can have a dramatic impact on the ability of the organisation to operate effectively and to respond to forces for change. Given this, recognising and understanding the culture that exists within an organisation is a key element of business architecture.

Prominent authors about culture include those who focused on organisational culture, such as Schein (2004) and Handy (1993), plus those who provided insights into national cultures, such as Hofstede and Minkov (2010) and Meyer (2016). Schein (2004) defines culture as: 'The basic assumptions and beliefs that are shared by members of an organisation, that operate unconsciously and define in a basic taken-for-granted fashion an organisation's view of itself and its environment.'

Culture is often subtle, as it is based on beliefs, values, experiences and priorities that are not explicitly communicated. Edward T. Hall's famous representation of culture as an iceberg showed how the 'invisible' factors, such as beliefs and values, developed into other invisible factors, such as thoughts and emotions, which were evident as 'visible' behaviours. The iceberg model is shown in Figure 4.11.

Figure 4.11 The Iceberg model of culture (Source: Paul and Lovelock, 2019, adapted from Hall, 1976)

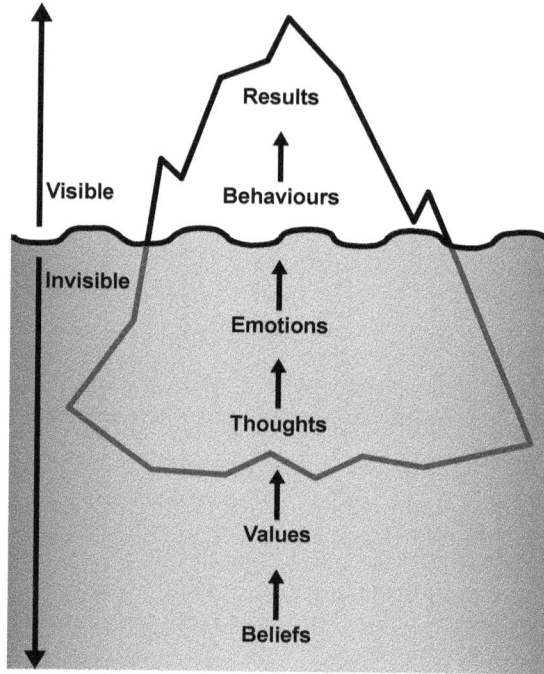

Whittington et al. (2023) defined the cultural web that included the dimensions that may be explored to understand the culture that exists within an organisation. These dimensions are described in Table 4.14.

Business architects need to work effectively with their organisation's stakeholders, and are more likely to succeed if they have a clear understanding of the organisational culture. Culture is rarely defined, so understanding an organisation's culture requires investigation and insight. Models can be particularly useful to clarify different elements and gain understanding. The culture pyramid is one such model and is shown in Figure 4.12. The levels that make up the culture pyramid are defined in Table 4.15.

Within an organisation, individual leaders of departments may have aligned or misaligned worldviews. Where worldviews differ, subtly different subcultures can develop within departments and lower-level teams. Through assessing the elements within the culture pyramid, the business architect can discover and potentially document the differences within the subcultures. This may be useful for the business architect as they attempt to navigate and facilitate strategic and tactical decision-making. The culture pyramid also provides a structure that may be used to acquire, retain and retrieve both tacit and explicit knowledge about an organisation's culture.

Table 4.14 Dimensions of the cultural web

Cultural web dimension	Description
Paradigm	The set of tacit assumptions held by those within an organisation that underpin aspects such as the demonstrated behaviours and physical artefacts.
Stories	The tales told by those within the organisation about the people and events within its history.
Symbols	The items and concepts that exemplify core beliefs, assumptions and values.
Power structures	The locations of power and influence within an organisation.
Organisational structures	The individual job roles, the designated areas of responsibility and the management and communication relationships within an organisation.
Control systems	The mechanisms deployed to monitor, enable and govern an organisation and its individuals.
Rituals and routines	The procedures and approaches applied to carry out the work of an organisation.

Figure 4.12 Culture pyramid (© Assist Knowledge Development Ltd)

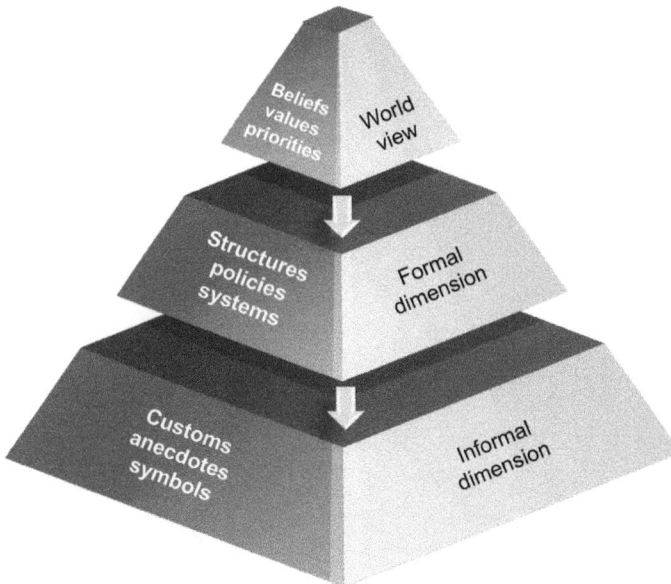

Table 4.15 Culture pyramid

Level	Definition
The worldview	The worldview drives the organisational culture and is based upon the leaders' values, beliefs and priorities regarding the organisation that underpin why it exists.
Formal dimension	The formal dimension level concerns the structures, policies and systems that are established within the organisation as a result of the worldview and govern the way the organisation operates.
Informal dimension	The informal dimension level concerns the customary ways of doing things within the organisation, the anecdotes told that reflect behaviours and the symbols used to represent the organisation.

CONCLUSION

The motivation and organisational views are key to obtaining a comprehensive understanding of an organisation's business architecture. When combined, these two views provide insight into the rationale that explains why the organisation operates as it does, the key components of the business model that form the basis for its operation and the structural and ecosystem elements that enable its continuing performance. The insights these views offer are essential if the business architect is to support and facilitate effective strategic and tactical decision-making. An understanding of the culture of the organisation is also a key element, as overlooking the impact of organisational culture can result in unexpected resistance to change initiatives and may ultimately pose challenges to the achievement of desired business outcomes.

5   CAPABILITY VIEW OF BUSINESS ARCHITECTURE

INTRODUCTION

This chapter introduces the capability view of business architecture. It covers the following topics:

- rationale for the business capability view;
- business capability modelling;
- elements of individual business capabilities;
- business capability analysis;
- leveraging business capabilities.

RATIONALE FOR THE BUSINESS CAPABILITY VIEW

A business capability represents a task or action that an organisation has the ability or motivation to perform. Tasks that organisations must perform include:

- strategy execution;
- employee recruitment;
- supplier engagement.

A business capability model is a blueprint that provides a static and conceptual view of the set of capabilities present within an organisation. This contrasts with the active view provided by the value stream diagrams (see Chapter 6), each of which represents the activities required to deliver a service offered by the organisation.

Organisations that make astute long-term investments in business capabilities have the potential to achieve a strategic advantage over other organisations in their domain. Sutton, in his book *Competing in Capabilities*, argues that the proximate cause of differences in wealth for nations and enterprises lies for the most part in the capabilities of firms (Sutton, 2012). Therefore, the business capability view offers significant insights when seeking to enhance the health of the organisation.

Table 5.1 suggests some of the key benefits that may accrue from applying a business capability view.

Table 5.1 Benefits of the business capability view

Potential benefit	Potential impact
Separates the strategic 'what?' from the tactical 'how?'	The business capability view is conceptual. It is essentially focused on 'what?' and not 'how?' Consequently, the view is agnostic of existing real-world organisational constraints. The view is also agnostic of legacy organisational elements such as people, organisation, process, information and technology (see POPIT in Chapter 3). The view is also agnostic of existing product or service provision.
	The conceptual nature of the business capability view allows for the organisation to be re-imagined in creative and innovative ways. This can be particularly useful if the organisation is seeking to build new or extend existing value propositions.
	This conceptual nature view with its focus on 'what?' is distinct from consideration of 'how?' capabilities are performed.
Supports holistic, strategic decision-making	The business capability view provides a representation of the entire organisation. As a result, this view supports strategic and tactical decision-making at an organisational level. Over time, this can support increased alignment of decisions with the organisational VMOST.
	For example, if an organisation has historically taken a fragmented or non-aligned approach when making investment decisions, variants of the same tasks or actions may exist in different areas of the organisation. The use of the capability view to identify and analyse these variations could highlight opportunities for increased alignment, consistency and efficiency, which could enhance customer and employee experiences.
	The capability view supports the evaluation of investment decisions within the context of the available organisational capabilities. For example, an organisation may have a strategic objective of enhancing the customer experience, but, if the investment strategy lacks significant investment in the organisation's customer experience capabilities, there may be a need to reconsider the objective or change the investment strategy.
Provides a consistent language for the organisation	The business capability model provides a language for the organisation. The names given to individual capabilities and their associated descriptions, provide a language that supports shared understanding and collaboration.
	In addition, the model and the language it applies can be used as a starting point for discussions regarding change initiatives within the organisation.
	For example, the capability model can help to standardise the language used in business analysis, service design and business change management activities (see Chapter 10).

BUSINESS CAPABILITY MODELLING

A business capability model represents all the tasks or actions that an organisation has the ability or motivation to perform.

When used to represent the current state, it depicts the tasks or actions that the organisation is currently able to perform. When used to represent the target state, it depicts the tasks or actions that the organisation wishes or is required to perform in the future.

Business capability taxonomy

A business capability model should be built using a taxonomy. This helps to ensure that the capabilities within the diagram are organised and presented in a clear and consistent manner. In general, capability models are organised into separate layers known as 'strata'. The strata are described in Table 5.2.

Table 5.2 Business capability model strata

Strata	Definition	Department store examples
Strategic: direction setting	Capabilities that are critical to the organisation's plan for success.	• promotion management; • customer insight; • supply chain management; • marketing management; • strategy development.
Primary: customer-facing	Capabilities that directly impact the organisation's interactions with customers.	• customer service; • customer loyalty; • store experience.
Support: non-customer facing	Capabilities that are non-customer facing that contribute towards the organisation's internal operation.	• facilities management; • human resource management; • IT management.

The following two levels can be used as a basis:

- Capability groups:
  - contains a minimum of two lower-level business capabilities;
  - may include other capability groups (known as nested capability groups).
- Business capability:
  - the lowest level building blocks of the capability model.

Figure 5.1 shows an example application of the business capability taxonomy, without the use of nested capability groups, for facilities management within a department store context and Figure 5.2 shows an example application of the business capability taxonomy, including the use of nested capability groups, for promotion management within a department store context.

Figure 5.1 Example application of the business capability taxonomy

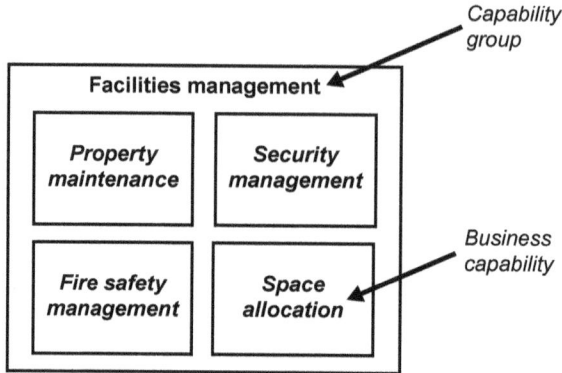

Figure 5.2 Example application of the business capability taxonomy including nested capability groups

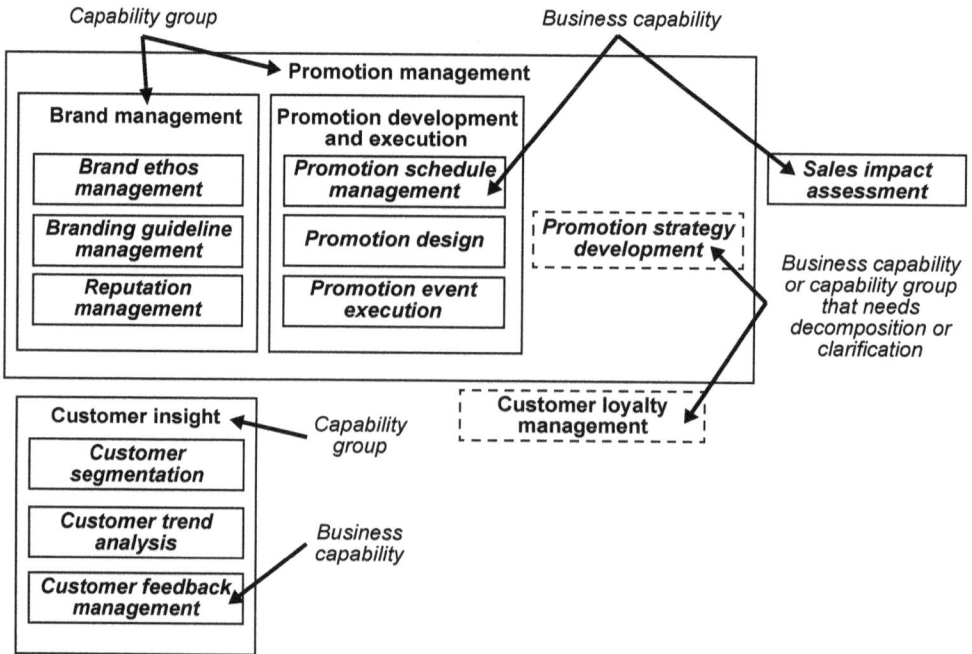

In Figure 5.2 both 'Brand management' and 'Promotion development and execution' are examples of nested capability groups. In contrast, 'Customer Insight' is a non-nested capability group. Figure 5.2 also shows that business capabilities can exist both inside and outside capability groups. The example shows that it is possible to document business capabilities or capability groups that require further decomposition or clarification.

The business capability model is usually shown as a single diagram with each of the levels of strata included. For display purposes, this has been split into Figures 5.3, 5.4 and 5.5. An example partial capability map for a department store focused on the strategic: direction-setting strata is shown in Figure 5.3, an example partial capability map for a department store focused on the primary: customer-facing strata is shown in Figure 5.4 and an example partial capability map for a department store focused on the support: non-customer-facing strata is shown in Figure 5.5.

Figure 5.3 Example partial business capability model for a department store focused on strategic: direction-setting strata

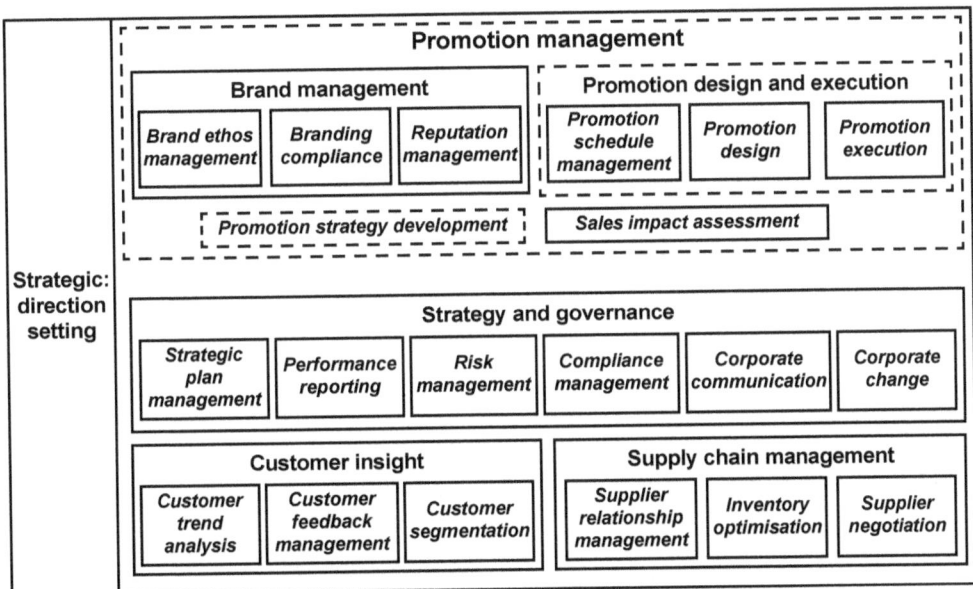

Figure 5.4 Example partial business capability model for a department store focused on primary: customer-facing strata

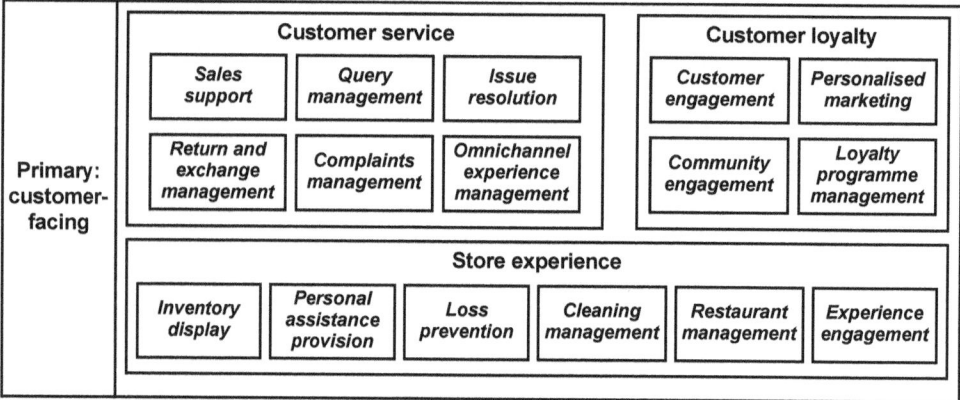

Key

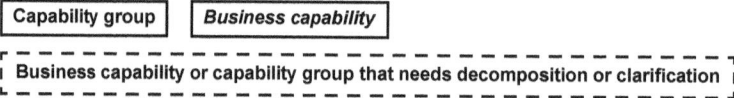

Figure 5.5 Example partial business capability model for a department store focused on support: non-customer-facing strata

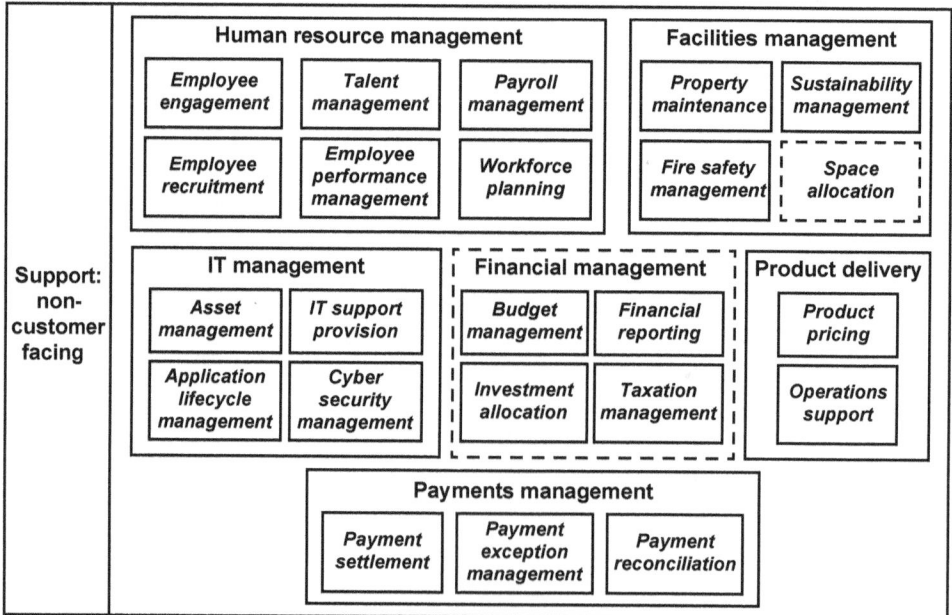

Key

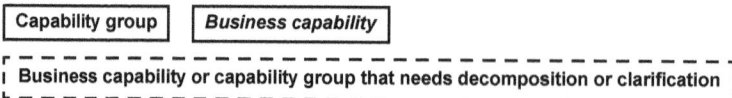

Business capability naming conventions

Value stream diagrams (Chapter 6) show the dynamic behaviour of an organisation, whereas a business capability model represents a static, structural view. Consequently, when naming business capabilities, the use of active language is avoided and the 'noun noun' is used.

For example, 'product selection' is a capability that meets the 'static' criterion through use of the noun noun format. In contrast, 'select products' does not meet this criterion as it uses an infinitive verb to convey the need for action.

When naming individual capabilities by applying the noun noun format, it is often tempting to qualify an area of work with the word 'management'. For example, product management, store management or strategy management. Alternative nouns are available that avoid repeating the term 'management'. Examples of alternative nouns that may be used to name capabilities are:

- process **verification**;
- component **production**;
- software **development**;
- document **maintenance**;
- customer **segmentation**;
- employee **allocation**;
- resource **provision**;
- stakeholder **engagement**;
- supplier **acquisition**;
- service **innovation**;
- regulation **compliance**;
- programme **governance**;
- strategy **execution**.

A gerund may also be used to name a capability. This is where a verb is used as a noun. An example is 'financial reporting'. The word 'reporting' on its own is a verb and as such describes an action. However, when combined with the noun 'financial', 'reporting' is no longer referring to the action of reporting but instead to the broader concept of 'reporting'. A further example is the capability 'strategic planning'. 'Planning', in this context, is not being used as a verb to describe the action of planning. Instead it is being used as a gerund to describe the concept of planning.

A means of determining whether a candidate name for a capability is appropriate involves putting the proposed capability name at the end of the following sentence stem: 'The organisation has the ability to execute ...'. For example, 'The organisation has the ability to execute talent' has a very negative connotation. In contrast, 'The organisation has the ability to execute talent management' would perhaps be appropriate.

Business capability quality criteria

Robust identification, modelling and evaluation of individual capabilities is essential if a business capability model is to represent an organisation accurately.

Each capability identified within the model should ideally be named and align with the business capability quality criteria defined in the SUAVE acronym. This is described in Table 5.3.

Table 5.3 Business capability quality criteria (SUAVE)

Quality criterion	Description
Stable	Each capability should represent a stable view of the tasks or actions that the organisation has the ability or motivation to perform.
	For example, the capability 'product selection' is applicable for a department store whether operating in 2005 or 2025, so the capability name may be retained. However, the way in which the organisation executes the capability could be vastly different.
Unique	Each capability is unique. Consequently, there should be zero duplicate capabilities within a business capability model.
	For example, 'accounts management' might initially be identified as a capability that is performed within the context of finance management. If at a later stage a capability with the same name is identified within the context of sales, it must be named in a way to make it unique. Alternatively, the originally identified capability could also be renamed. In this example the original capability could be named as 'financial accounts management' and the later capability as 'sales accounts management'.
Abstract	Each capability should be abstract or conceptual. It represents 'what' tasks or actions the organisation is able to perform rather than 'how' they are carried out.
Valuable	Each capability should offer value to a stakeholder of the organisation. This includes stakeholders such as customers, employees, managers, regulators, partners and suppliers.
	If the capability does not offer value to a stakeholder, questions should be asked as to why the organisation is concerned with performing the task or action identified.
Executive	Each capability should capture the interest of executive leaders of the organisation.
	If the capability is not of interest to the organisational leadership, or related to its chosen strategy, questions should be asked as to why the organisation is concerned with performing associated tasks or actions.

SUAVE can also be extended to SUAVED. The additional D requires that each capability is defined. The individual definitions help to build shared understanding when capabilities are used as a basis for discussion. For example, 'product selection' could be defined as 'the organisation's ability to identify, evaluate and select products and services to be offered to customers or to be used within internal operations'.

Organisations should adapt the SUAVE quality criteria to align with the use of business architecture in their organisational context. For example, the question of whether the capability is 'owned' might be deemed important for an organisation. This could therefore be added to the quality criteria (For example SUAVEDO – with the additional 'O' representing 'owned').

As discussed in Chapter 1, the use of business architecture should be outcome focused and context dependent. If business capability quality criteria are an impediment to value co-creation between stakeholders and the use of business capability thinking, consideration should be given regarding the need to adjust the quality criteria.

Business capability industry reference models

Identifying, modelling and evaluating individual capabilities can be time-consuming and expensive. In a worst-case scenario, stakeholders may become frustrated if they feel they are attending an endless series of workshops to discuss and agree their organisation's capability model. Where this type of situation occurs, stakeholders can quickly become disillusioned with the potential value of the business capability model. This is particularly the case where individual stakeholders have conflicting perspectives regarding capability names and where they are located within the model. This may be exacerbated when such conflicts are combined with the inflexible application of business capability quality criteria by business architects, and increased stakeholder resistance may result.

It may be helpful to refer to an appropriate industry reference model when developing a business capability model. These are available from organisations such as the Business Architecture Guild and can speed up the development of a business capability model and may also increase stakeholder buy-in.

Industry reference models contain high-quality content that has been subject to many hours of incremental research, debate and evaluation. Industry reference models often provide a view of the generic capabilities of an organisation that is operating within a chosen industry; however, caution should be exercised when using them. Potential disadvantages are that the resultant business capability model is not:

- representing the unique capabilities of an individual organisation;
- sufficiently robust – perhaps due to inappropriate quality criteria;
- sufficiently independent;
- representing the language of the organisation;
- encouraging sufficient buy-in from the organisation's stakeholders.

The motivation for the publication of an industry reference model should also be questioned. For example, a model may have been developed and published by an organisation that is seeking to sell its products or services. An example of this is a consultancy or technology provider creating or using an industry reference model to engage in discussions to sell their own consultancy or technology services. However, in contrast, a model may have been developed by an independent and objective industry body as a means of enabling collaboration among its members.

The motivation for creation of an industry reference capability model does not necessarily lead to its content being valid or invalid. However, the motivation that underpinned its creation may help to assess whether its content is relevant given the organisational context.

While time-consuming, the process of building a capability model with stakeholders, potentially supported by elements of industry reference models, can encourage stakeholders to be supportive and engage with the model.

ELEMENTS OF INDIVIDUAL BUSINESS CAPABILITIES

The term 'capability' is often used (mistakenly) to describe an individual's or a group's knowledge, skill or competency (see Chapter 8). However, the term 'competency' does not have the same meaning as the term 'business capability'. Business capabilities require skilled and competent actors to be available, but other dimensions also need to be present to form a business capability.

An individual business capability represents a task or action that an organisation has the ability or motivation to perform. Teece (2007) identified several elements that are required to fulfil a capability. Key elements include:

- skilled personnel;
- facilities and equipment;
- processes, routines and standards;
- authority;
- information.

Each element is considered further in Table 5.4.

The POPIT model (see Chapter 3) offers an alternative approach to analysing the elements that underpin a capability.

Business capability thinking

The business capability view offers a means from which to evaluate the implications of strategic and tactical decisions. In some instances, business architecture practitioners have become fixated with the completion and validation of a comprehensive business capability model for their organisation. It can be compelling to ensure that the business capability model follows appropriate naming conventions and other industry standards; however, efforts to build the model can stagnate where this approach is applied rigidly in a context of limited stakeholder understanding and support. This may result in the abandonment of the work to build the capability model and also the application of the capability viewpoint.

The business capability view transcends the business capability model. In other words, it is possible to think conceptually about business capabilities without the model. The

Table 5.4 Elements required to form business capabilities

Element	Description
Skilled personnel	These are individuals and teams with the knowledge and skill required to perform the tasks and actions of a capability; this includes employees and third-party suppliers.
	For example, within a department store, 'logistics management' might be a business capability. To execute this capability effectively, individuals with logistics management knowledge and skill are required. If these individuals are absent, the organisation cannot effectively execute the logistics management capability.
Facilities and equipment	These are the facilities and equipment required to support the execution of a capability.
	For 'logistics management' in a department store, the following facilities and equipment may be needed:
	• **warehouse space to store inventory:** shelving, refrigeration space for chilled goods and secure spaces for valuable inventory such as jewellery;
	• **a loading and shipping area:** a dedicated area for goods to be received and despatched between suppliers and customers;
	• **an inventory management system:** a system to support the monitoring and tracking of inventory levels and stock movement;
	• **stock-handling equipment:** equipment required to move stock within the warehouse; for example, forklift trucks, pallet trucks and conveyor systems;
	• **safety equipment:** equipment required for individuals working within the warehouse to remain safe; for example, helmets, safety glasses, high visibility vests and safety boots.
Processes, routines and standards	These are the processes, routines and standards required to perform tasks and actions when executing a capability.
	Logistics management within a department store may require a comprehensive set of processes, routines and standards that guide the execution of the capability.
Authority	This is the provision of authority or permission to execute the tasks and actions of a capability.
	For example, the logistic management team would require, or be delegated, the authority to make decisions regarding the movement of goods. Without this authority, the logistics management team cannot execute the capability.
Information	This is the supporting information and data required to execute a capability.
	For example, the logistics manager needs information and data about the suppliers, inventory, staffing levels and service levels. Without this information, the capability cannot be executed effectively.

aim in using the business capability view, and other business architecture views, should always be to enhance the outcomes of the organisation and its stakeholders (particularly customers) in alignment with the organisational strategy. The desire to complete the model and align with the notation and rules surrounding it should not distract from these outcomes. For example, when considering the capabilities of a house, 'heating provision' could be identified as a capability. Heating provision is a 'what?' task or action that the house needs to be able to carry out. Within the context of a hot summer day, the heating provision capability is likely to be inactive as additional heat is not required. In contrast, the heating provision capability is likely to be needed during a cold winter day.

When considering 'how?' the heating is provided within the house, there may be six different heating solutions available. Perhaps the house was extended or modified at various points in time leading to independent decisions being taken about the heating provision solution. Therefore, each heating solution is unique and not compatible with the others. In addition, each solution is subject to separate repair and maintenance schedules and requires specialist engineers and maintenance professionals. If inspections are required for safety or legal purposes, six different inspections would need to be completed within the required timescales. From the householder's perspective, changing the temperature of the house may require interaction with six independently configured temperature control systems. A pictorial representation of this current state situation is shown in Figure 5.6.

Figure 5.6 Example heating provision capability: 'what' and 'how'

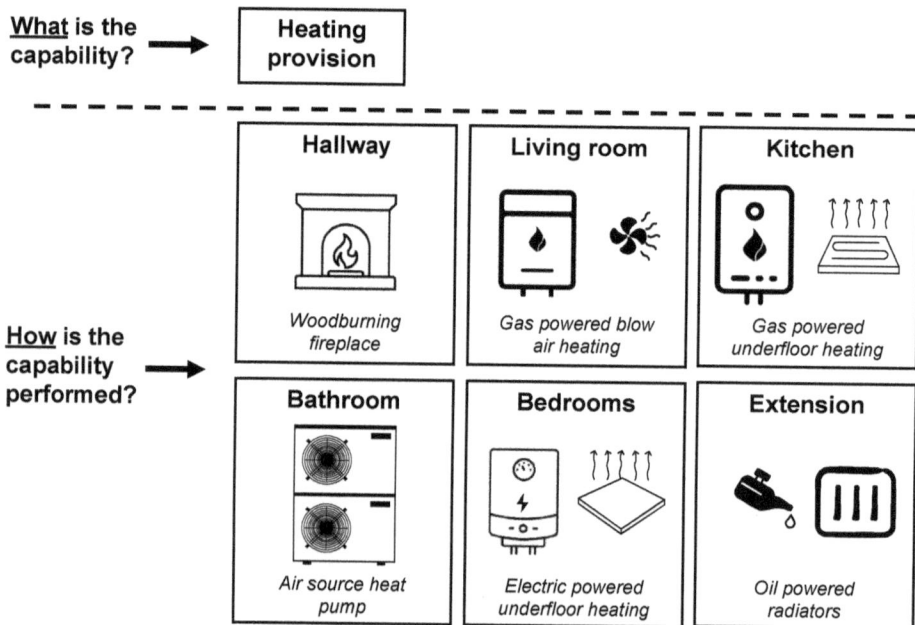

While this situation may seem slightly absurd within the context of a house, this is the situation regarding the business capabilities that exist within many organisations. Individual organisations may grow by acquisition or take non-aligned approaches to capability investment and development, and this can lead to multiple capability variants in areas such as human resource management, financial management, sales account management, procurement and payroll management.

A pictorial representation of the current state situation where there are many payroll management variants within an organisation is shown in Figure 5.7. This represents an organisation where each department has a unique configuration of POPIT elements (see Chapter 3) for the payroll management capability. Essentially, each department has a unique way of executing payroll management, as follows:

- **People:** each payroll team is required to hold different skills.
- **Organisation:** the payroll teams operate within different leadership structures. They each have unique strategies, priorities, policies and allocations of roles and responsibilities. They also work with different external partners.
- **Processes:** different ways of working are used to manage the payroll, including calculation and payment.
- **Information:** different approaches are used to capture payroll information and data.
- **Technology:** different technologies are used to support the payroll management activities.

Figure 5.7 Example payroll management capability: 'what' and 'how'

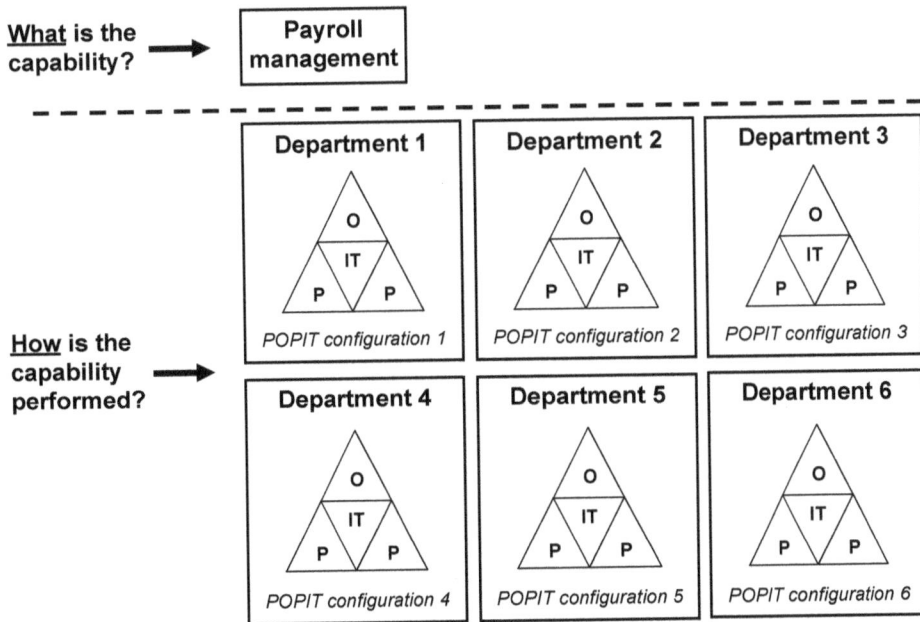

The complexity of the situation shown in Figure 5.7 would result in a significantly higher cost for providing payroll management services than within a similar size organisation that is unencumbered by the fragmented approach used to deliver this capability. The situation within Figure 5.7 is likely to lead to significantly higher staff salary costs due to the need for more individuals, across disparate teams, to deliver the payroll management services. The costs of providing IT solutions to support the suite of payroll management variants are also likely to be significantly higher.

If a need is identified to change payroll management, perhaps to comply with a change in government taxation policy, this change would need to be implemented for each of the six different payroll management teams. The cost of this change is likely to be higher than in comparison to an organisation with a single or streamlined approach to the delivery of payroll management services.

Analysing an opportunity such as that described above for the payroll management capability does not require a fully documented and validated business capability model. Instead, analysing situations by taking a capability perspective and thinking through the opportunities and issues can be invaluable to both business architects and their organisations.

BUSINESS CAPABILITY ANALYSIS

While having a business capability model is useful, it does not on its own provide insight into what the organisation should do to leverage capabilities in alignment with strategic goals and objectives. To provide this insight, business capability analysis is required. This includes: business capability maturity and performance analysis and business capability and business motivation analysis. When combined, these aspects provide a foundation for the organisation to maximise the potential value of the business capability model when conducting strategic and tactical decision-making.

Business capability maturity and performance analysis

The assessment and analysis of the maturity and performance of individual business capabilities provides insight into how well an individual capability is performing.

Analysing individual business capabilities provides insight into potential opportunities for enhancement of capability performance. For example, through analysis of an individual capability, an opportunity might be identified to enhance the way in which the capability is executed by changing the elements that form the capability.

One way to assess the performance or maturity of an individual capability is to assess it against a scale such as RAG (red, amber, green). This would lead to each business capability being categorised as:

- red – capability does not exist – maturity/capacity/performance significantly below expectations;
- amber – capability exists – maturity/capacity/performance needs some improvement to meet expectations;

- green – capability exists – maturity/capacity/performance meets or is above expectations.

Underpinning each of the RAG assessment levels are several elements, including whether a capability exists and its maturity, capacity and performance against expectations. Each of these elements is described within Table 5.5.

Table 5.5 RAG assessment elements

Element	Definition
Capability existence	This is an assessment of whether the capability exists or not.
	The capability can only be said to exist if it can be executed by the organisation. This requires that the following elements are available:
	<ul><li>skilled personnel;</li><li>facilities and equipment;</li><li>processes, routines and standards;</li><li>authority;</li><li>information.</li></ul>
	If these elements are absent, the organisation cannot currently execute the capability. In contrast, if these elements are in existence, the organisation is deemed to possess the ability to execute the capability.
Capability maturity	This is an assessment of the degree to which a capability is mature and established.
	For example, within a well-run and established finance department, the business capability of 'financial reporting' could be in an advanced and mature state. It is executed at regular intervals and there is limited variance in terms of both the approach and the quality of outcomes. When checking the capability elements the follow might be found:
	<ul><li>**skilled personnel:** competent and skilled personnel;</li><li>**facilities and equipment:** appropriate facilities and equipment;</li><li>**processes, routines and standards:** established processes and routines executed against agreed standards;</li><li>**authority:** established authority, clear ownership and accountability;</li><li>**information:** appropriate information available and in use.</li></ul>
	In contrast, for a new 'start-up' organisation, the capability of 'financial reporting' may not have been required previously so the capability elements may be absent or require improvement. Consequently, when assessing maturity, it is likely to be deemed immature.
	Where the capability has been executed in the past but capability elements require improvement, it may be deemed to need improvement.

(Continued)

93

Table 5.5 (Continued)

Element	Definition
Capability capacity	This is an assessment of the capacity (the maximum volume available) of a capability relative to the demand for that capability. For example, within the department store context, 'complaints management' could be a capability that has: • insufficient capacity to meet demand – the volume of complaints frequently exceeds capacity levels, which may lead to delays in processing complaints, staff complaints about being overloaded and complaints about the complaints management process; • sufficient capacity to meet demand – the volume of complaints is in alignment with current capacity levels, and there is some flexibility to meet any unexpected increases in complaint levels; • excess capacity to meet demand – the volume of complaints is frequently lower than capacity levels, so, while this may provide flexibility to meet unexpected increases in complaint levels, this indicates underutilisation of resources.
Capability performance	This is an assessment of the capability against performance expectations. This assessment requires consideration of whether capability performance: • is significantly below expectations; • needs some improvement against expectations; • is above performance expectations.

The assessed maturity and performance of each individual business capability can be displayed on a business capability model. This results in a blueprint that provides insight into the performance and maturity of the organisation. This is an input into business capability and motivation analysis.

LEVERAGING BUSINESS CAPABILITIES

Chapter 4 introduced the concept of analysing capabilities within the context of an organisation's VMOST. Given that the business capability model represents the tasks or actions that an organisation has the ability or motivation to perform, it is necessary that these capabilities enable and align with the organisation's vision, mission and objectives.

For example, the department store's vision is: 'To be the shopping destination of choice for the discerning customer.' However, an analysis of the organisation's core customer-facing capabilities uncovers that many are failing to enable the envisioned standard of service. This analysis highlights that the organisation is unlikely to achieve its vision unless a decision is made to invest in the core customer-facing capabilities.

Unfortunately for the organisation, it also highlights that the customer-facing capabilities do not offer a basis for organisational development and growth, further emphasising the need to invest in these capabilities.

Enhancement and investment in business capabilities have the potential to offer long-term strategic advantage. However, the capabilities need to align with the strategic vision and intent and must be leveraged effectively. Girvan and Paul (2024) suggest that this is a core element of business agility and highlight that capabilities possessed by an organisation should be understood, recorded and leveraged, with gaps addressed as required.

Several models and frameworks offer different perspectives that support leveraging and analysing business capabilities as well as assessment questions such as 'why?', 'what?' and 'how?' This includes the Zachman Framework (Chapter 3) the Integrated Architecture Framework (Van't Wout et al., 2010) and the Brown Cow Model (Robertson and Robertson, 2013).

Figure 5.8 CALM framework (© Assist Knowledge Development Ltd)

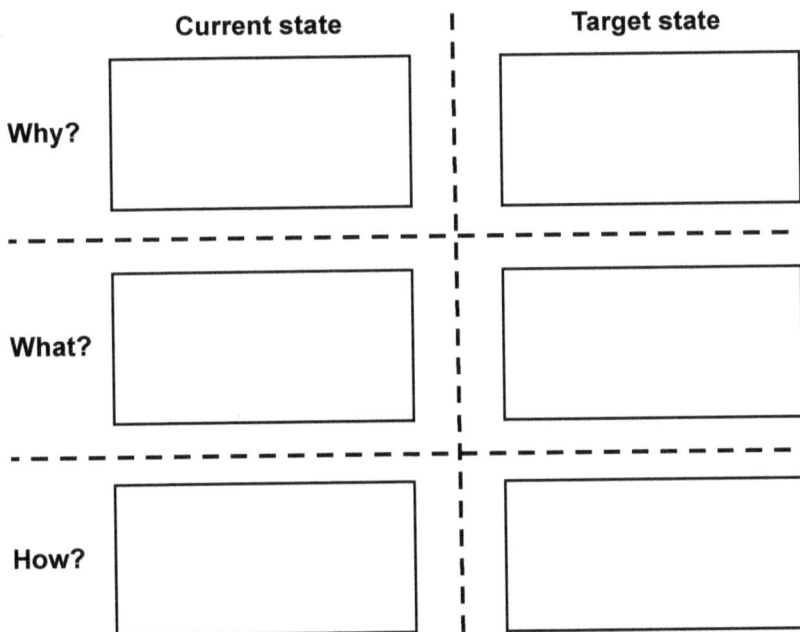

The capability analysis and leverage model (CALM) shown in Figure 5.8 provides a framework for analysing these questions regarding 'current' and 'target' states. The question 'why?' should be analysed for an individual capability by considering the underlying rationale for the current state of an individual business capability and the rationale for the required target state. The 'what?' question should be analysed by evaluating the title and objective of a business capability, both for the current and target states. The 'how?' question should be analysed by considering the elements required to establish the capability. The elements for the current state should align with the motivation, title and objective of the capability. The elements for the target state should be as envisaged by the answers to the 'why?' and 'what?' questions. This section is where the gaps that need to be addressed to move from the current state to the target state may be most evident. This analysis may also provide a basis for instigating business change or software development initiatives. An example of CALM being applied to an individual capability is shown in Figure 5.9.

Figure 5.9 CALM applied to an individual business capability (payroll management)

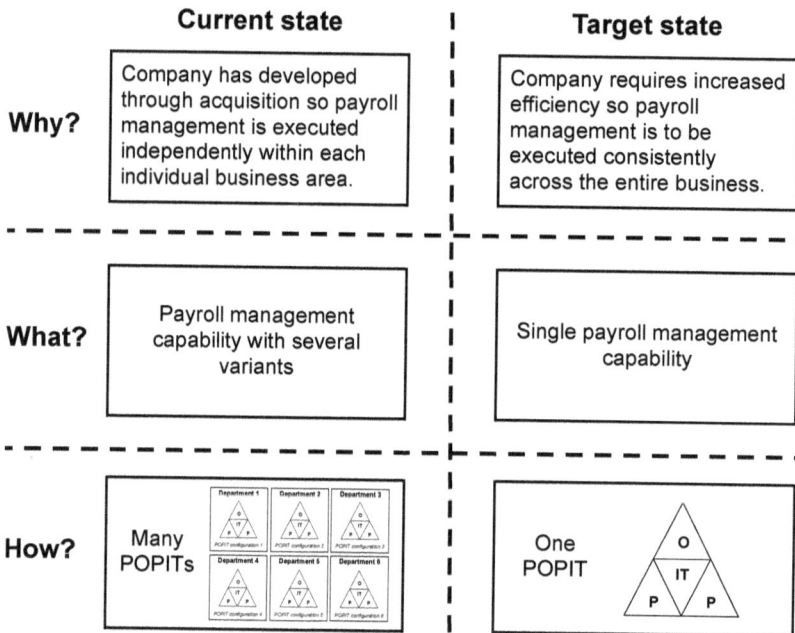

CALM can also be used to help identify and think through opportunities for innovation in the way that capabilities are leveraged. For example, an energy company may have several capabilities that enable the delivery and sale of petrol or diesel fuel to motorist customers. Moving forward, the energy company may wish to leverage these capabilities, and develop additional capabilities, to enable an electrical charging point service for customers who drive electric vehicles. The application of CALM to this example is shown in Figure 5.10.

CALM can be applied to other conceptual views, including value streams and business use cases (see Chapter 6).

Figure 5.10 CALM applied to an individual business capability (energy provision)

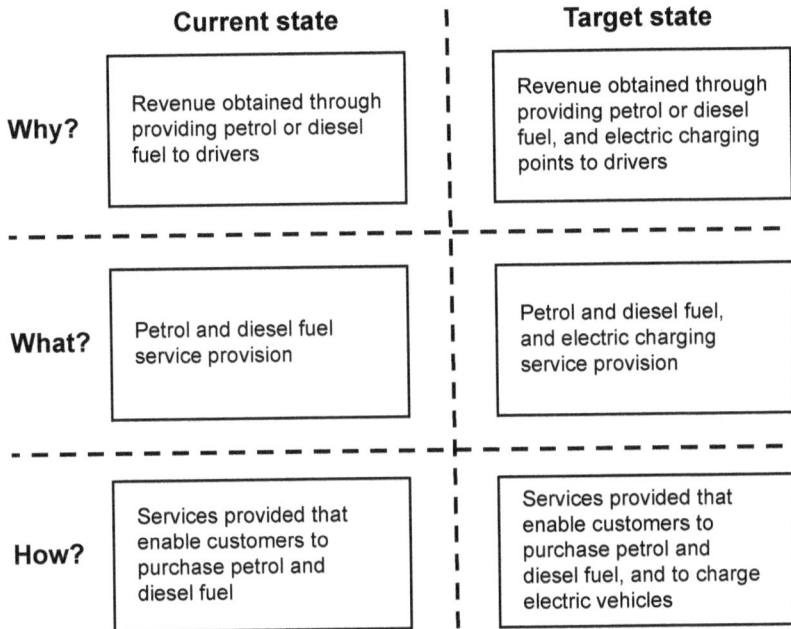

	Current state	Target state
Why?	Revenue obtained through providing petrol or diesel fuel to drivers	Revenue obtained through providing petrol or diesel fuel, and electric charging points to drivers
What?	Petrol and diesel fuel service provision	Petrol and diesel fuel, and electric charging service provision
How?	Services provided that enable customers to purchase petrol and diesel fuel	Services provided that enable customers to purchase petrol and diesel fuel, and to charge electric vehicles

CONCLUSION

Business capabilities are the areas of ability possessed by an organisation. They enable the organisation to carry out the activities within the organisation's value streams. They also provide a basis for organisations to respond to changes in the business environment and to develop innovative solutions and services.

The VMOST for an organisation should be supported by the business capabilities. Without this alignment, the VMOST may be undermined, and it may not be possible to achieve the organisation's business objectives.

6 PROCESS/SERVICE VIEW OF BUSINESS ARCHITECTURE

INTRODUCTION

This chapter covers the following topics:

- service concepts;
- service definition and value propositions;
- value stream analysis;
- customers, customer experience and customer journeys;
- network analysis.

The product/service view is a core dimension within an organisation's business architecture and represents the value streams of activities deployed to deliver the products or services provided to customers. Support activities that are required to enable these value streams may also be modelled. Understanding the nature of the offering made to customers, whether internal or external, is necessary to ensure that the activities conducted are in line with the strategic intent. Further, ensuring that the capabilities exist to enable the performance of the activities is also needed. This chapter examines the product/service view and the key areas of concern that should be understood if the work to depict and enact this view is to be successful.

SERVICE CONCEPTS

Organisations exist to create and deliver products or services that are required or desired by other organisations or by individuals. Each organisation needs to understand why it exists – and persists – as this rationale provides the basis for defining the target audience for the organisation and the offer made to that audience. The market targeted by an organisation may be a commercial or non-commercial group of potential customers or service recipients. For example, a government department focuses on a particular group of recipients. The service provided is concerned with the offering made to the market by the organisation and the ways in which the market's need – or promises to meet that need – are met by the organisation.

Products and services

Organisations decide on the individual products or services they create and provide to their customers. This may be within a commercial, government or non-profit context. Products are tangible items that offer specific features. For example, smartphones, lightbulbs, hair dye and board games all fall within the product category. Within the technology world, the term 'product' is also applied to intangible items such as software applications. Services are intangible processes that deliver specific features and are typically knowledge-based and require customer intervention. Training courses, management consultancy, car or rail transport and health care are all services. Within the technology world, services refer to the outputs provided by applications or components that enable the work of other products or services.

The service concept

The concept of service is of a higher order in that it is not just concerned with delivery – as in the case of products or services – but also encompasses other dimensions. These dimensions relate to quality factors and outcomes: dimensions that address the need for value or a beneficial outcome. Wieland et al. (2012) define the concept of 'service' as: 'The process of using one's resources to create value with and for the benefit of another actor.' This definition introduces the need for service to be beneficial to another actor and for the value arising from the service to be co-created.

Spohrer and Maglio (2010) define service as: 'Value co-creation phenomena that arise among interacting service system entities'. This definition introduces the notion that value is co-created, which is explored later in this chapter.

Another more practical definition is: the application and integration of resources to realise beneficial outcomes for both service providers and their customers.

The value concept

The term 'value' has been used in many contexts to communicate a worthwhile, beneficial outcome from a product or service. Service science research highlights the assumption that often underlies the use of this term: that the mere delivery of an item ensures the delivery of value. Vargo and Lusch (2008) contrasted two views on value, as follows:

- A **goods-dominant logic** that assumes value results from the delivery/purchase of an item.
- A **service-dominant logic** that requires value to be co-created and to be realised through use.

The purchase and deployment of software offers an example that has been experienced by many organisations. The steps in this scenario are:

- The software application is purchased and installed.
- Training is provided to the user community by the software supplier.

- The user community resist using the software as they don't understand the benefits that may arise from doing so.

- The user community gradually returns to original ways of working.

- The software product falls out of use.

A question arises: where is the value realised in this scenario? The software application has been delivered and installed, and training has been provided. The software supplier and the procurement team may consider that value has duly been delivered. However, without engagement from the user community, it is just a software product that has been delivered – the beneficial outcomes (or value) have not been realised.

Product vs service thinking

The advent of Agile has ensured that phrases such as 'deliver value early' have entered the business architecture and business change lexicon. There has also been an increasing focus on the development and speedy delivery of 'the product' and a corresponding increase in assumptions that 'value' results from delivery. This equates to the 'goods (or products)-dominant logic' described above and presents issues that may reduce the possibility of value realisation if they are not addressed.

The software scenario described above is a clear example of 'goods-dominant logic' or 'product thinking' and clarifies that, without any use of the product, it is unlikely that any beneficial outcomes will be achieved. On the contrary, the disruptive effect of installing the software may raise negative outcomes such as a reduction in productivity and deterioration in the customer experience provided.

Service thinking, based on service-dominant logic, offers a different, deeper perspective on customer engagement and product or service delivery. It considers that organisations need to understand the value their product or service offers and recognise that this value should be realised through collaboration with customers. The software scenario viewed through a service lens would look as follows:

- The requirements for business improvement are explored and analysed.

- A holistic approach to the business improvement is adopted. The POPIT model may be used to assess the business impact of a new software product.

- The stakeholders are identified and analysed, and relevant actions are taken to ensure stakeholder engagement.

- Software applications are evaluated. The selected product is purchased and installed.

- Processes are redefined in line with the features offered by the software and the needs of the business.

- Stakeholders, in particular the user community, are kept informed and are consulted throughout the change process.

- Training needs are analysed and training is provided to the user community. This may involve the software supplier and in-house business process analysts.

- Ongoing support is provided to the user community as necessary.

- Beneficial outcomes are evaluated after the change has been implemented, and adjustments are made as necessary. Stakeholders, in particular the user community, are consulted to ensure ongoing engagement and continuous improvement.

The essence of the service thinking approach is that all parties have a part to play. Capabilities need to be leveraged and stakeholders need to be engaged if the beneficial outcomes are to be achieved. The delivery of a product (in this case a software product) should not be confused with the realisation of value. Value assumptions based on product thinking are likely to undermine the service offering and the customer experience.

SERVICE DEFINITION AND VALUE PROPOSITIONS

Organisations should identify the services they offer their customers at an abstracted, conceptual level. Such services form a key component of the business architecture and are represented using value stream diagrams (discussed later in this chapter).

Value co-creation

The value item offered by each value stream requires analysis to define the nature of the value offered by the organisation and the extent and nature of the collaboration required with stakeholders, including external customers and suppliers. Figure 6.1 sets out a process for value co-creation that identifies the rationale and sequence of this collaboration.

Figure 6.1 Process for value co-creation (© Assist Knowledge Development Ltd)

The process shown in Figure 6.1 highlights the need for business architects to collaborate with other change professionals and stakeholders to co-create value and achieve the beneficial outcomes desired by the organisation. While this is shown as a linear process, in practice each stage is iterative and the entire process is also iterative. For example, prototypes may be used to demonstrate the features offered by a product or service and to obtain feedback, which is then used to make improvements.

Key roles engaged in possible collaborations within the process for value co-creation are described in Table 6.1. Other stakeholders, such as customers, managers and user researchers, may also participate in these collaborations.

Table 6.1 Role collaborations to co-create value

Stage	Roles engaged in co-creating value
1. Collaborating to identify where value might be achieved	Business analyst to analyse root causes of problems and define requirements. Business architect to develop value stream diagram. Service designer (see Chapter 10) to define service offering and value proposition.
2. Collaborating to develop a service that offers value	Service designer to clarify customer experience requirements, possibly using prototypes, and define the service blueprint (see Table 6.9). Business architect to identify capabilities needed to enable the value stream. Business analyst to support capability identification and gap analysis.
3. Collaborating to ensure that value is realised	Business change manager to assess business impact. Business architect to establish the required capabilities. Business analyst to conduct holistic analysis to identify where service changes are needed. Service designer to obtain customer feedback and adjust the service offering.

Collaboration helps to ensure the business architecture aligns with the customer value expectations and the organisation's service offering. It also avoids issues emerging from service and value assumptions.

Value propositions

The service view of an organisation is a key element in the business architecture. Each service aims to deliver the value proposition offered by the organisation and possibly realised by customers. A defined value proposition is a key element of a service description.

There are several frameworks that may be used to analyse value propositions. One framework, adapted from Kaplan and Norton (1996), considers three dimensions of value:

- **Suitability:** the features, pricing and quality level of the product or service.
- **Convenience:** the choices available to the customers that enable them to tailor the product or service to their requirements; the availability of the product or service in terms of timing and access.
- **Personal affiliation:** the sense of connection and affinity with the image of the product or service provider; the nature of the relationship between customers and the provider.

These dimensions and the individual elements are summarised in Figure 6.2.

Figure 6.2 Value proposition dimensions

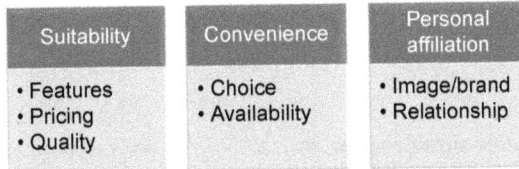

Suitability	Convenience	Personal affiliation
• Features • Pricing • Quality	• Choice • Availability	• Image/brand • Relationship

Osterwalder et al. (2014) have also defined a framework for designing value propositions. This framework focuses on two aspects: the pains to be overcome and the gains to be achieved. Each aspect is considered from the perspective of both the customer and the organisation. These perspectives are described in Table 6.2.

Table 6.2 Value proposition dimensions (Source: Adapted from Osterwalder et al., 2014)

Customer view	Organisational view
Pains: the pains experienced by the customer that need to be overcome or reduced.	**Pain relievers:** product or service features that resolve the root causes of customer pain or mitigate the impact.
An example pain is the customer being required to complete a complex and time-consuming task.	An example pain reliever is a product that provides features that simplify or speed up the work to complete the task.
Gains: the gains required to realise value. An example gain is a training service that could be enhanced by the provision of access to additional learning resources.	**Gain creators:** service features that enable the realisation of value. An example gain creator is ensuring all customers have access to additional resources that support and augment their learning.

This approach by Osterwalder et al. helps to address a dilemma often experienced in service delivery: the gap between the customer's value expectations and the organisation's value proposition. This gap may result from different areas of activity in the service definition, development and delivery process. This is represented in Figure 6.3.

The employee value proposition has gained focus in recent years and aims to highlight why an individual should choose to work for a particular organisation. A strong employee value proposition can help an organisation to attract, recruit and retain talent. It can also offer an advantage over competitor organisations that are competing to attract and retain highly marketable skills and expertise.

The service design gaps model

The service design gaps model has been adapted from the Gaps Model of Service Quality (Parasuraman et al., 1985; Bitner et al., 2010). The model is shown in Figure 6.3 and identifies five areas where there may be gaps between different activities within the process to design and deliver a service. The five gaps identified in the service design gaps model are described in Table 6.3.

Figure 6.3 The service design gaps model (© Assist Knowledge Development Ltd. Adapted from Parasuraman et al., 1985; Bitner et al., 2010)

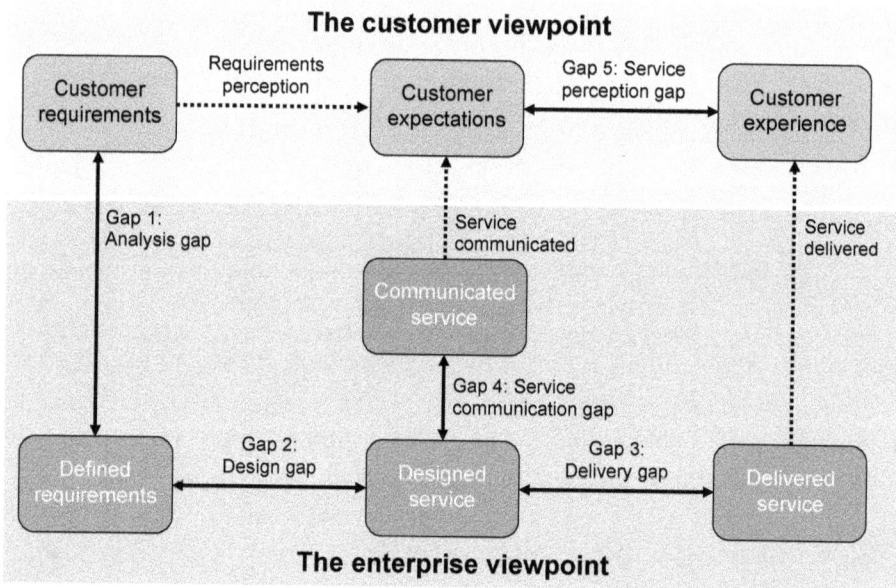

The service design gaps model helps to identify the root causes of problems with the customer perception of the product or service provided by the organisation. It raises questions such as:

- Was the analysis of the customers' requirements carried out effectively?
- Did the product or service design reflect the requirements accurately?
- Was the product or service delivered to optimise the design or to fulfil the design aspirations?
- Were promises communicated to customers that have not been fulfilled by the delivered product or service?

Ultimately, any or any combination of these gaps may have contributed to adverse perceptions by customers of the product or service, resulting in negative feedback and possibly a reduction in sales or engagement with the organisation.

Table 6.3 The five service design gaps

The service design gap	Description
Gap 1: The analysis gap	The gap between the customers' requirements regarding the service and how the service requirements are defined by the organisation. This results from a failure to apply effective requirements engineering techniques.
Gap 2: The design gap	The gap between the defined service requirements and the designed service. This results from a failure to understand the service requirements and, accordingly, to design the services that the customers want and expect.
Gap 3: The delivery gap	The gap between the designed service and the service delivered to customers. This results from a failure that occurs during service delivery, despite the service design meeting the customer needs.
Gap 4: The service communication gap	The gap between the designed service and the service promises made to customers. This results from a failure to communicate accurately the characteristics of the service offered by the organisation.
Gap 5: The service perception gap	The gap between the service expected by the customer and the service experienced by the customer. This may result from any of the other gaps.

VALUE STREAM ANALYSIS

Value stream modelling and analysis helps to identify the activities and key capabilities needed to fulfil the value proposition offered to customers by an organisation. There are several modelling approaches, each of which allows organisations to view the value offered and the value-enabling activities from various perspectives.

Four key value modelling approaches are described below. The value modelling approaches use a range of terms for the areas of work conducted. These terms include activity, process, task, stage, action and step. The descriptions of these models within this book use the term 'activity' in order to distinguish between other modelling approaches, such as business process modelling (described later in this chapter).

Porter's Value Chain

The value chain was first introduced by Michael Porter in his 1998 book *Competitive Advantage* and aims to represent both the activities directly related to the value offering plus the secondary or indirect activities needed to support the delivery of the organisation's products and services to customers.

Combining the direct (primary) and indirect (supporting) activities into a single model clarifies which activities are essential to achieving the value proposition and which activities support this goal. It also enables the analysis of the activities, including those

105

that are not directly concerned with delivering the value proposition, to identify where improvements are needed. Table 6.4 provides a summary of the primary and support activity categories identified in the value chain model and Figure 6.4 shows the primary and support activities that contribute to the execution of the sales value proposition in a department store.

Table 6.4 Descriptions of Porter's Value Chain activities

Activity group	Activity type	Description
Support activities	Procurement	The processes and standards applied to engage with external organisations to acquire resources required for the organisation's operations
	Technology	The processes and standards applied to establish and maintain the organisation's technology infrastructure, including the information systems and items of technology equipment
	Human resource management	The processes and standards applied to attract, recruit, retain and retire employees
	Firm infrastructure	The processes and standards applied to establish the premises, facilities and services that support those working for the organisation
Primary activities	Inbound logistics	The processes and standards applied to obtain the resources needed to perform the organisation's operations
	Operations	The processes and standards applied to create the products and services
	Outbound logistics	The processes and standards applied to deliver the products and services to customers
	Marketing and sales	The processes and standards applied to promote and advertise the products and services to customers
	Service	The processes and standards applied during pre- and post-sales contexts to engage with the organisation's customers

The value chain allows the business architect to see the proposition for a particular offering, which may involve the entire organisation. It provides an overview picture of how the organisation's activities connect and collaborate to deliver products and service to customers.

Figure 6.4 Value chain example for department store sales

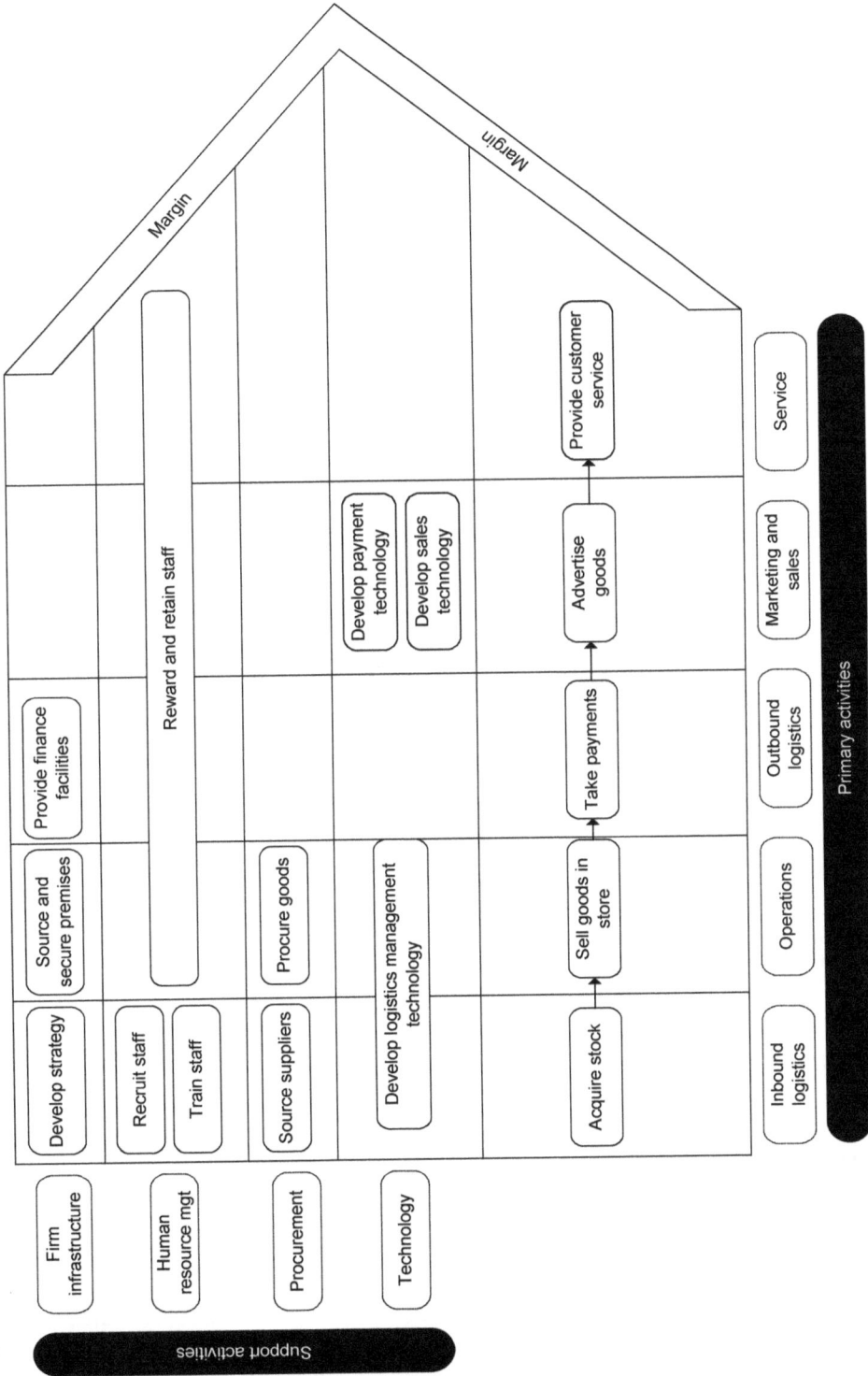

The value chain highlights the activities and business functions involved in creating and delivering the products and service to the customer with the aim of delivering the value proposition and ensuring a profitable return. The perspective it offers is an economic view of value. This focus on the financial return represents value for the organisation in the form of the profit margin, or for the customer through receiving the products or services at the appropriate price point.

Modelling the value-enabling activities holistically and at this overview level clarifies the zone of differentiation for the organisation. The activities required to ensure an operation is profitable while achieving the stated value proposition are represented at a macro level. This enables the organisation to gain a deep understanding of the factors key to its competitive and financial success. Comparing an organisation's value chain to its competitors' may also point to areas of competitive advantage and differentiation from rivals.

The value chain model, with its focus on the profit margin, may be criticised for focusing on commercial organisations. However, defining the primary and support activities required to deliver a product or service also supports the analysis of the costs incurred within the value chain. Accordingly, this approach may be used to analyse the expenditure incurred by government or non-profit organisations when delivering their products or services.

The value stream diagram

The value chain needs to be supplemented by other models when seeking to analyse and improve an individual product or service. The value stream diagram is a key value analysis technique in the business architect's toolkit. Table 6.5 shows the components included in a value stream diagram.

Table 6.5 Elements of a value stream

Value stream element	Description
Name	An active title (typically verb-noun format) for the value stream from the stakeholder perspective
Description	A short description of the value stream and its purpose
Trigger	The trigger for the value stream, which can be an internal, external or timebound trigger
Stakeholder/ customer	The recipient of the value item after all activities are complete
Value	A short description of the value item offered to the stakeholder by the value activities
Value activity	An outcome/name (typically two to four words) for the value stream activity

The value stream diagram allows business architects to represent the sequence of key activities undertaken to deliver a product or service and offer value to a customer. This diagram is an abstract representation of the activities conducted. It does not show the detailed tasks, actors and process flows. This is the province of a business process model, which may be developed to elaborate the value stream diagram, and is described later in this chapter.

The value stream is not constrained by the physical or environmental aspects within which the activities are conducted and just shows the sequence from the beneficiaries' perspective. A value stream diagram may include activities conducted by both internal functions and external organisations.

Value streams are used to represent the activities required to deliver a value item required by customers or stakeholders. They can be drawn to be more extensive than the activities represented in a value chain diagram. The value stream diagram transcends both the primary and support activities in the value chain and focuses on the delivery of the value item to the customer. The diagram may be used to represent a current or target state so offer a basis for gap and impact analysis.

Value stream diagrams are straightforward to create, requiring the business architect to represent the value-enabling activities that deliver the value item offered to customers. Given that the customer perspective underpins the value stream analysis, it is helpful to develop a deep understanding of the target customer prior to modelling the value stream. Service thinking techniques, such as empathy mapping or persona analysis, can help to inform the creation of value streams.

Figure 6.5 provides an example value stream for the sale of female fashion clothing within the department store context. Some of the value stream activities from this model are elaborated later in this chapter.

Additional information that extends the understanding of the value stream diagram is usually needed when analysing a value stream to identify improvements. An example of the additional information for the value stream in Figure 6.5 is provided in Table 6.6. A customer journey map related to the value stream and based on a particular persona is shown in Figure 6.11.

The number of value streams required to cover an entire enterprise varies as this depends on the size and complexity of the organisation, the volume of services and/ or products provided and the range of target customers. The environmental context for the organisation is also likely to be a factor in the overall number and complexity of an organisation's value streams.

For example, within a department store there are typically many different clothing ranges and associated product lines offered. However, at a macro level there will also be other value items offered such as household products, electronic and electrical items, gifts, cooking items, furniture and cosmetics. Each of these may require value stream analysis. An organisation may diversify to offer financial service items such as repayment plans, loyalty schemes or insurance/warranty products. These may all be subject to value stream modelling and the analysis of the underlying suite of capabilities and processes.

Figure 6.5 Example value stream for department store

Female clothing sales value stream

This value stream diagram shows the activities conducted to acquire the latest female fashion clothes and facilitate their sale to shoppers within the department store.

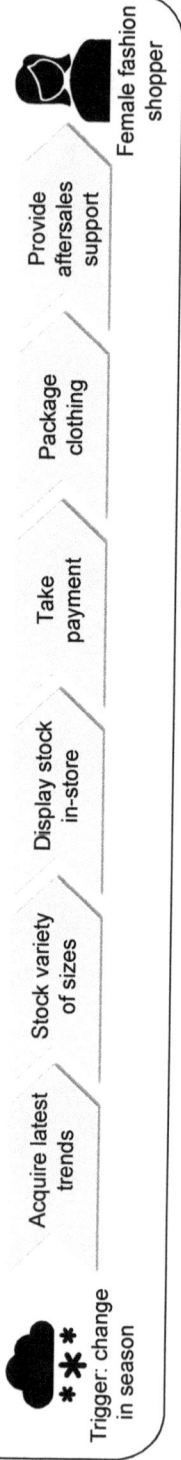

Trigger: change in season

Acquire latest trends

Stock variety of sizes

Display stock in-store

Take payment

Package clothing

Provide aftersales support

Female fashion shopper

Table 6.6 Value stream elaboration for the department store example

Value stream activity element	Description	Example
Value stream activity name	An outcome/name of the value activity (typically two to four words)	Display stock in a department store
Description	A short description of the value stream activity and its purpose	Shop assistant will place clothing in the women's section of the department store, allowing customers to view and try on items
Stakeholder/ customer	The recipient/beneficiary of the value item for this activity and/or the actors involved in delivering the value activity	Visual merchandise team Female fashion shopper
Activity entry criteria	A short description of the conditions that need to be true for the value stream activity to be triggered	Stock is delivered to store Stock display is permissible (space is available)
Activity exit criteria	A description of the conditions that need to be true for the value stream activity to be exited or concluded	Stock has been displayed and additional packaging removed
Value item	A description of the value delivered to the stakeholder/ customer by this value stream activity	Items are now available to view, try on and purchase

Value stream diagrams may also be developed, and analysed, for the delivery of value items to internal customers. The focus for business architects is often on those value streams that deliver external outcomes to customers, suppliers, regulators and partners. Understanding these external values streams helps to set the outer boundaries before exploring the internal value streams.

The business process hierarchy

Business process improvement is a core service offered by business analysts (Paul and Cadle, 2020). This service may also be undertaken or supported by other roles, such as business process analysts, business architects and service designers. The approach taken explores business processes at three levels: enterprise level; event–response level; actor–task level. These levels are defined in Figure 6.6.

Figure 6.6 Business process hierarchy

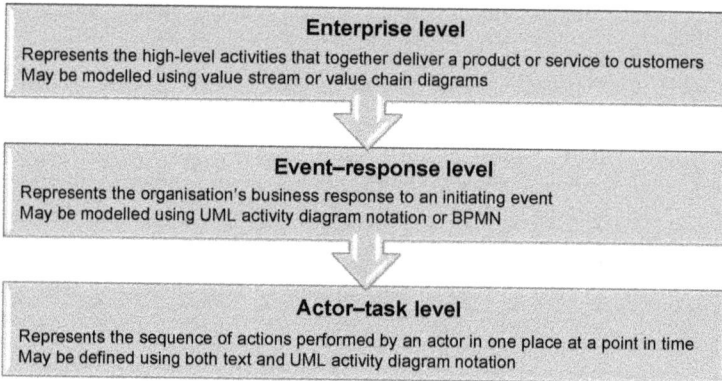

Enterprise level
Represents the high-level activities that together deliver a product or service to customers. May be modelled using value stream or value chain diagrams

Event–response level
Represents the organisation's business response to an initiating event. May be modelled using UML activity diagram notation or BPMN

Actor–task level
Represents the sequence of actions performed by an actor in one place at a point in time. May be defined using both text and UML activity diagram notation

A value stream or value chain model is typically used to define the enterprise level for an organisation. These models identify the activities that may be further investigated to identify potential areas of improvement.

The event–response level is modelled using business process models (Paul and Cadle, 2020), which represent the business event that initiates a business process and the flow of tasks that comprise the process. Each value stream activity is initiated by at least one business event. Three different types of event are considered:

- The event may originate from outside the organisation, for example from a customer; these events are known as external events.

- The event may be time-based and initiate a regular occurrence of an activity such as salary payments.

- The event may originate from inside the organisation; these events are known as internal events and typically involve a business decision.

The organisation responds to each event by carrying out the tasks shown in the business process model. This response is usually represented using a business process model that forms a basis for communication, analysis and improvement. Each task on a business process model is carried out by an actor, which may be an individual, department, business function or software application. Business analysis is used to investigate the tasks in order to ensure any opportunities for improvement are uncovered.

Mapping value streams to capabilities
The value stream should not be used in isolation as there is a direct relationship between the value stream diagrams, the capability model and the business processes for an organisation.

Each value stream activity invokes and is enabled by one or more business capabilities. Mapping the capabilities to the value stream clarifies which business capabilities have a direct impact on the value proposition. For example, the value stream in Figure 6.5

shows an activity to obtain new clothing in line with the latest trends. This activity requires several capabilities if it is to be enacted, including:

- clothing trends identification;
- clothing trends analysis;
- supplier procurement;
- stock acquisition.

This mapping helps to identify which capabilities are used to enact the value stream and the relative importance of those capabilities. Should a capability not be at the appropriate level of maturity, or not delivered to the right standard, it may have a substantial negative impact on the effective operation of the organisation and the delivery of the value item. Action may need to be taken to improve a capability in order to better support the value stream activity where the capability is applied. Chapter 5 discusses capabilities and capability modelling in further detail.

An understanding of the capabilities also enables organisations to identify where there are opportunities to extend their service offering or enhance the customer experience offered. For example, the department store's capabilities may offer the opportunity to provide customers with fashion trend guidance and help with building outfits for different occasions. This could be an addition offered with each purchase or could be the basis for additional commercial activities.

Organisations often encounter commercial or budgetary difficulties, such as from economic conditions, government funding limits, demographic changes within a target market or competitor innovation. These changes may require the organisation to revisit its products and services, or even its entire service provision. Analysing the potential offered by capabilities can offer a means of innovating the value streams while continuing to align with the organisation's business strategy.

Clarifying the relationship between value stream activities, capabilities and business processes helps organisations to understand how their value streams are delivered. If complex or substandard processes are in place, the ability of the organisation to deliver the products and services efficiently and to co-create value with customers is likely to be impaired. Equally, if efficient and effective processes underpin the value stream activities, a positive outcome is likely to ensue both for the customer and the organisation.

Streamlining and improving processes that relate directly to the value stream can have a far greater positive impact on the customer outcomes and the tangible and intangible value a customer is able to realise from engaging with the organisation. This can also provide a competitive advantage – as the likelihood of customer engagement increases, the organisation's reputation is enhanced and the costs associated with managing issues are reduced.

The activities within the 'Female Clothing Sales' value stream example each represent an aggregated summary of capabilities, business processes and organisational departments. A more detailed exploration of each activity would help to identify these aspects. Figure 6.7 summarises the capabilities, business processes and the organisational departments required to deliver the 'Take Payment' activity.

Figure 6.7 'Take Payment' value stream activity with related capabilities, business processes and organisational departments

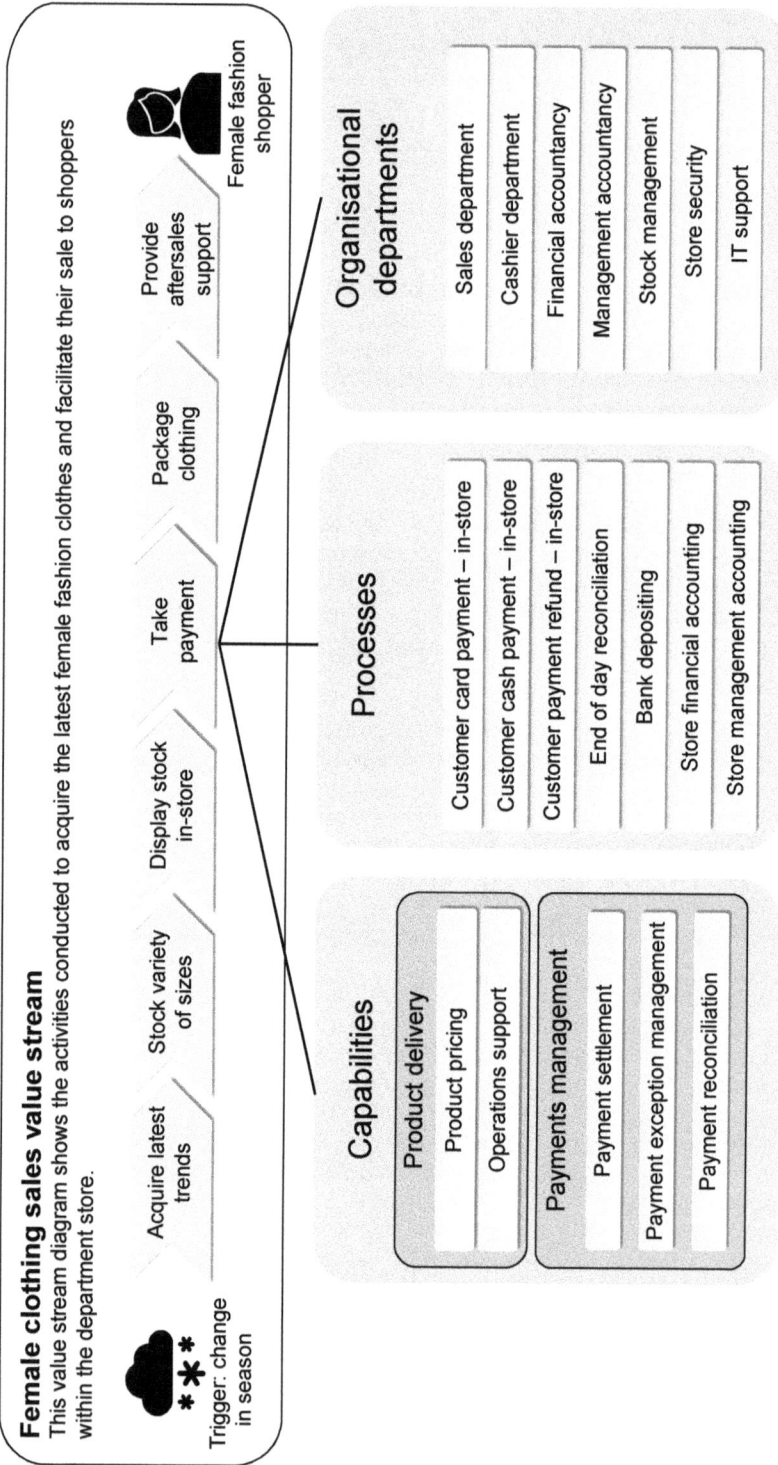

Female clothing sales value stream

This value stream diagram shows the activities conducted to acquire the latest female fashion clothes and facilitate their sale to shoppers within the department store.

Trigger: change in season

| Acquire latest trends | Stock variety of sizes | Display stock in-store | Take payment | Package clothing | Provide aftersales support |

Female fashion shopper

Capabilities

Product delivery
- Product pricing
- Operations support

Payments management
- Payment settlement
- Payment exception management
- Payment reconciliation

Processes

- Customer card payment – in-store
- Customer cash payment – in-store
- Customer payment refund – in-store
- End of day reconciliation
- Bank depositing
- Store financial accounting
- Store management accounting

Organisational departments

- Sales department
- Cashier department
- Financial accountancy
- Management accountancy
- Stock management
- Store security
- IT support

Mapping the value stream activities to the business processes and capabilities, plus adding the organisational departments involved, allows a business architect to understand the operating model from different viewpoints. It helps to identify areas for business improvement such as where there are capability gaps or organisational overlap and redundancy. The availability of capabilities can also highlight where value stream/business process improvement is possible. For example, there may be a capability that can improve process efficiency or remove bottlenecks.

Lean value stream mapping

The Lean manufacturing movement developed and applied a technique called value stream mapping. This technique has similarities with the value stream modelling and analysis approach applied by business architects. Lean value stream mapping is also known as material and information flow mapping, as the technique aims to show the information and flow of materials during the production of products.

One of the key aspects of this technique is the analysis of the main activities to identify where there are issues with the flow of the work and delays. These issues are known as 'waste'. The concept of 'waste', and the different perspectives where this might be identified, may be used by business architects when analysing value streams to improve efficiency.

The eight waste categories defined by Lean are shown in Table 6.7. These can be remembered using the mnemonic TIMWOODS, which represents the first letter from each waste category.

Table 6.7 Eight wastes of Lean

Waste	Description
Transportation	Wasted time, costs and resources used to move products and materials unnecessarily
Inventory	Wasted funds and space by holding stock and storing an unnecessary volume of materials or products
Motion	Wasted time and effort used to move people unnecessarily
Waiting	Wasted time waiting for the next process, task or step
Overproduction	Wasted effort, costs and materials making more products than will be required by the customer
Overprocessing	Wasted effort, cost and materials due to higher quality than required for the product
Defects	Wasted cost and effort needed to rework defects and products as they don't meet the required standards
Skills	Wasted ability due to underutilising peoples' skills, talent and knowledge

Accurate data is required to analyse the flow of information and materials throughout the value stream. For example, data about processing times, waiting times, inventory volumes and number of people involved in a task is needed to identify waste and support the process improvement.

A detailed level of information is required for this in-depth analysis, so it is unlikely to be suitable for use across the organisation. Business architects may wish to use this approach where particular problems occur or to inform change activities for a specific area within the organisation.

Figure 6.8 provides an example of a Lean value stream map for the 'Display stock in department store' value stream activity as shown earlier in Table 6.6. In this example, the total cycle time, which is the amount of time spent on value adding tasks for this process, is just over nine hours. The total lead time, which is the overall elapsed time for the process, is almost 50 days or 1,185 hours. This identifies that just 0.7 per cent of the process time is spent on activities that offer value to the customer and 99.3 per cent is wasted time.

The material and information flow mapping approach highlights the potential areas of waste within this value stream activity. These areas are shown in Figure 6.8 using a 'Kaizen Burst' (explosion icon). Waiting times between activities, transportation of the clothes and levels of inventory could also be reviewed in order to remove waste and increase the efficiency of this process.

Additional approaches to explore service, value and process improvement

There are numerous approaches, techniques and frameworks that may be used by business architects to model, analyse and improve their organisations. The specific approach adopted is context dependent.

Business use case diagrams

The business use case diagram provides a holistic and conceptual representation of the work (or functions) conducted by an organisation. The diagram shows the external actors that wish to access the business system and their interactions with the areas of work. The business use case diagram can be used to represent the entire organisation, but is also often used to model a business area within the organisation.

A context diagram offers a good start point for building a business use case diagram: the context diagram shows the interactions between actors and the business system under consideration. An example business context diagram for a coffee shop within a department store is shown in Figure 6.9.

A 'stripe' in the left corner of the elements may be used to differentiate between business and system use case diagrams. This convention is shown in Figures 6.9 and 6.10. Note that an actor may be an individual or group carrying out a particular role, or may be another business system (for example, the Bank actor shown in Figure 6.9).

The business use case diagram provides greater detail than the business context diagram and provides further insight into the interactions between actors and the work (or functions) conducted within the organisation. An example business use case diagram for a coffee shop within a department store is shown in Figure 6.10.

Figure 6.8 Example value stream map for 'Display stock in department store' process

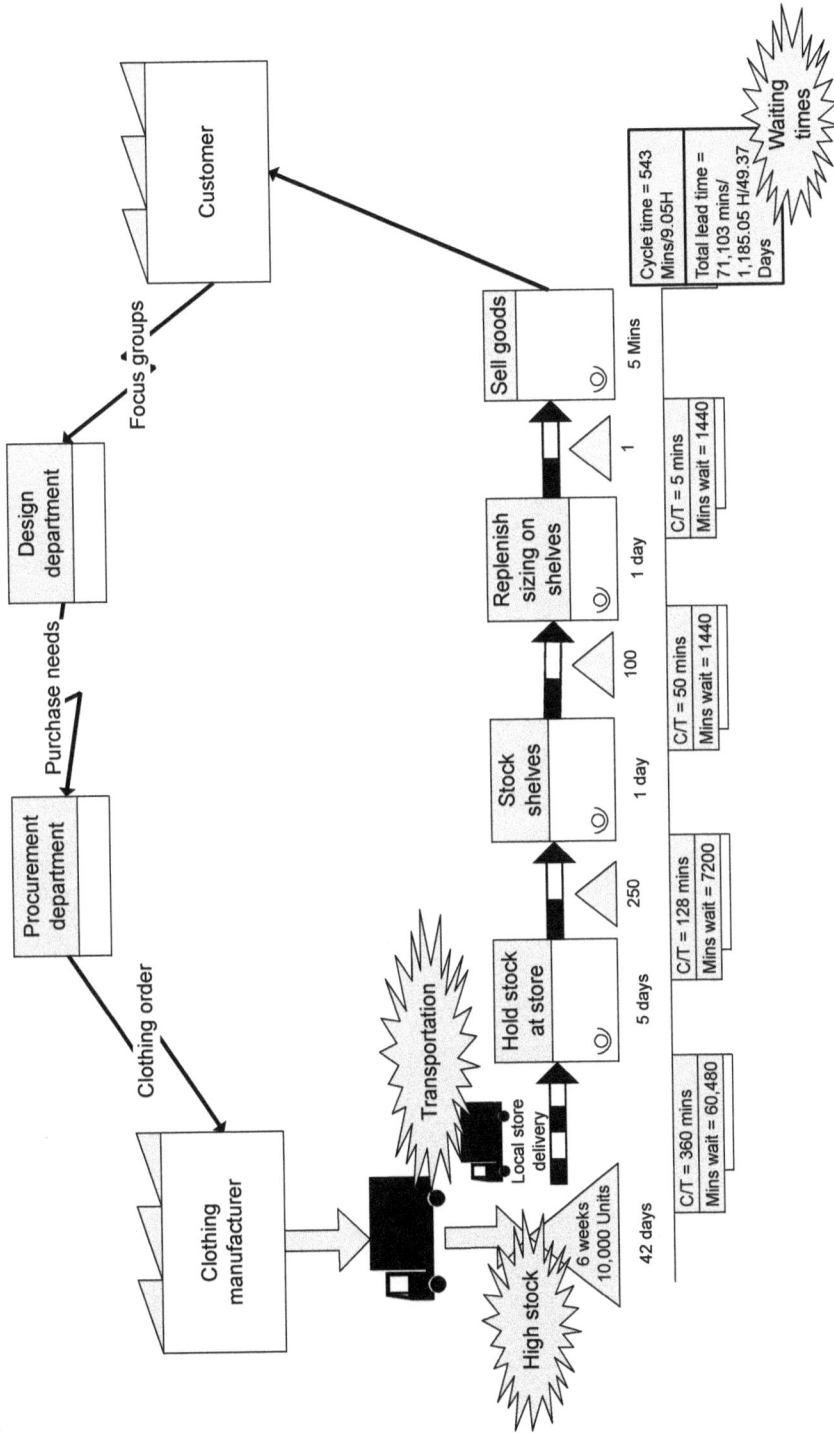

Customer

Focus groups

Design department

Purchase needs

Procurement department

Clothing order

Clothing manufacturer

Transportation

Local store delivery

High stock

6 weeks
10,000 Units

Hold stock at store

Stock shelves

Replenish sizing on shelves

Sell goods

Waiting times

42 days	5 days	1 day	1 day	1 day	5 Mins
	250	100	1		

C/T = 360 mins
Mins wait = 60,480

C/T = 128 mins
Mins wait = 7200

C/T = 50 mins
Mins wait = 1440

C/T = 5 mins
Mins wait = 1440

Cycle time = 543 Mins/9.05H

Total lead time = 71,103 mins/ 1,185.05 H/49.37 Days

Figure 6.9 Business context diagram for a coffee shop within a department store

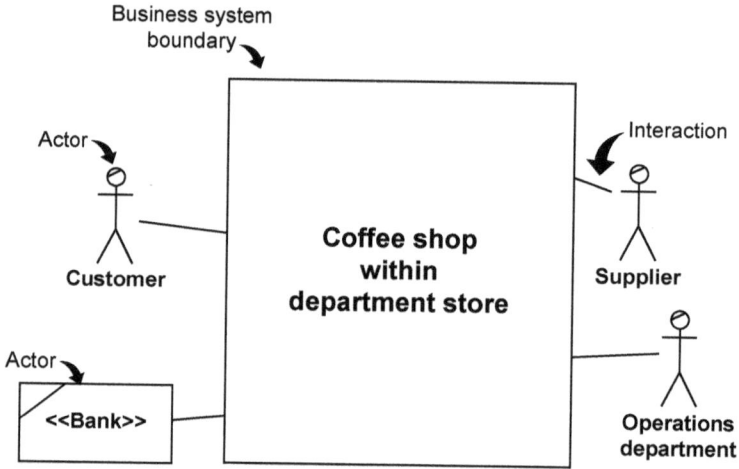

Figure 6.10 Business use case diagram for a coffee shop within a department store

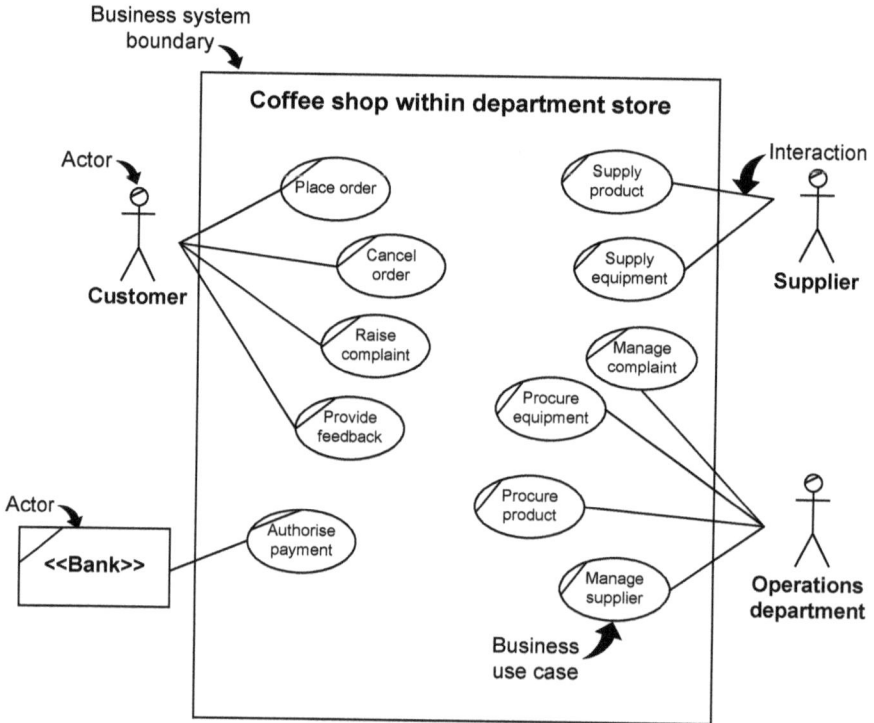

The business use case diagram on its own can be a useful artefact to support shared understanding. However, it may also be useful for the business architect to develop business use case descriptions. These provide further detail and insight into the content of individual business use cases.

A framework such as CALM, introduced in Chapter 5, can aid with ensuring differentiation between 'what' (the business use case) and 'how' (the business use case description). There are several techniques and frameworks that can be used to develop a business use case description, including POPIT (see Chapter 3) and SIPOC (see Table 6.8).

In addition to the development of business use case descriptions, business architects may find it useful to analyse and map business use cases to:

- value streams (see 'The value stream diagram' section above);
- business capabilities (see Chapter 5);
- customer journey maps and service blueprints (see Table 6.9).

The analysis and mapping of business use cases to value streams and business capabilities can support the identification and management of dependencies. This can be particularly useful for both scope and impact analysis.

Analysing a business use case to consider how it relates to the relevant customer journey map and service blueprint enables the business architect to take a customer-centric and outcome-focused approach. In turn, this may support collaboration with individuals offering service design and business analysis services (see Chapter 10).

Lean and Six Sigma

The Lean and Six Sigma process improvement methods offer a suite of frameworks and techniques that may be used to explore processes and identify improvements. They can also help business architects to focus on areas of challenge. Table 6.8 summarises some of the key approaches.

In addition, the service approach described earlier in this chapter has gained significant popularity in recent years, resulting in a suite of techniques that may be used to develop further perspectives. These techniques are highly relevant for business architects as they offer different ways of representing and analysing the process and service dimension and communicating with business executives. Table 6.9 summarises some relevant service design techniques.

CUSTOMERS, CUSTOMER EXPERIENCE AND CUSTOMER JOURNEYS

When establishing a business architecture, organisations should ensure that the strategic context is clear. The rationale for the organisation's existence (discussed in Chapter 4) should be understood as it underpins the organisation's VMOST and values. This also helps to identify the customer community for the organisation.

Table 6.8 Lean and Six Sigma frameworks and techniques used by business architects

Name	Description
SIPOC (supplier, inputs, process, outputs, customers)	This is a framework for documenting an organisation, process or service. The five elements defined in a SIPOC are: • The suppliers who provide resources or inputs to the process. • The inputs required to carry out the process – these may include data, funding or people. • The documented process. • The outputs from the process. • The customers who are the recipients or beneficiaries from the process.
DMAIC (define, measure, analyse, improve, control)	This is a five-step approach to process improvement. The steps are: • Define the problem to be improved. • Quantify the problem using measurable data to understand the root causes of problems. • Analyse the problem and identify waste that may be removed. • Identify and deploy potential actions for improvement. • Implement means of sustaining the improvements and enabling further improvements.
Kaizen (continuous improvement)	This is the practice of continuous improvement where the entire workforce are encouraged to identify and enact improvements.
PDSA (plan, do, study, act)	This is a four-stage cycle used to drive ongoing business improvement. The four stages are: • **Plan:** establish the objectives, the process to achieve the objectives and the measures required to evaluate success. • **Do:** implement the process and gather the data required to measure and analyse the outcomes. • **Study:** analyse the data and outcomes and compare with the success measures defined in the Plan stage. • **Act:** deploy corrective actions to remove differences between the planned and actual results.
Ishikawa diagram (fishbone diagrams)	This is a visual representation of a business situation that uses a 'fish' skeleton as its structure. The 'head' of the fish contains a statement of the problem under investigation. The aspects that are to be analysed regarding the problem are shown as major 'bones' emerging from the spine of the fish. Smaller 'bones' linked to the major 'bones' are used to identify specific issues.

Table 6.9 Service design techniques to support business process improvement

Technique	Description
Customer journey map	This is a model of the activities, experiences and emotions encountered by a customer persona when accessing a service in pursuit of a particular goal or outcome. This technique is described in more detail later in this chapter.
Service blueprint	This is a definition of the activities conducted and touchpoints encountered during the delivery of a service, and the resources used. The service blueprint distinguishes between the 'front stage' elements that are customer-facing and the 'back stage' elements that are concerned with aspects such as the processes, standards and data needed to deliver the service. The service blueprint is usually developed from a customer journey map and is used to analyse the customer experience and identify where 'back stage' improvements may be made.
Service safari	This is a personal engagement with a service offered by an organisation. This technique is used to obtain an experience of a service and acquire knowledge about the approach taken to its delivery. It is used to gain insights into how an organisation engages with customers during the delivery of its services.
Storyboard	This is a visualisation of the activities conducted to deliver a service. The storyboard may be used to represent a particular customer journey or service blueprint and aids understanding of an entire process. A storyboard may be used to visualise manual or automated activities within a customer journey.
Empathy map	This is a two by two matrix used to explore and record a customer's perspective on a service. Four dimensions are considered: what the customer sees; what the customer hears; what the customer says; what the customer does. These dimensions are used to interpret how the customer is thinking and feeling about the situation.
Persona	This is a sub-category of a user role that represents customers with common characteristics, such as their behaviours, preferences and requirements.
POPIT	This is a framework for analysing business situations, value streams and business processes. It ensures that the five key dimensions are investigated: people, organisation, processes, information and technology.

The target market

One element that requires consideration is the market or market segment served by the organisation and the characteristics of the customers. Some organisations are established to provide products and services to a particular customer population. For example, BCS, The Chartered Institute for IT serves the professionals working within the technology industry and their employers.

Commercial organisations often clarify their target market by defining the characteristics of their customers. For example, using demographic characteristics based on age, gender or nationality. Consumer preferences are also analysed to determine the customer base. These include specific brand preferences related to company image, service quality or product durability.

An understanding of the customer community informs the organisational decision-making. It also enables the business architect to define the business architecture principles and governance mechanisms, plus the organisation's services, value streams, capabilities and information needs.

Customer experience

Customer experience has been recognised as a key contributing factor to business success (www.accenture.com/us-en/insights/song/customer-experience-index). It is described as 'multi-dimensional', encompassing aspects such as how those engaging with an organisation feel, think and behave, and relating to the interactions with an organisation across the 'entire customer journey' (Lemon and Verhoef, 2016).

Customers want to feel that their engagement with an organisation has satisfied their needs from several perspectives. They want:

- their needs to be addressed where possible – if this is not possible, they want to have been 'heard' so that their needs are understood and available options are presented;
- the product or service to meet their requirements;
- to be treated with the expected level of courtesy and respect by the staff of the organisation with whom they are engaging, and know that their custom is valued;
- the purchased product or service to provide the level of quality they expect;
- timely communications and a high degree of responsiveness to queries.

Where the brand encourages customers to feel part of a community, they may also wish to feel a sense of belonging and recognition.

In summary, customer experience is a complex area for organisations to navigate. When delivering products or services, every interaction is an opportunity for a customer to be pleased or dissatisfied with the customer experience encountered. Business architects, as custodians of the value streams and capability models, need to understand the issues associated with customer experience. They also need to appreciate the strategic context for customer experience and be able to identify where there are gaps in the available organisational capabilities.

Customer journeys

Customer interactions with organisations are opportunities for successful, or less successful, engagement. These interactions are known as 'touchpoints', and a customer may engage in several touchpoints during a customer journey. A poor experience at one touchpoint may create a negative impression about an organisation even if the delivered product or service has met the customer needs.

Customer journey maps are developed to explore the actions conducted by a customer, and the experience encountered, when engaging with an organisation. Figure 6.11 shows an example customer journey map, including the range of elements documented and analysed about a customer journey.

Figure 6.11 Example customer journey map

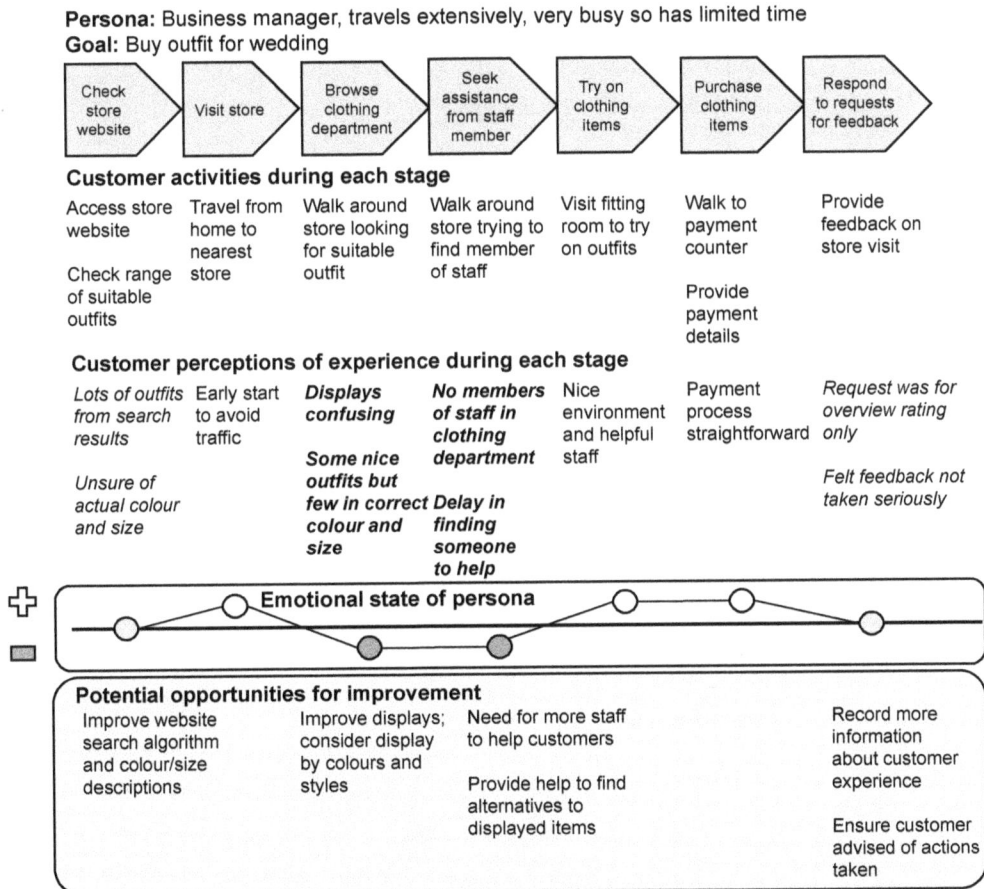

Persona: Business manager, travels extensively, very busy so has limited time
Goal: Buy outfit for wedding

Check store website	Visit store	Browse clothing department	Seek assistance from staff member	Try on clothing items	Purchase clothing items	Respond to requests for feedback

Customer activities during each stage

Access store website Check range of suitable outfits	Travel from home to nearest store	Walk around store looking for suitable outfit	Walk around store trying to find member of staff	Visit fitting room to try on outfits	Walk to payment counter Provide payment details	Provide feedback on store visit

Customer perceptions of experience during each stage

Lots of outfits from search results *Unsure of actual colour and size*	*Early start to avoid traffic*	*Displays confusing* *Some nice outfits but few in correct colour and size*	*No members of staff in clothing department* *Delay in finding someone to help*	Nice environment and helpful staff	Payment process straightforward	*Request was for overview rating only* *Felt feedback not taken seriously*

Emotional state of persona

Potential opportunities for improvement

Improve website search algorithm and colour/size descriptions	Improve displays; consider display by colours and styles	Need for more staff to help customers Provide help to find alternatives to displayed items	Record more information about customer experience Ensure customer advised of actions taken

Customer journey analysis is used to investigate, analyse and improve customer experiences encountered as they navigate the organisational value stream activities to fulfil a desired goal. The relevant value stream provides additional information to support this analysis. The activities in the value stream that require touchpoint engagement with customers may be explored to uncover how well the activities are carried out during each touchpoint. The capabilities that enable the value stream may be analysed to identify how well they support the activities and customer touchpoints.

When combined with value stream and capability analysis, customer journey analysis offers the potential to identify the following areas of concern:

- The touchpoints where customers were not satisfied or actively dissatisfied.
- The touchpoints where customers felt the engagement met their needs but the organisation has the capability to exceed those needs.
- The capabilities or capability factors that cause issues, typically because of capability gaps or limitations that needed addressing.

These areas of concern may require the business architect to review the value stream activities and the value proposition offered and to consider improvements or additions to the organisational capabilities.

VALUE NETWORK ANALYSIS

Verna Allee developed the value network analysis technique, which is explained in her book *The Future of Knowledge* (Allee, 2002). It is a modelling approach that allows the exploration of both tangible value and non-tangible value exchanges within an ecosystem, organisation, department or specific process or value stream. There are two types of value network analysis: those that focus on the internal exchanges within an organisation and those that include external parties such as suppliers, competitors, customers and partners.

The value network approach requires a deep understanding of the business and is created using roles as the key building blocks, represented by 'nodes'. Allee stresses the importance of using roles rather than people to ensure a level of repeatability and stability in the model. The roles can be identified from an organisation structure, ecosystem model, business process or other organisational view (see Chapter 4).

Once the roles are captured, formal value exchanges can be added. The tangible value items are explicit and measurable, and are represented by solid lines. Tangible items such as contracts, service level agreements, reports, data, products and services are observable, often involve money and are typically documented and managed.

The informal value items can then be added to the model using dashed lines. These fall into two categories: knowledge and intangible benefits. These intangible concepts are much harder to assess, are unstructured and are often difficult to identify. Items such as reputation, assumptions, informal feedback, loyalty, favours, know-how, benefits and motivation allow the organisation to understand what hidden value the product or service can offer.

Figure 6.12 Value network for the 'After Sales Support' value stream activity

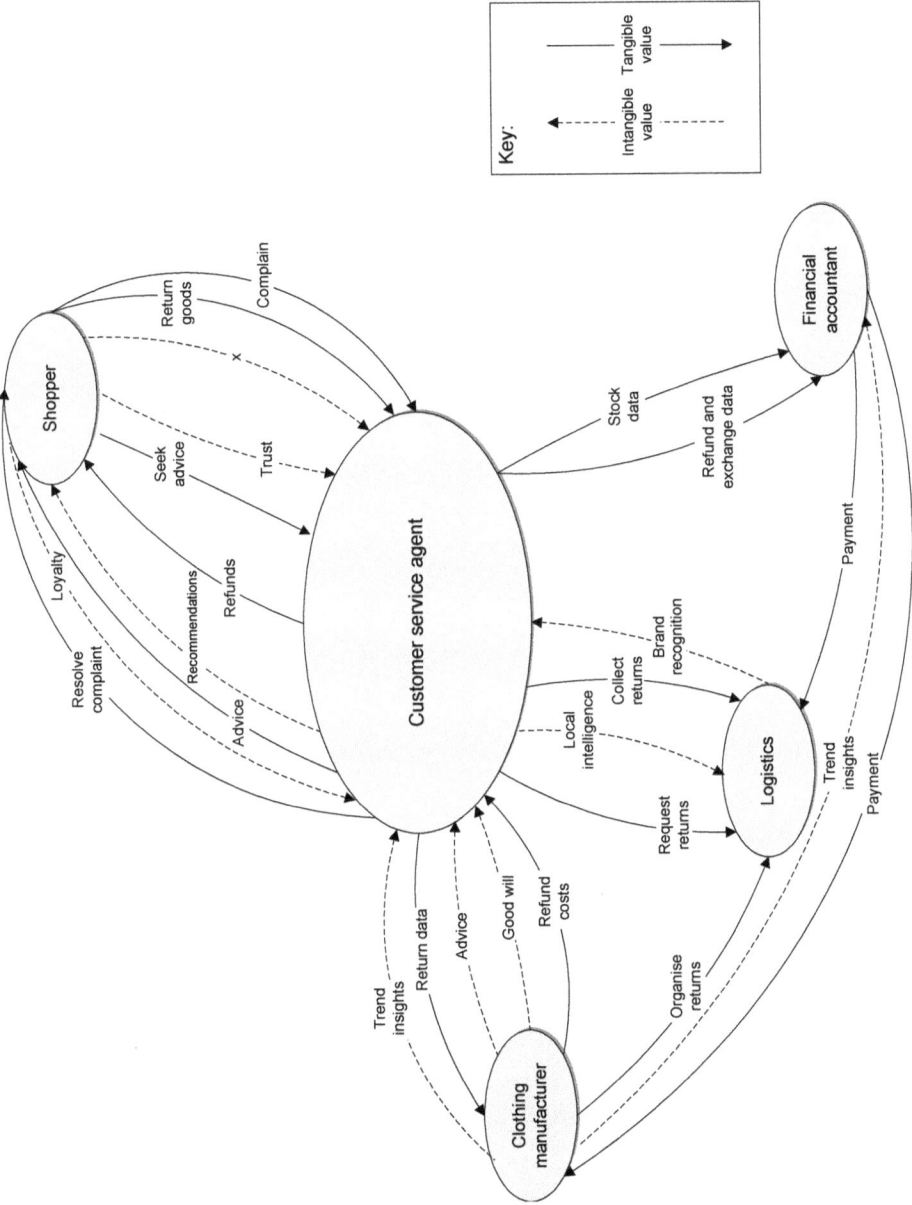

The final step is to record the value items, typically in a table, and use this as a basis for analysis. The aim is to understand and potentially transfer value items from being hidden to offering visible and measurable value that may be realised by the beneficiaries.

The example provided in Figure 6.12 explores the value network for the 'After Sales Support' value chain activity from the department store.

CONCLUSION

This chapter has explored the meaning of value, including how value can be used for competitive advantage and how the business architect can represent value intentions and offerings from a variety of perspectives.

Value-oriented diagrams highlight the links between the business services, value streams, business capabilities, business processes and the overall operating model. They help business architects to communicate with business leaders so that they appreciate the activities that enable customers to co-create value when engaging with the organisation.

The models may represent an entire enterprise, a particular business unit or a specific product or service. They support a range of actions, including customer analysis, business impact analysis and process improvement. They help to identify where beneficial operating model changes may be made, such as the removal of business activities that are not contributing to the achievement of the value proposition.

The creation of the models and diagrams discussed in this chapter is time-consuming and requires expertise. However, they offer a meaningful and customer-centric view of an organisation and highlight where there are opportunities to improve customer outcomes and there is the potential for significant competitive advantage.

7   INFORMATION VIEW OF BUSINESS ARCHITECTURE

INTRODUCTION

This chapter covers the following topics:

- the importance of the information view;
- metadata, data and information;
- business information modelling;
- links with other business architecture artefacts.

THE INFORMATION VIEW

A small proportion of the world's information is now paper based. With the growth of the internet, cloud computing, artificial intelligence (AI), digital resources, social media and collaborative platforms such as YouTube and TikTok, the volume of available data and information is growing at an astounding rate. A staggering amount of new information and data is generated and created on an hourly basis, and this rate of generation is set to continue and to accelerate.

This explosion of information provides an opportunity to both individuals and businesses alike. Organisations that have a good understanding of the information they hold, and the data that supports business decision-making and insights, can gain a competitive advantage over rivals, decrease the time to market and more quickly and easily co-create value with customers.

However, information and the relationships between capabilities, operating models, processes and people is an important yet underrated element of a business's architecture. This chapter explores the importance of the information view, how it relates to business data, approaches to model the data and how this may be utilised to gain insights and understanding. The chapter also discusses the fundamental issues that need to be addressed, such as ensuring the accuracy and privacy of information, if data is to be a positive asset for an organisation.

The nature of information

Information is the lifeblood of an organisation. It enables the value stream activities and is a key element within the business capabilities. Organisations cannot operate without information as it is required by the business processes and is the key input to every business decision. For example, within a department store, information is needed about the products, the equipment, the staff, the store facilities and the sales levels. If the store didn't have information about the products available, it would not be possible to make a sale, advise customers on product features or decide the price to be charged.

Information is an abstract concept that is generated from raw data values and is interpreted to gain knowledge. Typically, it summarises a number of different elements or aspects and is the basis for the collective interpretation of the ecosystem, organisation, products, services, data, processes and customers. It is often confused with data but is much broader and less tangible. While data concerns the raw values that are collected, organised and recorded by organisations, information results from reporting on the data within given parameters that enable interpretation or offer insight. As a result, information is often defined as 'data in context'.

While this distinction is often drawn between the terms 'data' and 'information', many organisations use them as substitutes rather than distinguishing between them. For example, the DAMA International Data Management Body of Knowledge (DMBOK) states that it uses the terms interchangeably.

Well organised and high-quality information is a benefit to business owners, managers and employees, and supports the delivery of the organisation's value proposition. It helps organisations to employ their business capabilities in the most efficient and effective way. An organisation that can exploit its information to inform action and decision-making is well positioned to adapt and evolve its ecosystem in response to a fast-paced modern business environment.

Information concepts are a core notion in the software industry, and technology solutions are often used to capture, store, retrieve and report on the information an organisation holds. This may be information about a wide range of stakeholders, including employees, partners, customers and competitors, plus the products or services delivered by the organisation. However, information may also be present in physical forms in the work environment – printed advertising materials, video or audio recordings, employee comments and verbal customer feedback are all examples of information that would not be held or indexed using a formal mechanism such as a software application, as would be the case for data regarding financial or sales records.

Information concepts represent 'what' a business knows. It is an aggregation of items, and, for this reason, it can be problematic to capture and document some information. It is often tempting to focus on the tangible elements of information, such as that related to products or services, organisational policies or business rules, but the items that are less tangible, such as reputation, know-how, experience and feedback, are equally important to support the achievement of customer outcomes and profitable return on investments.

The importance of the information view

The information view supplements and enhances the other business architecture views. Information supports and enables both the business capabilities and the value stream activities. Therefore, the information view has the potential to provide important insights regarding an organisation, its business environment and the products or services it offers. It is a key business architecture perspective.

Business architects use the information view to clarify the products, services, activities and actors (or service systems) of interest to the organisation and the terminology used when conducting the work of the organisation. These clarifications underpin understanding of the organisation's ecosystem. They also provide assurance regarding the capabilities possessed by the organisation and the value stream activities conducted to deliver products and services to customers.

The information view answers the following questions:

- What do those working for the organisation or engaging with the organisation need to know about?
- How can consistency of terminology and understanding be assured within the organisation?
- How is the organisation's knowledge communicated effectively?
- What information is held that is subject to data protection and how is data security accomplished?
- What information might be exploited to enhance or extend the products and services offered by the organisation?

Where information is sourced, created, applied and harnessed effectively, it can enable strategic superiority for an organisation.

METADATA, DATA AND INFORMATION

Data, metadata and information are all related concepts but are different in the way they can support the understanding of an organisation and its architecture. Figure 7.1 shows the hierarchy of information, metadata and data.

Figure 7.1 Hierarchy of information and related types

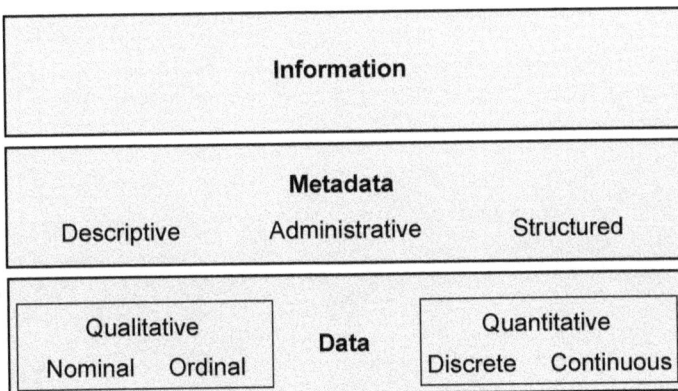

Information

Metadata		
Descriptive	Administrative	Structured

Qualitative	Data	Quantitative
Nominal Ordinal		Discrete Continuous

Metadata

The term 'metadata' was first trademarked by Jack E. Myers in 1969. Metadata is data about data. It is an aggregated view of individual pieces of data and allows for the sorting, categorising and understanding of the data elements. It provides contextual description and structure about the data.

Bruce Schneier recently highlighted the importance of metadata to organisations and business architects in his book, *Data and Goliath* (2016) stating: 'Data is content, and metadata is context. Metadata can be much more revealing than data, especially when collected in the aggregate.'

There are three main types of metadata:

- Descriptive metadata enables discovery, identification and selection of resources. It can include elements such as title, author and subjects.

- Administrative metadata facilitates the management of resources, such as file names, versions and storage locations.

- Structural metadata describes the data types, formats, versions and relationships between data groups and items. Structural metadata may optimise search engines, provide context and organise data. A class on a class model is an example of structural metadata.

Data

Data is collected and recorded by organisations and is used to generate information. The use of data can be traced back to the Palaeolithic era, when early humans used bones to count and record values.

Data refers to a specific piece of evidence or a fact. The data held by an organisation consists of raw values and is often meaningless without a context. For example, the number 111213 could be a product identifier, an account number, an invoice number or a date. If it is used within the format PI 111213, it may be assumed to be a product identifier; if it is reported using the format 11/12/2013, it may be seen to represent a date. The format provides context and so can convert the raw data into information, although it is always vital to check any interpretation.

The raw data values may be numerical, alphabetical or a combination. For example, RD22 6PH is a combination of numerical and alphabetical values; the format suggests that this is a car registration number (in the UK).

The concept of structured data was pioneered originally by Pfleumer in the late 1920s (Engel, 1999) and has grown and evolved substantially over the intervening decades. Data may be structured using a defined format, as shown in the car registration number, or may be unstructured, such as data that is contained within written text or video.

While data may be recorded on paper, it is more typical for data to be stored within computer databases. However, the potential usage of data recorded on paper should not be overlooked.

The creation and advancement of the World Wide Web in the late 1980s by Sir Timothy John Berners-Lee substantially increased the volume and nature of the data available to organisations.

Data may be qualitative or quantitative, and within each of these categories there are two further types of data. The types of metadata, qualitative data and quantitative data are described in Table 7.1 with examples from the department store context for each category.

Table 7.1 Definitions and examples of data and metadata

Concept	Description	Example
Metadata	This is data that describes the characteristics of the data.	This might be a model of the data, listing the groupings, individual data items and the links between the data groups.
Descriptive metadata	Descriptive metadata is information that provides a detailed description of a data resource, helping users to understand its content, context and characteristics.	This might be the dimensions of an image file, such as the resolution and size of a photograph of a product.
Administrative metadata	Administrative metadata refers to information that pertains to the management and administration of a dataset or digital resource. This type of metadata provides details about the logistical and operational aspects of data, helping to organise, track and maintain the dataset throughout its lifecycle.	This might be the format of a file that ensures compatibility with a software application used to conduct the business of the department store. For example, the.xls extension indicates the format for a Microsoft Excel file.
Structural metadata	Structural metadata provides information about the organisation and relationships within a dataset or a digital resource.	This might be the class model and XML schema definition for the data stored within the department store's website.
Qualitative data	Qualitative data refers to non-numeric information that describes and categorises attributes or characteristics of a subject. There are two types of qualitative data: nominal data and ordinal data.	Textual reports or audio and video recordings that capture verbal and non-verbal communication, providing insights into tone, emotion and context.

(Continued)

Table 7.1 (Continued)

Concept	Description	Example
Nominal data	Data that uses language (labels) to distinguish between different categories but does not have an order or rank. Nominal data is used primarily for classification and grouping.	This might be a report listing the home locations of visitors to the department store over a given month.
Ordinal data	Ordinal data uses language to distinguish between different categories and has a pre-determined order or rank that indicates the relative position of each category.	This might be a report listing the age ranges of visitors to the department store on a particular day, or a summary of responses to a customer satisfaction survey using the Likert scale: strongly disagree, disagree, neutral, agree, strongly agree.
Quantitative data	Quantitative data refers to information that is expressed in numerical terms and can be quantified or measured.	Reports that provide data using numerical values.
Discrete data	Discrete data can be counted and has a fixed set of values; for example, number of employees in a company, number of attendees in a class and the population of a city.	This might be a report listing the number of staff members employed on particular dates.
Continuous data	Continuous data refers to information that can take any value within a given range, is obtained by measurement rather than by counting and can be measured with a high level of precision.	This might be a report listing electronic product dimensions, such as screen size and weight, that are used to label items sold within the department store's technology section.

Data tends to be a stable resource for organisations, so the information it generates offers a long-term view for an organisation. The information provides insights into various aspects of an organisation's operational context so is usually deemed a beneficial resource or asset. However, the value of the information asset depends upon whether or not it is accurate, organised and accessible. Many organisations hold data that cannot be used to generate information because it is not sufficiently well organised – which makes reporting difficult and time-consuming or completely inaccurate, resulting in information that is unreliable and does not offer insights and support to the organisation.

Organisations record, store and report data in its raw form. They use this raw data to conduct operational processes, such as responses to customer service queries, and to create tactical and operational information that supports executives and managers when making business decisions. Today's world of constant change requires organisations to ensure data is correct so that it generates accurate information that offers advantages for the organisation and its customers.

Information

Information is a summarised view of both data and metadata and usually presents data in a form that is business relevant. Information may present the results of tangible data, using structured reporting formats, or may include less tangible items, such as a decision that requires experience to interpret and analyse the reported information. It is a key dimension of a business architecture for an organisation. Business architects need to record the information that underpins the capabilities, and is required by the business processes and decision makers, to ensure it supports the information needs at all organisational levels.

The three levels of information required by organisations are:

- strategic information;
- tactical information;
- operational information.

Table 7.2 describes these three levels of information and provides an example at each level using the department store context. The information levels described are also represented in Figure 7.2, using Anthony's Triangle (based on Anthony, 1965).

Table 7.2 Levels of information within the organisation

Concept	Description	Example
Strategic information	Strategic information is used to support long-term, intentional decision-making within an organisation.	Market trends and analysis: information about emerging trends, consumer behaviours and market dynamics to inform product development or market entry strategies.
Tactical information	Tactical information is used to support tactical (managerial) decision-making within an organisation. It's focused on achieving specific short- to medium-term goals.	Female clothing quarterly sales reports: information on sales figures over a period to help adjust inventory levels or employee numbers.
Operational information	Operational information refers to data that is used to carry out the daily processes that are conducted to carry out the work of the organisation.	Inventory/stock levels in the electronics department: real-time information on the quantities of products or materials in stock to support re-ordering and deliveries.

Figure 7.2 Anthony's Triangle information levels

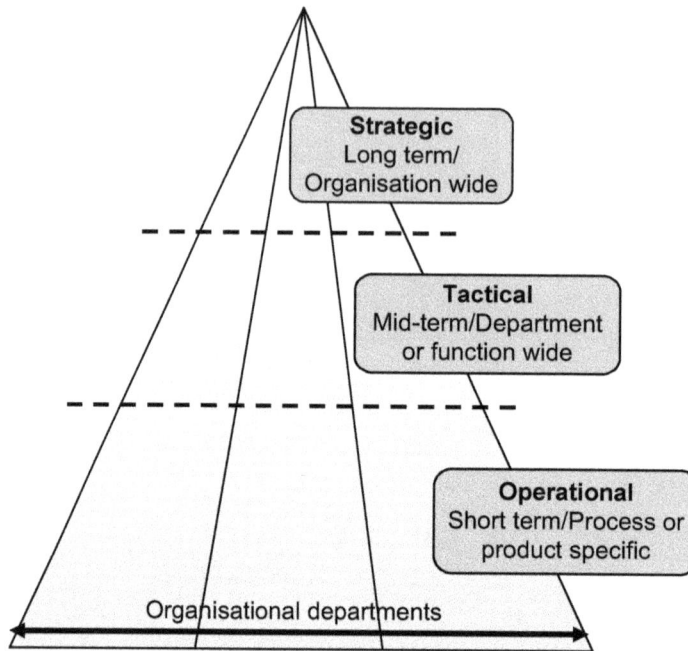

Accuracy and privacy of information

With the increasing volumes of data and information available to organisations, and the potential value this asset offers, information must be managed and processed in a sensitive and protected way. The accuracy and consistency of the data and information is critical, as is ensuring the safety and security of information on behalf of employees, suppliers and customers. Having rigorous data management policies and procedures in place helps to build trust between the stakeholders providing data and the organisation.

In recent years there has been an increasing focus on ensuring the privacy of every individual's personal data and aligning with the principles that underlie data protection, such as accuracy, storage, currency and relevance. The need for data protection and privacy has been driven by a dramatic increase in criminal activity relating to data, such as identity theft and fraud, plus the growth of misinformation and disinformation dissemination. This has led to a shift in public opinion as more cases are publicised and awareness has grown. Stakeholders need and wish to be assured that their data is protected when they engage with an organisation.

The UK Data Protection Act, 2018, a variety of legal requirements from the US, in particular the California Consumer Privacy Act (CCPA), and the General Data Protection Regulation (GDPR) in Europe are measures introduced by legislators to protect consumers from data misuse and exploitation. These laws aim to ensure transparency about how data is gathered and used, with the aim of maintaining confidentiality and integrity.

Organisations now have both a legal and a moral obligation to ensure the accuracy of the information they hold and use. Good, accurate data enhances decision-making at all levels of the organisation. It ensures that customer requests are processed effectively, managers are able to make decisions about their domains and executives can identify the opportunities, trends and patterns that enable them to predict organisational or product performance and determine where strategic changes are needed.

The growth in popularity and utilisation of AI to process global data resources and provide requested information requires business architects to have a good understanding of the information concepts available to the organisation. The development and increasing use of technologies such as large language models, machine learning, generative AI (such as ChatGPT) and the advancement of neural networks provide new opportunities for product or service enhancement and value co-creation with customers. It is inevitable that the use and popularity of these technologies will grow and that this will raise data protection (and information) challenges for organisations. Given this, it is likely that the use of AI technologies will be governed by new legislation that is added to the existing legislation mentioned above.

Sources of information

An organisation's data may be sourced from a range of service systems within the organisation's ecosystem. This is a key factor for consideration by the business architect. Information sources are varied and wide reaching and so it is vital that information is obtained from reputable, reliable sources. The cost, level of detail, relevance and timeliness are also important factors to take into consideration.

Information sources are typically categorised into three main groups. Table 7.3 describes the primary, secondary and tertiary groups.

Table 7.3 Sources of information

Type	Description	Example
Primary information sources	First-hand accounts or original materials sourced from the creators. They are typically new discoveries, materials or information.	Original art works, academic or medical research papers, photographs, surveys, interview records and verbal or written feedback.
Secondary information sources	Second-hand accounts or summaries of a single source or multiple primary sources. They interpret or aggregate the original sources to add additional details or build upon the original information concepts.	Textbooks, biographies, commercial data, competitor analysis, sales reports and databases.
Tertiary information sources	Third-hand sources that summarise and aggregate secondary data sources. They simplify and combine other information without specific references or recognition of the original information source.	Guidebooks, manuals, handbooks and some textbooks.

When looking to gather information or support business decisions with secondary and tertiary information, it is essential to ensure the provenance and reliability of the data provided.

Should business decisions be made using flawed or inaccurate data, any conclusions reached could be undermined, harm may be caused to customers or prospective customers and reputational, regulatory or criminal repercussions may result. For example, when applying for a property loan, a bank may utilise the following data sources to inform an underwriting decision:

- financial records from a credit reference agency, including loans, savings, income and other debts;

- nationality information from the Driver and Vehicle Licensing Agency or Passport Office;

- address validation services to confirm location information;

- government statistics regarding flood risk and crime information;

- financial crime databases to screen for politically exposed persons, suspicious activity reports and sanctions;

- valuation reference data for the property and local area.

These factors enable the business architect to support sourcing and use of accurate information for decision-making at all levels of the organisation.

Ethics and information

Business ethical considerations are complex and must be applied to all aspects of a business architecture. In relation to the information a business uses, there are several areas that should be given particular attention to ensure an ethical, legally compliant and fair approach is applied to all business activities and decision-making processes:

- **Social responsibility:** how the information business practices affect stakeholders and support positive ethical business outcomes.

- **Legal responsibility:** how legal and regulatory requirements are met. Legal compliance requirements, such as those concerned with data protection, may be relevant across all organisations. However, other requirements, such as those concerned with financial services regulations, may be associated with a particular sector or industry.

- **Intellectual property:** how intellectual property rights are protected and due consideration and care is given regarding external intellectual property used by the organisation.

- **Fair representation:** how information maintains fairness and avoids favouritism or discrimination so that access to information is equal.

- **Bias:** how awareness is raised regarding biases that may influence the interpretation or presentation of information. Organisations should strive to maintain objectivity and consider diverse perspectives to mitigate the impact of bias on decision-making processes.

Through ensuring ethical considerations are imbedded in information used in the decision-making processes, businesses can build trust with stakeholders, promote responsible decision-making and contribute to the long-term success of the enterprise.

BUSINESS INFORMATION MODELLING

A model provides a pictorial representation of a particular perspective on an organisation or system. Chapter 5 discussed business capability models, which represent the strata and levels of capabilities possessed by an organisation. Chapter 6 explored value stream diagrams, which provide a view of the key activities conducted within an organisation in order to deliver a value item to customers. These two views are complemented by business information models, which provide a view of the information held and utilised by an organisation.

The business information model is also known as an 'information concepts model' or 'enterprise data model' and is a key business architecture artefact. The model provides an overview of the sets of information (or 'information concepts') used within an organisation.

Information may be modelled at three distinct levels of abstraction: conceptual; logical; physical. These levels are described in Table 7.4.

Table 7.4 Three levels of information modelling

Level	Description
Conceptual	This is the highest level of abstraction. Conceptual models provide an overarching view of the areas of information that are of interest or concern to an organisation. The associations are shown between the information areas (or concepts), and the rationale for each association is indicated using terminology that is recognised by those conducting the work of the organisation.
Logical	A logical information model typically focuses on the data requirements for a particular system. This model may also be developed to represent the data requirements of an entire organisation. However, for most organisations, a corporate logical model is too complex, containing a wealth of information that is difficult to assimilate and use.
	At the logical level, the model represents groupings of data rather than information concepts. It provides detailed information about the attributes (or individual data items) within each grouping and the business rules governing the associations between these groupings. The attributes may also be defined to ensure consistency of terminology and understanding.
Physical	At the physical level, the data is modelled such that it may be used as a basis for the development of a database design. This requires the model to be fully defined and normalised with any duplication and redundancy removed. The data definitions are more detailed and formal, including information such as format, structure and validation rules about the individual attributes.

A business information model shows a conceptual view of information and identifies the key information areas that enable an organisation to function. The overview nature of the business information model helps business architects to gain a mental map of the information needs of the organisation. The model uses terminology that is recognisable within the organisation and so enables consistent communication and understanding.

A business information model is developed as follows:

- Define the scope to be modelled. This may be the entire organisation, a business unit or a support service area. For example, a business unit may concern a particular product line or service offering, and a support service area may concern the finance or procurement functions.

- Identify the information concepts of interest to the organisation that are within the defined scope.

- Represent the information concepts using a standard notation (described below).

- Consider the business associations between the information concepts. Represent and name the associations between the information concepts.

- Validate the information concepts against the other business architecture views.

These stages are discussed in further detail in the following sections.

Define the scope to be modelled

There are several techniques that may be used to model the scope to be covered by the information model.

A partial ecosystem diagram (see Chapter 4) may be used to identify the service systems that interact with the area of concern. This can be a helpful initial step before exploring the scope in further detail. A mind map, such as that shown in Figure 7.3, offers a way of structuring the scope definition, showing how the central area interacts with other actors. This model is also useful to generate ideas regarding the relevant information concepts.

A context diagram is often used to model the scope of an area of interest. The diagram has limited notation and so is straightforward to develop and can be communicated easily to business stakeholders. The context diagram has the following elements:

- a central box or circle that represents the area of interest;

- external actors, typically represented as named ellipses or stick people;

- lines between the central area of interest and each external actor, indicating the business association.

Figure 7.4 shows an example of a context diagram.

Figure 7.3 Mind map of scope for information modelling

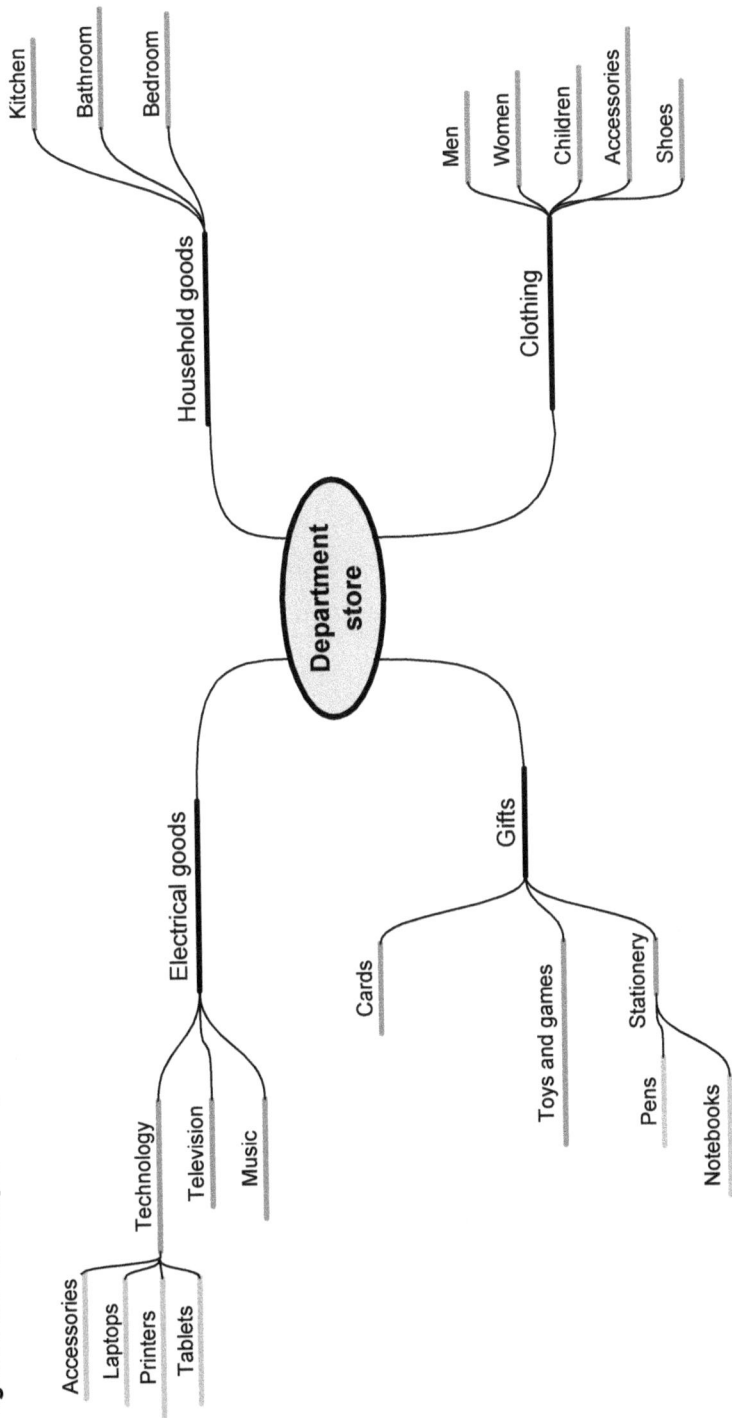

Figure 7.4 Example context diagram representing scope for information modelling

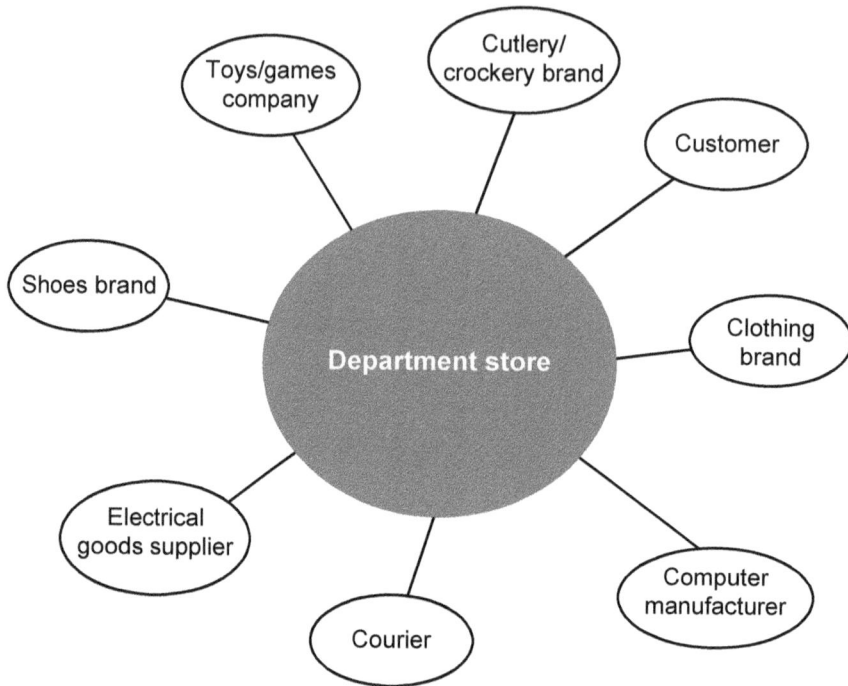

Identify the information concepts

The information concepts of interest to the area to be modelled may be identified by considering the following:

- **The nouns in the capability model:** this helps to identify the concepts that the organisation needs to hold information about. For example, within the department store, the business capability 'Product management' indicates that Product is an information concept of interest to the organisation.

- **The activities in the value streams:** for example, within the department store, the activity 'Take payment' indicates that Payment is an information concept of interest to the organisation.

- **The product structure represented in the mind map:** for example, within the department store, the products shown may indicate an information concept such as Product Type.

- **The actors and service systems represented in the context diagram:** for example, within the department store, Customer and Supplier are information concepts of interest to the organisation.

Represent the information concepts

The information concepts of interest that have been identified are represented using a box for each information concept. This is shown in Figure 7.5.

Figure 7.5 Information concepts for the department store example

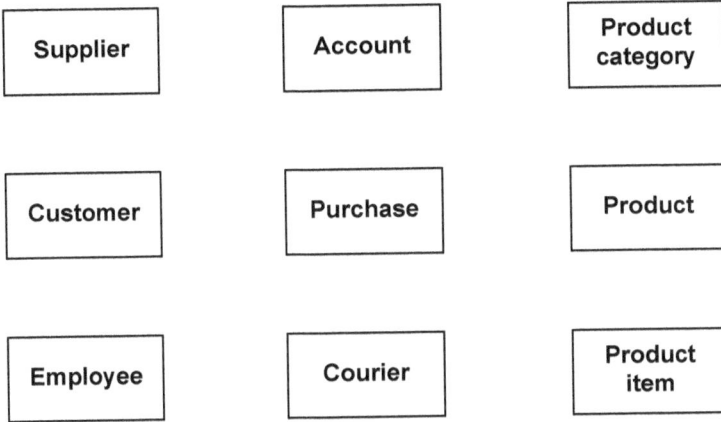

Consider the business associations

The links between the information concepts are analysed to determine if there is a relevant business association between each pair of concepts, and, if so, the nature of the association. Figure 7.6 shows a business information model containing the business associations between the information concepts for the department store example.

Figure 7.6 Business information model for the department store example

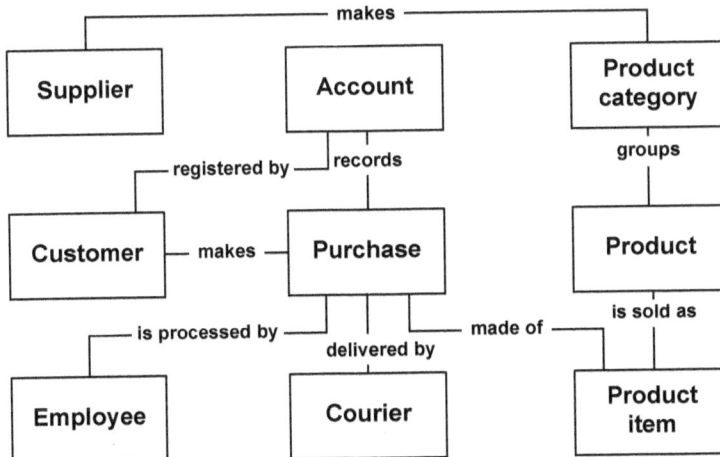

Validate the information concepts

Each of the information concepts should be used to carry out a value stream activity and to support the establishment of a business capability. Therefore, each concept should be analysed against the other artefacts to identify where there is an alignment and to validate that the information concept is required by the organisation. A matrix may be used to do this, as shown in Figure 7.7.

Figure 7.7 Matrix mapping information concepts from the department store example to a value stream diagram

Information concept/ value stream activity	Acquire latest trends	Procure stock	Display stock in-store	Take payment	Package purchase	Provide after sales support
Supplier	X	X				X
Customer				X		X
Courier		X		X		X
Product category	X	X	X			X
Product	X	X	X			X
Product item	X	X	X	X	X	X
Purchase				X	X	X
Account				X		X
Employee		X	X	X	X	X

This matrix provides a basis for analysing where information is used. It helps to uncover the following:

- where information is not linked to a value stream activity and so does not seem to be used – this may mean that an information concept is not required or a value stream activity has been missed;

- where a value stream activity does not have any related information concepts – this may mean that the activity is not required or that information concepts have been missed.

A matrix may also be used to map information concepts to organisation structures/ functions (see Chapter 4) and to business capabilities (see Chapter 5). These links are discussed further below.

LINKS WITH OTHER BUSINESS ARCHITECTURE ARTEFACTS

The models used to represent a business architecture should not be viewed in isolation, as they show different views of the same organisation. Figure 7.8 provides a visualisation of three views and how they offer different perspectives on a particular enterprise.

Figure 7.8 Three perspectives on an organisation

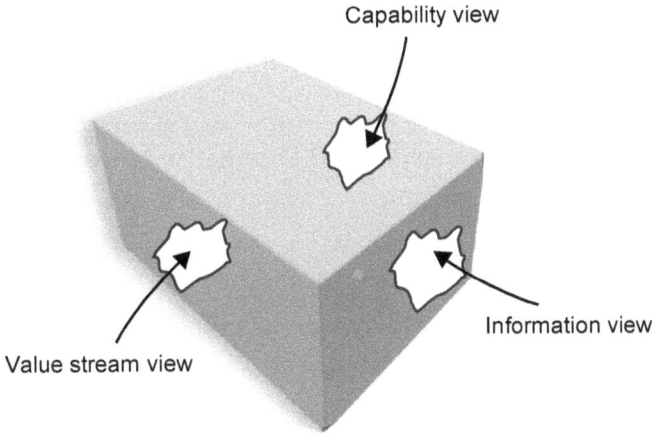

There are direct links between the three key artefacts developed by business architects: the business capability model, the value stream diagrams and the information concepts model. The reciprocal links between the three pairs of models are described in overview in Table 7.5.

Table 7.5 Links between the key business architecture artefacts

Linked artefacts	Nature of the relationship
Information concepts model and business capability model	Information is a key element of a business capability. Understanding the information concepts and the terminology used by the organisation supports the achievement of a business capability.
	For example, the business capability 'strategy analysis' requires information about the business environment within which an organisation works. Relevant information concepts may concern legal frameworks and customers and their preferences.
Information concepts model and value stream diagrams	The activities in a value stream usually require information for their operation. Understanding the information concepts used by an organisation clarifies the work carried out within a value stream and the information used within the activities.
	For example, a value stream activity 'Answer customer query' may require several information concepts, such as Customer, Product and Order.
Business capability model and value stream diagrams	The activities in a value stream diagram are enacted using capabilities. Value stream activities may be undermined if there are gaps in the capabilities.
	For example, the 'Procure stock' activity within the female clothing value stream for the department store may be performed ineffectively if the Procurement business capability does not contain defined standards.

Linking value streams to information concepts and capabilities

An example of the relationship between a value stream activity and the business information model is shown in Figure 7.9. The 'Take payment' activity and the associated information concepts are highlighted.

Figure 7.9 Linked value stream activity and information concepts

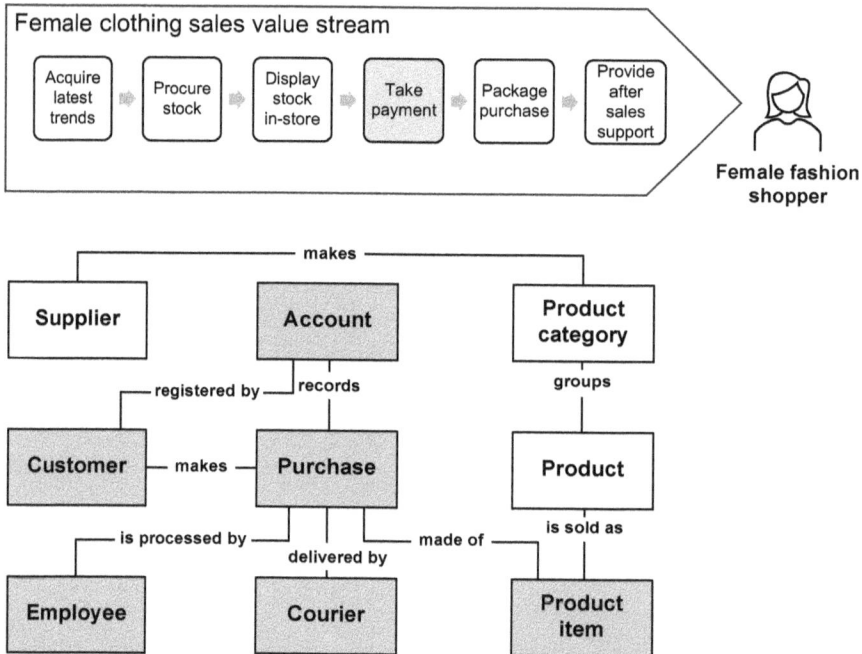

Analysing the links between business capabilities, value stream activities and information concepts provides a basis for representing an organisation's information requirements. Understanding the location, range and scope of information used within an organisation informs decision-making and supports internal service activities such as data protection and regulatory compliance. In addition, it offers insights when analysing proposed change initiatives.

CONCLUSION

This chapter has discussed the information view of a business architecture and the concepts, principles and techniques relevant to a business architect. Information is summarised from raw data collected by organisations during the course of their daily operations and may be used to inform organisational decision-making. Accordingly, it is essential that data is managed in an ethical manner and is consistent, accurate and complete.

The information view offers insight into a valuable asset that may be exploited by organisations to improve efficiency, engagement with customers and business competitiveness.

8 PEOPLE/ORGANISATIONAL COMPETENCY VIEW OF BUSINESS ARCHITECTURE

INTRODUCTION

This chapter covers the following topics:

- definition of competency terms and concepts;
- organisational competency analysis;
- situations and the organisational competency view.

PEOPLE/ORGANISATIONAL COMPETENCY VIEW

An organisation needs to possess business capabilities to deliver its products and services. Various elements need to exist for a business capability to be established, with skills at defined levels of competence being a key element within each business capability. Chapter 5 explored capability modelling and explained how business capabilities enable an organisation to conduct the activities identified in its value streams and deliver its value propositions.

Business architects are concerned with ensuring their organisations possess the capabilities that are needed to achieve the strategic vision and direction. Therefore, business architects should be aware of the competencies that underpin each capability in order to identify where organisational competency is required, where there are competency gaps and how these gaps may be addressed and the organisational competency elevated.

This chapter examines two key areas:

- the nature of organisational competency, much of which is embedded in the skills, knowledge and experience of those employed by the organisation and the wider ecosystem;
- the business architect's responsibilities in supporting their organisation to achieve the required competencies.

DEFINITION OF COMPETENCY TERMS AND CONCEPTS

The terms capability, competency and capacity are often used interchangeably and may be misunderstood or used inconsistently. These three terms are associated with ability or skill

145

and may be associated with either an individual or an organisation. A further complication arises regarding the term 'competence', as this is often used in place of competency.

These terms, and the meanings attributed to them in this book, are defined in Table 8.1.

Table 8.1 Key terms related to the competency view

Term	Definition
Capability/ capabilities	A task or action that an organisation has the ability or motivation to perform.
Competency/ competencies	A specific area of skill at a required level of ability. Competency concerns a skill at the level of ability needed to perform a particular task. Organisational competency is typically aggregated from competencies held by a group of individuals.
Competence/ competences	A general level of ability. Competence and competences are broad concepts that tend not to be focused on the achievement of a particular task.
Capacity	The volume or quantity of items that may be delivered or tasks that may be carried out.

Capabilities describe what a business needs to be able to do to operate and deliver products and services to customers. They are focused on the required business outcomes. However, an organisation's employees must possess the competencies required within each capability if the organisation is to be able to perform the defined tasks and actions. Therefore, a competency is concerned with the level of skill that is possessed within an organisation and is available to conduct the organisation's work. Competency is not concerned with the business outcomes to be achieved but with having the level of ability within the organisation such that it is possible to achieve the business outcomes.

A related concept concerns 'sufficiency' – the extent to which an organisation has competency in a particular area or the volume of employees who can provide a required level of skill. Sufficiency may be defined as the 'required capacity of organisational competency'. An organisation cannot be said to have 'sufficiency' regarding a particular skill if there is not sufficient competency within the organisation to meet the need. For example, a consultancy company may employ individuals who have significant competency in the areas of strategic analysis and execution, but, if these competencies are only held by a small number of consultants, the organisation may only be able to fulfil its value proposition for a limited number of customers. This insufficiency regarding the strategic analysis and execution competency may have a negative effect on the organisation's ability to offer services in this area. If the situation persists and customer demand for this service is high, this may have a negative effect on the organisation's reputation and finances.

However, the alternative is also problematic. Extensive competency may risk skills wastage and cause underutilised employees to seek opportunities elsewhere. Lean thinking originally identified seven wastes that were focused on identifying where a process may be inefficient. This was expanded to include an additional waste that is concerned with the underutilisation of talent and skills. Where waste occurs, an organisation may consume scarce financial resources paying salaries to employees who are not sufficiently utilised or may lose highly proficient staff who feel dissatisfied with their work situation.

Sufficiency is closely linked to scalability, which is concerned with the future growth of an organisation. While the level of competency within an organisation may be sufficient for its current business level, it may not provide a basis for service or product expansion. A balance needs to be attained between underutilising skills and being ill-prepared for the influx of additional business opportunities. For example, in the department store case study, if a new service is offered to customers, the quantity of employees with the ability to provide this service needs to be estimated. Should the service prove popular and have the potential to attract a high volume of customer interest, the store may find that the scalability of the service is not possible due to insufficiency of the competency. The demand management competency is required by the department store to ensure that sufficient resources are available to plan for and address such situations. These concerns and the effect on organisational competency are visualised in Figure 8.1.

Figure 8.1 Levels of organisational competency

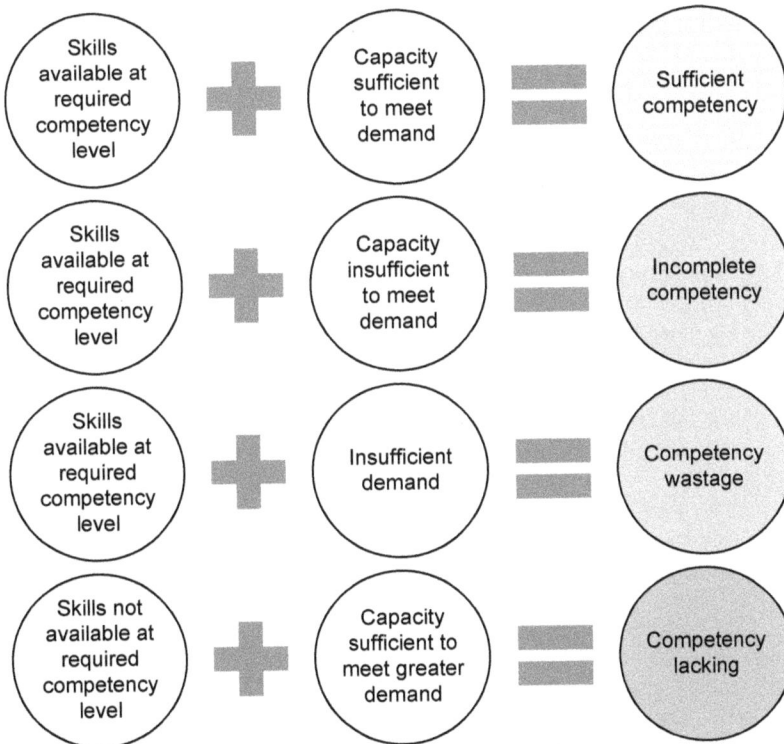

ORGANISATIONAL COMPETENCY ANALYSIS

Organisation development applies behavioural science to design and deliver change, focusing on organisational culture, values, capability, behaviours, relationships and ways of working (see https://cipd.org/uk). While business architects do not have entire responsibility for this work, they play a significant role in providing architectural views and insights that help to ensure resource optimisation and support achievement of the strategic goals.

Clarifying the relationships between an organisation's goals, value stream activities, capabilities, information concepts and business processes helps executives and managers to understand how their services are delivered and to ensure the strategic goals are achieved. Service delivery and strategy execution can be undermined if elements are not available or underperform. For example, if complex or substandard processes are in place, the ability of the organisation to deliver the products and services efficiently, and to co-create value with customers, is likely to be impaired. Alternatively, if efficient and effective processes underpin the value stream activities, a positive outcome is likely to ensue both for the customer and for the organisation.

However, well-defined, efficient value streams and processes can be severely compromised if there are issues with the required organisational competency. Specifically, if the organisational competency needed to carry out value stream activities is limited or unavailable, there is likely to be a diminished service to customers and the organisation.

Business architects should have an awareness of the importance of organisational competency and, working with other specialist professionals such as the learning and development function, should offer two documented views of organisational competency:

- definitions of the skills and the associated competency levels;
- definitions of the functions and roles performed within those functions, and the relevant skills and levels of competency they encompass.

Skill and competency level definitions

Each capability defined for an organisation is formed from several components, including people skills, standards, processes, equipment, information and technology (see Chapter 5). Where an organisation is said to possess a capability, all these components must exist and be available. Should any of the components be missing, the capability is likely to be less effective. For example, if the capability 'stock management' is defined within the capability model for the department store example, there is an assumption that the organisation possesses the relevant information, equipment, processes, standards, financial resources and competent people, all of which are needed to fulfil this capability.

Stating the skill requirements that underpin a capability does not guarantee that the competency level required for that capability exists. In the 'stock management' example, the standards and processes may be in place, but, if the employees do not know how to apply them to carry out the work effectively, the capability is likely to be weakened and require improvement.

Business architects can support the people/organisational competency view by defining the standard structure to be used for skill and competency definition and ensuring the structure is established within the organisation and used to validate the people skills elements of the business capabilities.

There are many standards available, but they are often extremely complex and require several levels of definition and, as a result, are difficult to implement, use and maintain. A more straightforward structure is usually beneficial, as this enables effective deployment within the organisation. Table 8.2 sets out a structure that may be used as a basis for defining a skill and the associated competency levels for that skill. The levels may be used to clarify the competency needed to establish the people/skill aspect required for a particular capability.

Table 8.2 Structure for defining a skill and levels of competency

Skill name	The name given to the skill.
Skill definition	An overview description of the skill, setting out the key qualities related to that skill.
Competency level	**Competency definition**
Aware	Has knowledge and understanding of a particular skill, and is able to apply the skill within straightforward contexts, typically with guidance and under supervision
Proficient	Can apply a skill without guidance or supervision within contexts that are not highly complex
Expert	Sets standards for the application of a skill across all contexts and provides direction for applying the skill within highly complex contexts

Standard skills frameworks are available for several business domains, and they can help to determine the skills and associated competency level required to establish a capability. The Skills Framework for the Information Age (SFIA) provides 'the global common reference for skills and competency for the digital world' (The SFIA Foundation, 2024), defining the key skills and competency levels across six categories.

Each SFIA category is divided into several sub-categories. For example, SFIA 9 includes the 'Strategy and architecture' category, which is divided into five sub-categories: Strategy and planning; Financial and value management; Security and privacy; Governance risk and compliance; and Advice and guidance. Each sub-category contains a set of skills, and each skill is defined at the relevant levels of professional competency. For example, the skill 'Enterprise and business architecture' is defined to three levels of professional competency.

SFIA provides a basis for determining competency within the digital professions in an organisation. However, other domains also require clear skills and competency level definitions. While frameworks may be available from professional bodies such as the Chartered Institute of Personnel and Development (CIPD), this is not the case for all functions and roles within an organisation. Therefore, business architects may need to collaborate with other specialists to help define organisational competency requirements. This work often involves reviewing the organisation structure (see Chapter 4) to determine and analyse the various functions and roles.

Analysing functions and roles

Analysing the work of a function, and the roles within the function, provides information about the organisational competency requirements and helps to identify where there are gaps. Without this knowledge, an organisation struggles to understand the competencies required to deliver the desired service offering.

The organisation view (see Chapter 4) provides outline information about the functions, roles and actors employed to carry out the work defined in the value streams. However, this is a limited view that provides an overview representation of the organisational structure and ecosystem. While the organisation view is useful for clarifying reporting lines and functional hierarchies, it doesn't provide a view of the competencies to be provided by the functions and roles that collectively form the organisational competency and enable the delivery of the products and services.

Each of the other business architecture views raise a similar issue. Value streams (see Chapter 6) provide a visualisation of the activities to be performed at an enterprise level. These may be decomposed into business process models, but they do not clarify the competencies needed to perform the value stream activities. The capability model defines the capabilities of the organisation, of which competency is a key component, but does not clarify the extent of the required competency. Therefore, the people/organisational competency view is needed to augment these views and clarify the organisational competency requirements.

Business architects can provide a competency view that states the required competencies, the level of competency needed and where the competencies reside within an organisation or may be sourced, possibly via third parties. This view also offers insights about improvement requirements, clarifying when there is a need to enhance, increase or replace competencies. It also provides a basis for deciding whether competencies are core to the organisation, so should be developed or recruited, or can be outsourced to external entities within the organisation's ecosystem.

This information is invaluable to senior leaders as it enables them to manage and maintain ongoing operations while having awareness of the available competencies that may be leveraged or replaced to gain competitive advantage.

Functions
Each organisation contains an internal ecosystem that consists of the core functions of the organisation. These functions may carry out the core activities of an organisation's value streams or may offer support services that enable the core activities. Some functions also manage the associations with entities from the organisation's external ecosystem.

Functions provide an abstract means of structuring and understanding an organisation. They are formed from logical groupings of processes and activities that conduct the work of the organisation. Function definitions describe the work conducted within each function and the knowledge, skills and competencies needed to perform that work.

An analysis of the different functions, and the associations with other functions, within the internal ecosystem for an organisation helps to identify where competency may be found. It also helps to identify where competency is required but is not available. A template for a function description is shown in Table 8.3 and an example function description is shown in Table 8.4.

Table 8.3 Template for a function description

Section	Description
Title	The title or name given to the function.
Rationale	The reason for the function and its purpose in overview.
Key goals	The defined objectives and outcomes to be achieved by the function.
Critical success factors/key performance indicators	The key measures by which the function's performance is evaluated.
Structure and roles	The line management structure and the roles that are tasked with carrying out the work of the function.
Key services/tasks	The services to be delivered by the function and the work areas for which the function is responsible.
Key applications/ artefacts	The key software applications used to conduct the work of the function and the documents used or created by the team members.

Table 8.4 Example function description

Title	HR management
Rationale	To ensure all HR responsibilities are fulfilled in line with the company's HR strategy, the organisation's policies and relevant employment law.
Key goals	• Implement the company's HR strategy. • Maintain the organisational and employment policies. • Provide HR services to all employees while they are employed by the company.

(Continued)

Table 8.4 (Continued)

Title	HR management
Critical success factors/key performance indicators	CSFs: • excellent and timely support for business executives and managers; • excellent and timely support for all employees; • compliance with policy and legal requirements. KPIs: • % accuracy in responding to HR queries; • # hours taken to respond to HR queries; • % accuracy when implementing policy and legal requirements.
Structure and roles	HR director HR manager HR assistant
Key services/ tasks	• employee recruitment service; • employee personal record maintenance; • employee appraisal process service; • learning and development service; • disciplinary service; • general HR queries service; • employee redundancy service; • payroll service (via outsourced provider).
Key applications/ artefacts	HR records system Payroll system

Table 8.4 gives a description of a human resource management function, which is likely to be found in every organisation. The work of this function may be conducted by a separate team or even an entire department. In a large organisation, several people may be employed within the HR team, each of whom may specialise in specific areas. In small organisations, HR may be combined with other functions, such as general administration, or the work may be assigned to managers of individual teams. However, where a small company requires individual managers to oversee HR matters, some activities could require competencies that are not available within the organisation; instead, it might be necessary to engage external specialist consultants or even employment lawyers.

While there could be different business models for HR, typically these include activities that are concerned with employee recruitment, development, welfare and performance. These standard activities require the same competencies irrespective of the size of the organisation.

Once the key responsibilities of a function are understood, the required competencies are evident and so may be defined. In addition, the basis for obtaining these competencies can be decided.

Linking the functions, and the competencies they require, to the capabilities and value streams offers extensive information that supports:

- the accurate assessment of risk related to the competency and staffing requirements;
- the development of staff development and management plans;
- the identification of opportunities for organisational competency enhancement and minimisation of waste;
- the targeted allocation of resources to improve collaboration between functions and the effective delivery of value streams;
- the generation of insights into the available competencies, the capabilities they enable and the ability to innovate the organisation's value proposition to its customers.

Organisations need to collect, store and access data about the functions within their internal ecosystem to develop a clear understanding about the people and the competencies they possess.

Roles

Organisations define roles to clarify the expected behaviours and responsibilities from those performing a set of tasks. Roles may be centralised, so are based within a particular function, or may be decentralised, so apply across the organisation.

The concept of a role emerged originally from the theatre, where a role is scripted and directed, making the expected behaviours clear (Biddle, 1986). Examples of actors playing film roles are shown in Table 8.5.

Table 8.5 Actors and example roles

Actor	Roles
Daniel Craig	James Bond in the *Bond* series of films
	Detective Benoit Blanc in the *Knives Out* series of films
Margot Robbie	Tonya Harding in *I Tonya*
	Barbie in *Barbie*

However, while film and theatre roles are clearly defined and directed, this is not the case for business roles. Business actors may perform different roles, often at the same time. The Open Group's ArchiMate specification provides the following definition of a business role:

A business role represents the responsibility for performing specific behavior to which an actor can be assigned, or the part that an actor plays in a particular action or event. (The Open Group, Business Layer: ArchiMate 3.2 specification)

ArchiMate 3.2 also states that 'business roles with certain responsibilities or skills are assigned to business processes or business functions'.

Within organisations, there may be little clarity about the expected behaviour of the individual performing a role and, while roles may have a stated title, there may only be vague description of the work to be performed. Role theory assumes that role participants (the 'actors') have the skills to carry out the activities defined within the role responsibilities (Broderick, 1998). This is essential if an organisation is to be successful in providing its services.

An actor who has the responsibility for conducting a business role has to ensure that the required tasks and behaviour are performed and that the required performance standard is achieved. To perform the role effectively, the actor must possess the required skills at the required levels of competence. However, this requires that the actors, and the organisation, are clear about the role, its responsibilities, the skills and competence levels and the relevant performance measures.

Role clarity concerns 'the extent to which individuals clearly understand the duties, tasks, objectives and expectations of their work roles' (Henderson et al., 2016, p. 1,718). However, many role definitions are unclear and do not offer specific, unambiguous information about the behavioural and associated competency requirements. Where role clarity is not available, there may be a clash of expectations between the actor performing the role and other actors within the organisation, which may add further confusion to the competency requirements.

The people/organisational competency view of business architecture should enable the introduction of enterprise-wide standards that serve to increase the clarity of the role definitions. These standards include templates for role definition and role profiles that set out the skill/competency requirements for each role. This helps to clarify the competencies required to conduct a role, providing a basis for gap analysis and ensuring the required people/organisational competency is present.

The human element is invariably a factor in understanding the skills and levels of competency required by an organisation. Business architects develop and maintain the business capability model, as described in Chapter 5, and the value stream diagrams, as described in Chapter 6 – both techniques support the analysis of organisational competency. In addition, a resource audit for an organisation may be applied to evaluate human resources and identify whether they offer the organisation strengths or weaknesses. This technique also reviews the motivation and commitment of employees when performing their roles. Where actors are not motivated to perform their roles to the best of their ability, the organisational competency may be diminished.

SITUATIONS AND THE ORGANISATIONAL COMPETENCY VIEW

Business architects should work with senior executives to understand the direction of their organisation, the desired outcomes and goals to be achieved and the services to be delivered. An organisation's value proposition, services and products can only be delivered successfully to customers if the organisational competency is present and sufficient. Understanding the competency view supports key organisational processes such as recruitment, performance management and demand management.

There are several scenarios where a business architect may advise strategists and other senior stakeholders about the organisational competency requirements. Techniques such as Porter's Five Forces model, PESTLE (political, economic, socio-cultural, technological, legal, environmental) analysis, scenario analysis, market trend analysis and stress testing also help to identify where organisational competency is needed and where there are competency gaps to be filled.

These techniques, in combination with other business architecture views, may be required to manage a variety of situations and scenarios. Key business situations requiring competency analysis are described in Table 8.6.

Table 8.6 Key business situations and competency activities

Business event/situation	Competency activities
Organisational change	Organisational change may be driven by many factors. For example, external environment developments identified using PESTLE analysis, competitor action identified using Porter's Five Forces analysis or new initiatives proposed by executives. Responses to such changes may necessitate the introduction of new functions, roles and skills. The level and capacity of the organisational competency is likely to be critical in achieving the organisational response to these changes.
Acquisition, mergers and divestments	The acquisition of an organisation or the merger with another organisation are two events that typically introduce additional capabilities. New skills or a greater volume of existing skills are likely to reside within these capabilities. This may mean that the organisational competency has been enhanced or augmented, creating opportunities for new or extended offerings to customers. However, it is also possible that the skills provided by the acquired or merged organisations are not aligned with the organisation's core values and purpose, or are redundant within the expanded organisation.
	Divesting the organisation of departments, functions or roles also requires analysis of the impact on the organisational competency and the available capabilities. The impact may be negligible given the services and products offered by the organisation. However, care is needed to ensure that there isn't a reduction in competency that exposes the organisation to external threats from competitors or other environmental forces.

(Continued)

Table 8.6 (Continued)

Business event/situation	Competency activities
Employment requirements	The way in which business is undertaken and the types of contracts that are available when engaging an individual employee have changed dramatically in recent years. There has been a move away from stable, secure employment – the 'job for life' construct that offers security and dependability – to contracts based on constructs such as zero hours, daily contract renewal and fixed term.
	Each type appeals to individuals who have a requirement for a particular work–life model. Executives need to decide whether they wish to apply these approaches and if they suit the operating model.
	Flexible employment contracts can raise challenges when considering the people/organisational competency view. Where many people are available to conduct the work, the flexibility can offer a valid commercial proposition for obtaining the required level of organisational competency in a timely manner. This can be of significant help with demand management during periods of demand fluctuations. However, where the volume of the available workforce is limited, organisations may find that the required competency is not available and may limit its ability to respond to market requirements for the products and services.
Role evaluation	There may be a need to establish a new role or change an existing role if the activities required to achieve business outcomes require improvement; for example, if they need to be performed more effectively. Role analysis (described above) offers a means of identifying where there are competency gaps.
Major world events	While techniques such as PESTLE analysis help executives to identify where there are developments within the external business environment, some major changes occur with little warning. These events have the potential to require new organisational competency or for the competency that is available to be leveraged within new contexts. Significant benefits can be offered where the business architect has defined and evaluated the competency view of an organisation. These benefits include enhancing the ability of the organisation to respond to major world events at pace and to ensure that the organisation remains operational in the face of these events.

Organisational culture

Chapter 4 described the organisation view, including the aspect related to organisational culture. The culture that is present within an organisation or business area may have a significant effect on the ability of the individuals to conduct their work effectively.

Culture is an area that has been researched extensively, and there are many theories and approaches that can be applied to understand the culture of an organisation (see Chapter 4). A definition of culture that is particularly relevant to the competency demonstrated by an organisation is:

> The unwritten shared values and beliefs that drive the strategy of an organisation and influence the behaviours of its members. (Paul and Lovelock, 2019)

Given the behavioural influence, a prevailing culture may result in an enhanced or diminished level of competency within an organisation or business area. The level of competency is a key element within each business capability, so the potential impact of the organisational culture on capability must be considered when analysing the business architecture and instigating change.

Business architects should understand the nature of organisational culture and the impact this may have on performance and competency if they are to navigate and influence decision-making. The intangible nature of culture can cause this dimension to be overlooked or misunderstood; applying the available frameworks and models can help to overcome any issues.

The culture pyramid included in Chapter 4 identifies how the worldview of an organisation's leadership is instantiated via formal standards and informal behaviours. This model is reproduced in Figure 8.2 and the impact of the three levels of the culture pyramid on behaviour and competency is defined in Table 8.7.

Figure 8.2 Culture pyramid (© Assist Knowledge Development Ltd)

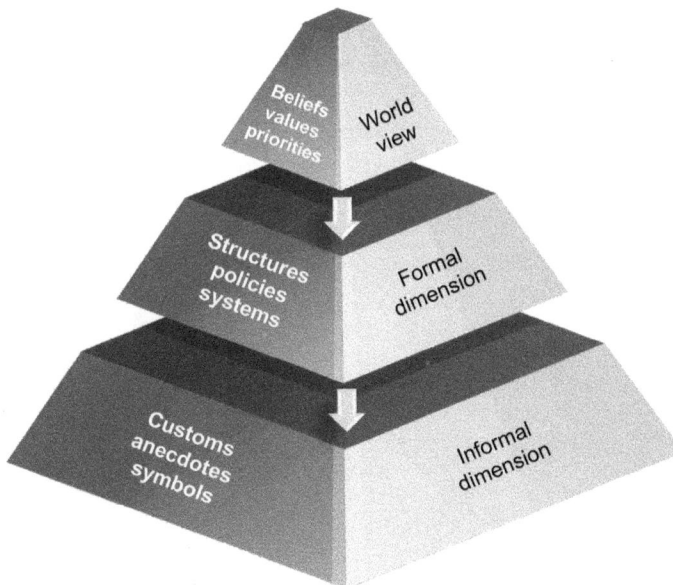

Table 8.7 Culture pyramid impact on competency

Level	Definition and impact on competency
The worldview	The leaders' values, beliefs and priorities about the organisation form the worldview they hold and set the vision for the organisation.
	This level helps to determine the nature of the behaviour and skill expected from the employees. For example, the department store VMOST in Chapter 4 described the customers as 'discerning' and the products as 'exclusive'. This vision and mission requires a significant level of organisational competency if they are to be fulfilled. Employees must be knowledgeable and supportive if they are to ensure customer satisfaction.
Formal dimension	The structures, policies and systems define the governance approaches within the organisation and determine the ways in which the organisation operates.
	This dimension sets the rules and performance measures for the employees, which are visible aspects of the organisational culture. For example, the department store has an objective 'to achieve a 98% customer satisfaction rating in the annual customer satisfaction survey'. This objective is part of the organisation's performance measurement system. It reflects the customer-focused culture of the organisation, generating performance measures that drive employee behaviour to work effectively and competently with customers.
Informal dimension	These are the customary behaviours within the organisation, the anecdotes told that reflect the demonstrated behaviours and the symbols used to represent the organisation.
	This dimension is where the tacit knowledge about the organisational culture lies and employees interpret the worldview and formal dimension.
	The subtlety of this dimension is reflected in the effect on competency. For example, within the VMOST for the department store, terms used include 'work proactively' and 'collaborate', which provide insight into the desired culture of the organisation. The interpretation of these terms drives employee behaviour and determines the competency required to manage the everyday business situations encountered, without the need for formal measures and procedures.

The culture pyramid provides a basis for analysing an organisation's culture. While executive and senior leaders set the tone for the organisation and determine which values are instilled within the culture, the interpretation of the leaders' worldviews has an effect on employee behaviour and competency.

A complication can arise where individual leaders of departments or functions have misaligned worldviews, as subtly different subcultures may develop within their teams. The levels of the culture pyramid can also help the business architect to analyse the organisational culture in detail and identify where the different worldviews and resulting subcultures exist. This can support further analysis of the behaviour demonstrated by employees within individual teams and the effect a particular manager's worldview has on the competency of the team.

CONCLUSION

Skills and competency levels are key components within an organisation's business capabilities. They enable the enactment of the value stream activities that deliver the organisation's services. Therefore, the people/organisational competency view of an organisation is a key component within the business architecture, and business architects need to understand and support the definition of this view.

Organisational competency is concerned with an organisation possessing the required skills at the required level of competency in the required volume. Analysing organisational competency requires an investigation and analysis of the functions and roles within the organisation. Each function delivers all or part of a service, and the skills/competency levels required to do this need to be recorded. Each role contributes to service delivery and so requires the holder of the role to possess a set of skills at the required competency level.

The required skills and the competency levels may be identified using skills frameworks such as SFIA. Such frameworks support the definition of role profiles, potentially at several grades, that show the combination of skills at the defined competency levels required to carry out each role effectively. The selection, implementation and ongoing use of a skills framework typically falls outside the role of the business architect, typically being decided by managers and HR specialists. However, business architects should have awareness of such frameworks and understand how they may be applied.

Culture is also a factor that contributes to organisational competency. When evaluating the competency available to deploy a business capability, it may be necessary to consider cultural factors and the impact they can have on the organisational and individual performance.

9 BUSINESS ARCHITECTURE AS A SERVICE

INTRODUCTION

This chapter covers the following topics:

- the service concept;
- the value proposition concept;
- the business architecture service framework;
- business architecture and the business change lifecycle.

THE SERVICE CONCEPT

The need for a business architecture service framework to clarify the role of the business architect was introduced in Chapter 2 and in later chapters the range of frameworks and techniques available to business architects have been explored. This chapter examines the characteristics of a service thinking approach and the nature of the value that may be realised from the work of business architects. It defines the services within a business architecture service framework in terms of their value propositions, value streams, techniques and blueprints. The different business architecture services are represented using a key business architecture blueprint: the value stream diagram.

The nature and characteristics of 'service' have been the subject of research and discussion for many years. Traditionally, it has been assumed that services are delivered in the same way as products and that value results from delivery.

The term 'service' is used in a variety of contexts, including:

- a task undertaken for a customer that concerns a largely intangible rather than physical product;
- a task to offer support and guidance to customers during and following a sales process;
- a task to perform routine maintenance or repair work on a vehicle or piece of equipment.

However, the focus within these examples is on delivery rather than outcome, so can result in a limited view. The concept of 'service' does not just focus on delivery but on achieving customer outcomes, including the desired customer experience.

A more abstract view of service considers it to be an offering that is mutually beneficial and results from collaboration and integration of resources. One definition of this view is 'The application of competences for the benefit of another' (Vargo and Akaka, 2009). Another, more specific, definition is 'The process of using one's resources to create value with and for the benefit of another actor' (Wieland et al., 2012).

Business architects are employed by their organisations to offer services – to collaborate with other professionals such as business analysts, service designers and solution architects, to enable their organisations to leverage their capabilities (or resources) and achieve desired business outcomes. These outcomes may concern the execution of a business strategy or the achievement of tactical intentions. Whichever the case, if business architects view their work from a service perspective, they will ensure that the focus is customer-centric and is on achieving the desired outcomes. They will understand the need to deliver the value proposition offered to customers. In addition, they will ensure that the available capabilities are deployed effectively in pursuit of the organisational objectives.

THE VALUE PROPOSITION CONCEPT

A service approach is customer-centric so has to begin by gaining an understanding of the customer requirements. These requirements can be wide-ranging, from focusing on the features of the product or service to stating the less-tangible requirements relating to the experience encountered when engaging with the organisation.

Understanding the customer

The first step in determining the value proposition to be offered by a service is to understand the customers and their requirements. Given that business architecture is an internal function within an organisation, the customers may fall into several distinct categories, as follows:

- Internal customer categories: the executives and managers of the organisation who wish to improve or regulate the internal operations, update existing products or services or introduce new products or services.
- External customer categories: the partner organisations within the organisation's ecosystem, the regulators that impose compliance requirements or the consumers of the organisation's products and services.

Business architects have to work with other professional disciplines and approaches to ensure that the needs of the customers are understood. Such collaboration can be advantageous, helping to ensure different perspectives and techniques are used to analyse the customers. Techniques that may be particularly relevant are role analysis, persona analysis, power/interest grid and RACI (responsible, accountable, consulted, informed) matrix. These techniques are described in Table 9.1.

Table 9.1 Customer analysis techniques

Technique	Technique definition
Role analysis	Role analysis explores the business and IT system access requirements of specific groups of individuals or organisations (the 'actors' within a business system context).
	A 'role' (sometimes known as a 'user role') is a title given to a group of actors who share common tasks and so require access to a distinct set of system services. For example, the Employee role may be the collective name for all the employees of an organisation who need access to the human resources services; the Supplier role may be the name for the set of organisations that provide products or services to an organisation.
	Individuals or individual organisations are viewed as adopting a 'role' when interacting with a business system. It is possible for an individual to adopt more than one role where they wish to access two distinct sets of services. For example, an individual may adopt the Employee role when accessing HR services and may also adopt another role that is relevant to their particular area of responsibility. This could be Sales Manager for an individual with sales decision-making responsibilities or Finance Officer for someone with financial control responsibilities.
	Role analysis applies analytical thinking to identify the roles that need to interact with a business system. The Customer role is present for most business systems, but may be decomposed to identify sets of customers where they have different access requirements. For example, Shareholders may be deemed customers with specific access requirements to financial reports; Consumers may be deemed customers who purchase (or consume) the products or services offered by an organisation.
Persona analysis	Persona analysis explores the distinctive characteristics of individuals or individual organisations that have been grouped together within a role.
	Personas are identified by examining a role and considering the different 'types' within that role. For example, the Consumer role is often investigated by organisations that wish to analyse the nature and characteristics, and the attendant requirements, of separate groups of consumers interacting with the organisation. These groups may be identified by characteristics that include:

- age band;
- disposable income;
- value perceptions;
- motivations and goals;
- behaviour and attitude;
- accessibility and usability needs.

(Continued)

Table 9.1 (Continued)

Technique	Technique definition
	A persona that has been identified through anecdotal evidence and team discussion is known as a '**proto persona**'. This is a persona that has been created from the observations and perceptions of those who have engaged with a particular role. A persona that has been identified using user research data is known as a '**validated persona**'. Persona analysis applies analytical thinking to determine which different personas are evident (whether through research data or anecdotes) and how the service delivery may be tailored to meet the needs of each persona. Two persona examples are shown in Figure 9.1.
Power/ interest grid	Stakeholder analysis comprises three stages: stakeholder identification; stakeholder analysis; stakeholder management. The power/interest grid (P/IG) provides a means of analysing stakeholders and determining the relevant stakeholder management strategy. The P/IG contains two scales: 1. The level of Power of a particular stakeholder or stakeholder group. 2. The level of Interest of a particular stakeholder or stakeholder group. Once the stakeholders relevant to a particular business context or project have been identified, they may be analysed to determine their level of power and interest in the situation. The placement helps to identify the management strategy that should be deployed for each stakeholder. For example, a stakeholder with a high degree of power and influence should be managed closely, to ensure their views are known and taken into account where possible. Where some stakeholders are customers, the PI/G helps to identify the level of engagement required to collaborate effectively with customers on a particular initiative. The PI/G is shown in Figure 9.2.
RACI matrix	A RACI matrix is used to analyse the tasks or blueprints required by a business function or project. The key tasks/blueprints are listed on the left hand axis and the actors are listed along the top axis. Each task/blueprint is then analysed to determine which actors have any involvement in the completion of the task or creation of the blueprint. The nature of an actor's involvement is analysed using the following RACI categories:

(Continued)

Table 9.1 (Continued)

Technique	Technique definition
	Responsible: the actor who is responsible for performing the work of a task or producing a deliverable. For example, a business architect is likely to be deemed responsible for developing a business capability model.
	Accountable: the actor who is answerable to senior management and owns the success or failure of a task or deliverable. For example, a project sponsor is likely to be deemed accountable for the business case for a project.
	Consulted: the actor who is able to provide information that supports the work of the task or development of the blueprint. For example, relevant business actors may be consulted about the problems with their area of work.
	Informed: the actors who are informed about a task/blueprint but do not contribute directly to the work. For example, a senior executive may need to be kept informed about the progress of a project.
	An example RACI matrix is shown in Figure 9.3.

Figure 9.1 Two example personas

	Jane	Barney
Narrative	• Retired schoolteacher • Keen traveller • Active grandparent	• Self-employed management consultant • Online gaming enthusiast • Active social media user
Character	• Enthusiastic and extrovert	• Self-styled maverick
Tagline	• 'Life is too short – enjoy it'	• 'There must be a better way to do this'
Motivation and goals	• Loves reading • Does part-time volunteering to meet people • Likes to visit new places	• Driven by success for his business • Loves being creative and pushing boundaries • Wants to retire in his early 50s to become a comedian
Content preference	• Likes travel magazines • Enjoys novels	• Likes technology • Enjoys attending shows
Social media and communication tools	• Radio, television • WhatsApp • Smartphone	• Instagram, X, LinkedIn • Smartphone, smart speaker

Figure 9.2 The power/interest grid

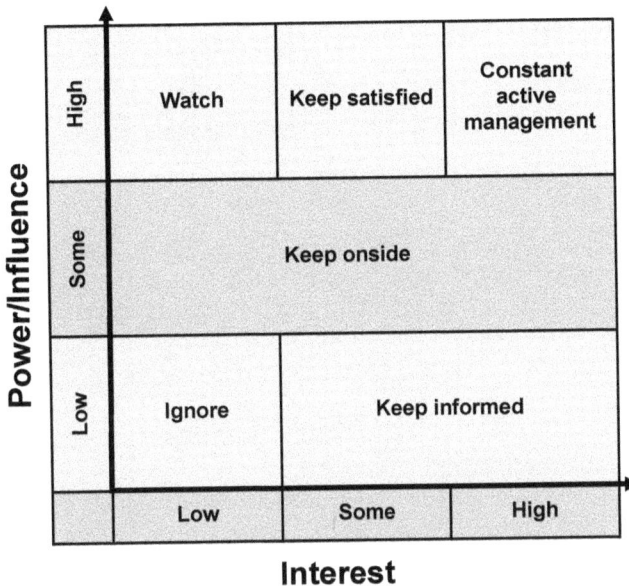

Figure 9.3 Example RACI matrix

		Project manager	Business analyst	Business architect	Manager
	Develop business case	A/R	R	R	C
	Investigate business problem	I	A/R	R	C
Tasks	Define required capabilities	I	R	A/R	I
	Design processes	C	A/R	R/C	C
	Decide priorities	C	R	C	A

Value proposition analysis

Value proposition analysis explores several distinct aspects related to a product or service offered by an organisation. Kaplan and Norton (1996) defined the key elements to be considered when defining a value proposition:

- Product/service attributes concern the item purchased and the aspects of performance related to timeliness. These attributes cover the following areas:

- functionality: the features offered by the product or service;
- price: the amount charged for the product or service;
- quality: the level of performance offered by the product or service, which includes performance areas such as robustness, accuracy and speed – these vary depending upon the functionality of the product or service;
- choice: the potential for customising and personalising the product or service;
- availability or timing: the level of responsiveness when faced with a customer request or purchase.

- Image/reputation concerns how the organisation presents its image or reputation and the way in which this is viewed by consumers and commentators. Some products or services are considered to offer increased value because they are provided by an organisation with a highly regarded image/reputation.
- Customer relationship concerns the experience offered to customers by an organisation throughout the customer journey.

These elements are represented in Figure 9.4.

Value proposition analysis helps to clarify:

- the service offered by an organisation, and the elements that make up that service;
- that what is delivered to customers will achieve what they desire or need;
- why organisations differ from their competitors.

A value proposition is a powerful mechanism when applied thoughtfully. It provides a means for an organisation to analyse the service available, given the organisation's values, core purpose and capabilities. This analysis provides insights into what an organisation believes its customers want and value and the ways in which this understanding is translated into the customer experience offered.

Figure 9.4 Elements of a value proposition

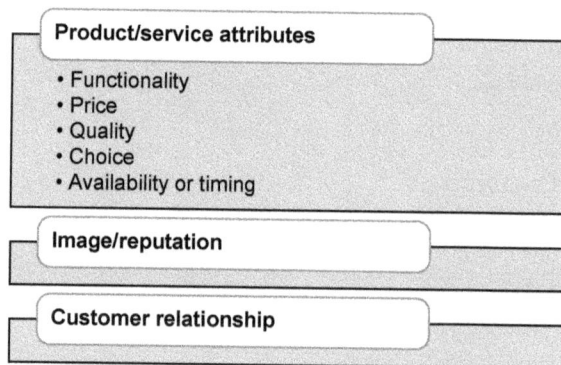

Product/service attributes

- Functionality
- Price
- Quality
- Choice
- Availability or timing

Image/reputation

Customer relationship

THE BUSINESS ARCHITECTURE SERVICE FRAMEWORK

The concept of a service framework was developed originally by Paul (2018) in the form of the Business Analysis Service Framework. This framework applied the service perspective to the business analyst role. Since this framework was launched, other disciplines have expressed concern about role clarity and the need for the level of clarity offered by a service framework. The business architecture service framework shown in Figure 9.5 has been developed to address this need.

Figure 9.5 Business architecture service framework

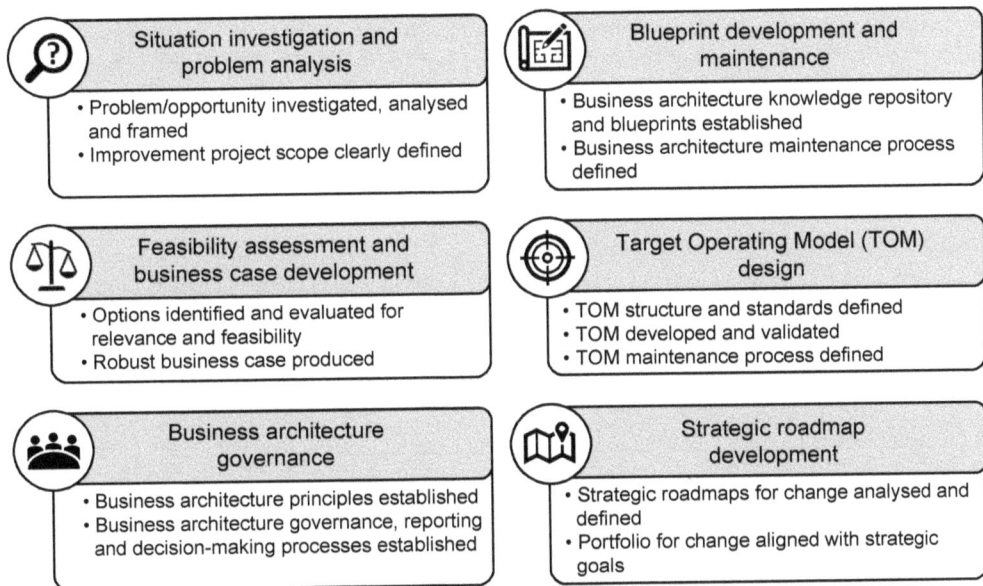

Situation investigation and problem analysis	Blueprint development and maintenance
• Problem/opportunity investigated, analysed and framed • Improvement project scope clearly defined	• Business architecture knowledge repository and blueprints established • Business architecture maintenance process defined
Feasibility assessment and business case development	Target Operating Model (TOM) design
• Options identified and evaluated for relevance and feasibility • Robust business case produced	• TOM structure and standards defined • TOM developed and validated • TOM maintenance process defined
Business architecture governance	Strategic roadmap development
• Business architecture principles established • Business architecture governance, reporting and decision-making processes established	• Strategic roadmaps for change analysed and defined • Portfolio for change aligned with strategic goals

Stakeholder engagement is an auxiliary service.

The business architecture service framework was described in overview in Chapter 2 as a basis for identifying the competency requirements for business architects. This chapter provides further detail regarding the framework, defining business architect service patterns through the definition of the value stream activities for each service.

Situation investigation and problem analysis

This service is required when a business situation has been identified as problematic or requiring improvement. The business architect, as custodian of the business architecture blueprints, works with other change professionals, such as business analysts, to investigate where there are issues, identify the problems and their root causes, and define the scope and shape of the required change initiative. Where problems are identified within a business area, stakeholders may identify where they feel the problems lie. However, it is often the case that the symptoms are identified rather than the root causes. It is incumbent upon the business architect to challenge any assumptions made about the situation, ask questions of the stakeholders and review the available business blueprints to ensure the actual problems are identified.

Business architects have to be able to collaborate with the stakeholders involved in the business situation to elicit and investigate the issues. This may require them to review various aspects of the situation, such as the processes and information, to identify where problems originate and which elements of the business architecture need to be reviewed and improved.

Stakeholder engagement is key to the success of this service. Different stakeholders are able to offer their views and experiences about the issues, and analysing these different perspectives provides a holistic view that helps to enrich the business architect's understanding.

The value proposition offered by the situation investigation and problem analysis service is that the business area is investigated and analysed with care, to provide a clear statement of the business problem to be addressed and a definition of the scope of the improvement project that is required to resolve the problem.

Situation investigation and problem analysis value stream

The activities required to carry out the situation investigation and problem analysis service are shown in the value stream diagram in Figure 9.6.

Figure 9.6 Value stream: situation investigation and problem analysis service

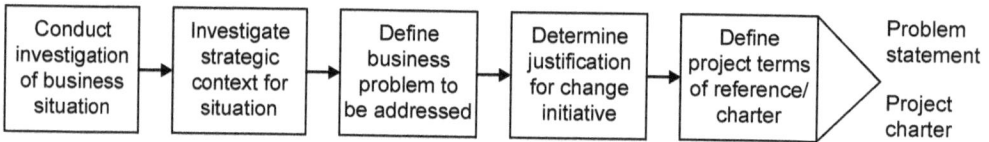

| Conduct investigation of business situation | Investigate strategic context for situation | Define business problem to be addressed | Determine justification for change initiative | Define project terms of reference/ charter | Problem statement

Project charter |

The context for this service is often unclear, with significant ambiguity regarding the issues affecting the situation and the ways in which they might be addressed. Accordingly, business architects need to have a toolkit of techniques that enable them to contend with the ambiguity and work effectively with both the stakeholders and their business change colleagues.

There are many techniques available that support the work of this service, including:

- business situation investigation techniques such as interviews, workshops, focus groups, observation and scenario analysis (qualitative research techniques); surveys, sampling (record or activity) and document analysis (quantitative research techniques); analysis techniques such as context diagrams, fishbone diagrams, business process models and the 5Ws and 1H questions (what, why, when, where, who and how);

- strategic analysis techniques such as VMOST and SWOT (strengths, weaknesses, opportunities, threats) analysis;

- business architecture techniques such as capability modelling, value stream analysis and information concepts modelling;

- problem definition techniques such as problem framing and problem statement definition;

- project definition techniques such as project charter/project initiation document (PID) creation using OSCAR (objectives, scope, constraints, authority, resources).

The products created during this service are:

- investigation records such as meeting reports, documented observations and survey results;
- business models such as context diagrams and business process models;
- problem statement;
- project charter or PID.

These techniques are defined within the Glossary and references to further guidance are provided.

Feasibility assessment and business case development

This service is concerned with evaluating the options to improve a business situation and identifying which option offers the best way forward. Each option should be considered from the three feasibility perspectives: business, financial and technical feasibility. Aspects to consider for these three perspectives are shown in Figure 9.7 and the activities required to carry out the feasibility assessment and business case development service are shown in the value stream diagram in Figure 9.8.

Figure 9.7 Three dimensions for feasibility assessment (Source: Paul and Cadle, 2020)

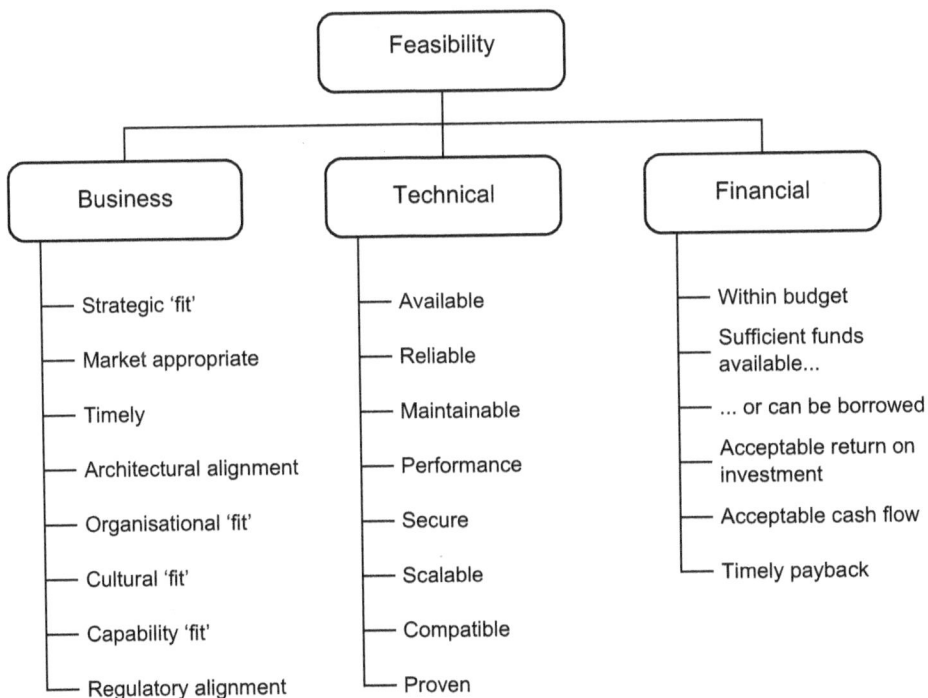

Figure 9.8 Value stream: feasibility assessment and business case development service

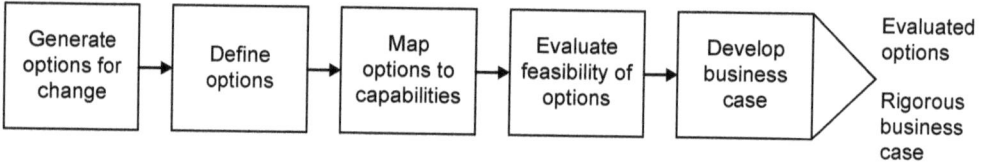

Assessing the business feasibility focuses on the alignment of an option with the organisational context. This may require the business architect to consider aspects such as the values and core purpose of the organisation, and whether the option would be likely to succeed given this context. The culture pyramid (see Chapter 8) can help to clarify where there are cultural issues that may affect an option, both positively and negatively.

The business architect, as custodian of the capability model, should analyse the organisation's capabilities when evaluating each option. This analysis should map the capabilities to each option, showing where they fall into one of the following four categories:

- capabilities available within the organisation that could be leveraged to support an option;
- capabilities that are available but would need to be enhanced to support an option;
- new capabilities that an option requires but are not currently available;
- capabilities that are not relevant to an option.

An example option/capability evaluation matrix is shown in Table 9.2. The evaluation categories are: L: leveraged (category 1); E: enhanced (category 2); N: new (category 3); I: irrelevant (category 4).

Table 9.2 Option/capability evaluation matrix

Option / Capability	Option 1	Option 2	Option 3
Strategic capability A	L	L	I
Customer-facing capability A	I	L	L
Customer-facing capability B	E	E	L
Customer-facing capability C	I	N	I
Support capability A	L	L	L
Support capability B	I	L	E
Support capability C	N	N	I

The example mapping in Table 9.2 indicates the following:

- Option 1 leverages some capabilities but also requires one customer-facing capability to be enhanced and an added support capability to be established.
- Option 2 leverages some capabilities but also requires one customer-facing capability to be enhanced and two new capabilities, one customer-facing and one support, to be established.
- Option 3 can be achieved by leveraging and enhancing existing capabilities.

Enhancing existing capabilities and establishing new capabilities is likely to require investment in one or more of the capability features defined in Chapter 5. For example, this may require additional people skills or technology. Using capability mapping to evaluate the feasibility of options ensures that all three feasibility perspectives are considered. Evaluating the technology required to enhance an existing capability or establish a new capability underpins the technical feasibility assessment. Identifying expenditure on enhancing or establishing capability features provides a basis for assessing the financial feasibility of an option.

The key techniques required for this service include:

- idea generation techniques such as brainstorming, brainwriting and affinity analysis;
- option definition techniques such as a context (scoping) diagram and business process model;
- capability mapping using a business capability model and option/capability evaluation matrix;
- option feasibility assessment using the areas defined in Figure 9.7, cost–benefit analysis and investment appraisal techniques such as payback and discounted cash flow;
- business case development techniques such as investment appraisal, risk analysis and impact analysis, and benefits planning techniques such as benefits categorisation and a benefits dependency network.

Business architecture governance

This service is concerned with the effective definition, communication and maintenance of the principles and standards that underlie and govern the business architecture. These principles and standards clarify the content of a business architecture and how it is applied to support organisational business decision-making.

The activities required to carry out the business architecture governance service are shown in the value stream diagram in Figure 9.9.

Determining the principles and standards that govern the business architecture helps to ensure clarity and consistency. This aids communication and understanding among executives and employees, supporting decision-making at all levels of the organisation. Areas to be covered by business architecture principles and standards are described in Table 9.3.

Figure 9.9 Value stream: business architecture governance service

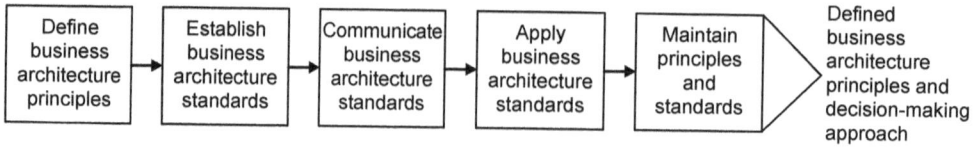

| Define business architecture principles | → | Establish business architecture standards | → | Communicate business architecture standards | → | Apply business architecture standards | → | Maintain principles and standards | ▷ | Defined business architecture principles and decision-making approach |

Table 9.3 Business architecture principles and standards

Principle dimension	Description
Ecosystem	The principles that govern the organisation, the relationships with third-party service systems and the expected service quality. For example:
	• The ecosystem scope encompasses the organisation itself, the partner organisations and the third-party suppliers.
	• All ecosystem operations and relationships must align with the company vision and values.
	• All ecosystem organisations must demonstrate compliance with the organisation's regulatory obligations.
Blueprints	The principles that govern the business architecture. For example:
	• The views to be included in the business architecture include the organisation's vision and mission, structure and functions, value streams, capabilities and core information concepts.
	• The notational standards to be applied include naming conventions, documentation templates, terminology conventions/codes and branding/styles.
	• The characteristics to be applied when developing the blueprints, such as the view offered, should be conceptual, holistic, technology agnostic and at a defined level of abstraction/detail.
	• The behaviour and values that underpin the service standards of the organisation are included.
Processes	The principles that govern the use of the business architecture within the organisation. For example, the application of the business architecture blueprints in the following situations:
	• to investigate business problems or opportunities;
	• to enable business decision-making;

(Continued)

Table 9.3 (Continued)

Principle dimension	Description
	• to identify and define options for business improvement and change; • to support strategy execution and communication. These principles may also state the roles to be involved in conducting the processes and the techniques to be applied. For example, when evaluating options for change, the principles may determine that any change programme requiring investment above a prescribed limit will require financial appraisal using specific techniques and confirmation of accuracy from identified individuals or roles.

Having defined the principles and standards to be applied, mechanisms should be developed to ensure that the information is communicated across the ecosystem and is applied consistently. There is also a need for ongoing review and maintenance of the principles and standards to ensure compliance and relevance.

Blueprint development and maintenance

This service is concerned with the development of the blueprints that make up the business architecture, including blueprints that define the organisation's motivation, organisational structure, value streams for the services offered by the organisation, the capabilities that enable these value streams and the operation of the organisation, the information concepts used to conduct the work of the organisation and the roles and people characteristics. These blueprints define the different dimensions that form the business architecture for an organisation. The business architect is responsible for investigating these dimensions, developing the blueprints and ensuring they are kept current and relevant.

The activities required to carry out the business architecture blueprint development and maintenance service are shown in the value stream diagram in Figure 9.10.

Figure 9.10 Value stream: blueprint development and maintenance service

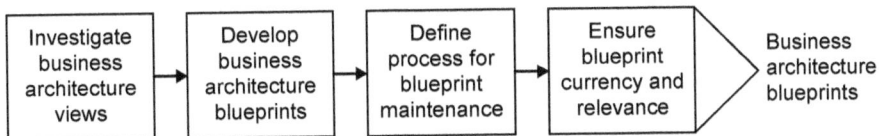

Investigate business architecture views → Develop business architecture blueprints → Define process for blueprint maintenance → Ensure blueprint currency and relevance → Business architecture blueprints

This service is closely aligned with the earlier services, as the blueprints must align with the principles and standards defined for the business architecture and are used to identify the need for change and evaluate options. This service is also closely aligned with the services described below, as the business architecture blueprints will be key inputs to the design of the target operating model, and the strategic change roadmap is likely to require changes to the business architecture blueprints.

173

Target Operating Model (TOM) design

This service is concerned with designing and defining the TOM for an organisation or business area. The work to define the process for applying and maintaining the TOM is also included within this service. The activities required to carry out the TOM design service are shown in the value stream diagram in Figure 9.11.

Figure 9.11 Value stream: Target Operating Model design service

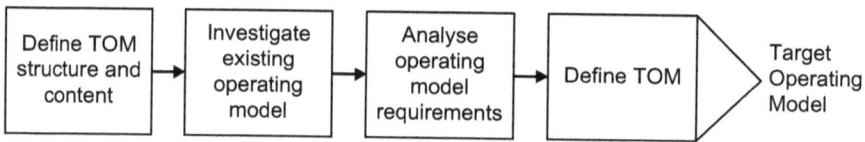

```
┌──────────────┐    ┌──────────────┐    ┌──────────────┐    ┌──────────────┐
│  Define TOM  │    │ Investigate  │    │   Analyse    │    │              │  ╲   Target
│ structure and│ →  │  existing    │ →  │  operating   │ →  │  Define TOM  │   ╲ Operating
│   content    │    │  operating   │    │    model     │    │              │   ╱   Model
│              │    │    model     │    │ requirements │    │              │  ╱
└──────────────┘    └──────────────┘    └──────────────┘    └──────────────┘
```

A TOM describes the required future state of an organisation's operating model. There is often debate about the content of a TOM, so the first activity within this service focuses on the definition of the structure and content of the TOM.

This activity is typically organisation specific as the TOM has to be relevant to the context and must align with the organisation's principles and standards. Where specific standards are absent, the POPIT elements may be used as a starting point. Ross et al. (2006) define an operating model as 'The necessary level of business process integration and standardization for delivering good and services to customers.'

Figure 9.12 Business process hierarchy (Source: Paul and Cadle, 2020)

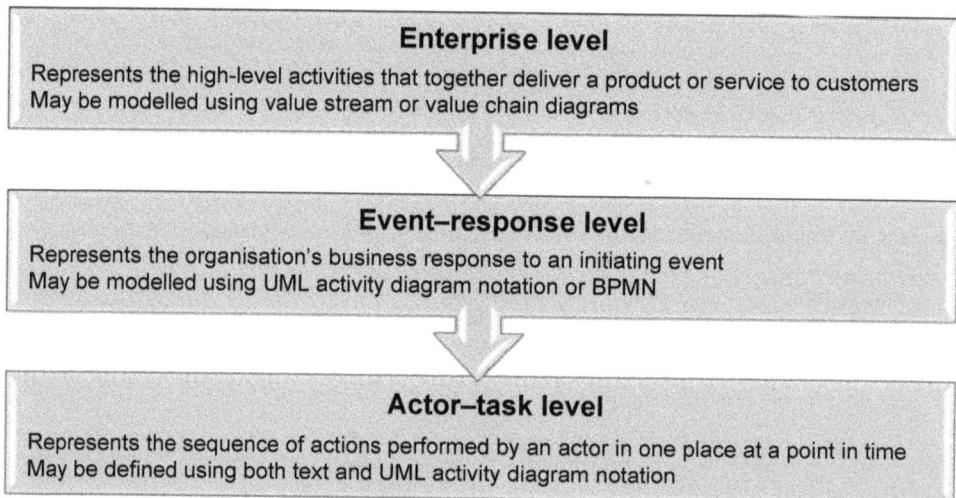

Enterprise level
Represents the high-level activities that together deliver a product or service to customers
May be modelled using value stream or value chain diagrams

⇩

Event–response level
Represents the organisation's business response to an initiating event
May be modelled using UML activity diagram notation or BPMN

⇩

Actor–task level
Represents the sequence of actions performed by an actor in one place at a point in time
May be defined using both text and UML activity diagram notation

The business process hierarchy that enables the operation of an organisation is defined at three levels, as shown in Figure 9.12 (see Chapter 6 for the hierarchy description). This hierarchical approach enables the integration, standardisation and consistency envisaged by Ross et al. (2006) as follows:

- Each product or service is delivered via a value stream that comprises a linked set of activities.

- Each activity within the value stream is triggered by one or more business events, each of which requires a business response. This response is documented using a business process model. The organisational principles and standards for documenting processes – such as the Unified Modeling Language™ (UML) activity diagram technique – are applied when creating the event–response models.

- Each task within a business process model is evaluated for further exploration and definition. Where a task is defined, the information recorded includes the business event triggering the task, the actor who conducts the task, any information input to the task, the output from the task and the rules applied when performing the steps of the task.

The TOM may also include descriptions of:

- the organisational units or functions to clarify areas of responsibility and key roles;
- the capabilities that enable the tasks within the business processes;
- the information shared when conducting the tasks; the information requirements may be defined using data maps that show the data classes and attributes used when undertaking the business processes and tasks.

Strategic roadmap development

This service is concerned with the execution of strategic change. The business architect, in collaboration with other business change roles, investigates a new or revised business strategy to determine where there is a need for executable projects that will translate the strategy into operational reality. This project portfolio is used to define a strategic change roadmap for the organisation. The activities required to carry out the strategic roadmap development service are shown in the value stream diagram in Figure 9.13.

Figure 9.13 Value stream: strategic roadmap development service

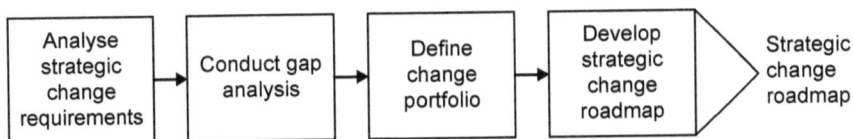

175

Drivers for change may originate from a variety of sources. For example:

- global events;
- regulatory change;
- competitor action;
- ideas generated by senior executives.

Each of these drivers may instigate strategy revision leading to tactical and operational change. The business architect has the responsibility for analysing the effect of any strategic change on the business architecture. This analysis should consider:

- the capabilities to identify where there are gaps that need to be addressed;
- the value streams to identify changes to the value propositions, activities and outcomes;
- the organisation's ecosystem to identify where new service systems are needed or the service offered by suppliers requires change;
- the information used within the organisation to identify information gaps.

The analysis of the business architecture within the context of the change drivers, generates high-level requirements that are reviewed and used to develop a portfolio of change projects or programmes. The business architect, in collaboration with senior management, prioritises the portfolio and uses the prioritised projects to develop a strategic roadmap for change.

Stakeholder engagement

The stakeholder engagement service is not included in the business architecture service framework because it is an auxiliary service that must be applied when conducting any of the core services. This is the case for all of the business change professions where stakeholder engagement is a relevant service irrespective of the particular role.

Stakeholders are affected by every business change initiative. However, the impact on individual stakeholders or stakeholder groups varies depending upon their position in the organisation's ecosystem. For example, some stakeholders may be affected directly by the changes, while there may be a minimal, indirect impact on others. Some stakeholders may have specific perspectives about the business problems or opportunities and the nature of relevant solutions, while others may disagree or be indifferent. It is the responsibility of the business architect and other change professionals to engage with the stakeholders and understand the rationale for their perspectives. Without this understanding, there is a risk of stakeholder resistance or even opposition.

The stakeholder engagement service offers the following value proposition: 'To support the achievement of business change success through effective stakeholder relationship management and communication.'

Figure 9.14 Stakeholder engagement activities

The activities required to carry out the stakeholder engagement service are varied. Some are proactive, while others are responses to events, but this is rarely a service where a linear process can be followed. Figure 9.14 sets out the range of activities within the stakeholder engagement service.

BUSINESS ARCHITECTURE AND THE BUSINESS CHANGE LIFECYCLE

The business change lifecycle clarifies the key stages required to execute change successfully. While represented as a sequential model, the lifecycle should not be interpreted as imposing a restrictive linear approach. Instead, the flow between the stages indicates an overall direction of activity. The business change lifecycle is shown in Figure 9.15.

Business architects work throughout the stages of the business change lifecycle, collaborating with other change professionals to ensure the successful execution of strategic change projects. Table 9.4 sets out the business architect's contribution to each of the business change lifecycle stages.

Figure 9.15 Business change lifecycle (Source: Paul and Cadle, 2020)

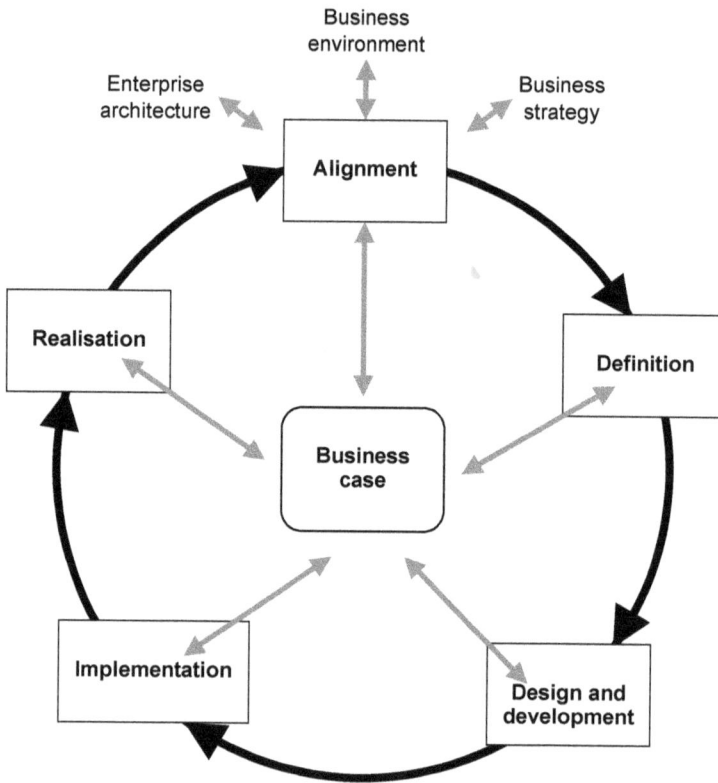

Table 9.4 Business architect responsibilities within the business change lifecycle stages (Source: Adapted from Paul and Cadle, 2020)

Stage	Business architect responsibilities
Alignment: concerned with ensuring proposed changes are aligned with the organisation's objectives and strategy, the external business environment, and the enterprise and domain architectures.	Confirm alignment between proposed changes and the organisation's objectives and strategy, the external business environment and the enterprise and domain architectures.
Definition: concerned with analysing a business situation in order to uncover root causes of problems, recommend relevant, feasible changes and define requirements for change.	Explore the issues inherent within a business situation and identify where there are implications for the business architecture; for example, this may require the development of existing or new

(Continued)

Table 9.4 (Continued)

Stage	Business architect responsibilities
	capabilities, reviewing the value stream activities required to deliver a service or product, enhancing the available information or proposing changes to roles.
Design and development: concerned with the detailed specification, development and testing of the business changes.	Ensure the business architecture changes are aligned with the requirements and are clearly defined within the blueprints.
Implementation: concerned with the planning, preparation and deployment of the business changes.	Support the deployment of changes by ensuring the enhanced or new business architecture dimensions are established within the organisation.
Realisation: concerned with reviewing the business benefits predicted regarding a business change to ensure that further action is taken if necessary to realise the benefits.	Contribute to the benefits review by identifying where business architecture changes may be required to enable the realisation of benefits, or where leveraging business architecture elements (such as capabilities) may provide a basis for benefits realisation.

CONCLUSION

The role of the business architect as the custodian of the business architecture blueprints has been clear for many years. However, the contribution that business architects can make to their organisations through applying their expertise and architectural mindset continues to require further investigation and clarification.

The business architecture service framework has been developed to offer a service view that clarifies the business architect role. This chapter has described the business architect services, including a set of value stream activities that collectively offer a value proposition for each service.

While the business architecture service framework is intended to clarify the business architect role, it is anticipated that it will be subject to revision by each organisation. The organisational context is key when defining roles, and the business architect role is no exception. Therefore, the framework offers a start point from which an organisation can clarify the business architecture services and develop its business architecture capability. This clarity also provides insights into business architects' responsibilities within the business change lifecycle.

10 BUSINESS ARCHITECTURE AND THE BUSINESS CHANGE ECOSYSTEM

INTRODUCTION

This chapter focuses on the relationship between business architecture and the business change ecosystem. It covers the following topics:

- The rationale for the service system and ecosystem view of business architecture.
- The relationship between business architecture and:
  - business analysis;
  - service design;
  - change management;
  - project management.

In addition, the chapter introduces several case studies that provide insight into the application of business architecture.

RATIONALE FOR THE SERVICE SYSTEM AND SERVICE ECOSYSTEM VIEW OF BUSINESS ARCHITECTURE

The concept of service systems – entities that interact in order to co-create value – was introduced in Chapter 6. Service science suggests that value is co-created because of interactions between multiple service system entities (Spohrer and Maglio, 2010). If this logic is applied to the business architecture service (described in Chapter 9), it can be viewed as a service system interacting with other service systems.

A service ecosystem is defined as a 'relatively self-contained, self-adjusting system of resource-integrating actors connected by shared institutional arrangements and mutual value creation through service exchange' (Vargo and Lusch, 2016, p. 11). Within the business change ecosystem, these actors include business analysts, service designers, change managers, project managers, business architects and enterprise architects.

Shared understanding is a foundational element for resource integration among actors. Service frameworks define the service portfolio offered by a particular role, including the value proposition offered by each service. These frameworks are a starting point for discussion and agreement of the services offered by individual entities, and as such provide a basis for the development of shared understanding.

The business architecture service framework was introduced in Chapter 2 and explained in further detail in Chapter 9. The service framework approach is extended in this chapter to explore the service portfolio offered by the other service systems and actors within the business change ecosystem.

Each proposed service framework is intended to establish the core services and value propositions offered by each role, and to provide a starting point for discussion with the other interacting roles. Exploring the services offered by each role, and the connections or dependencies between roles, provides a basis from which to understand the various roles and the ways in which they may collaborate to co-create value.

BUSINESS ARCHITECTURE AND BUSINESS ANALYSIS

The business analysis service framework (Paul, 2018), shown in Figure 10.1, identifies the range of services offered by business analysts and clarifies the business analyst role. This framework was developed from empirical research and is intended as a basis for customisation to each organisational context. Each of the services shown within the business analysis service framework is described in Table 10.1.

Figure 10.1 The business analysis service framework (© Debra Paul)

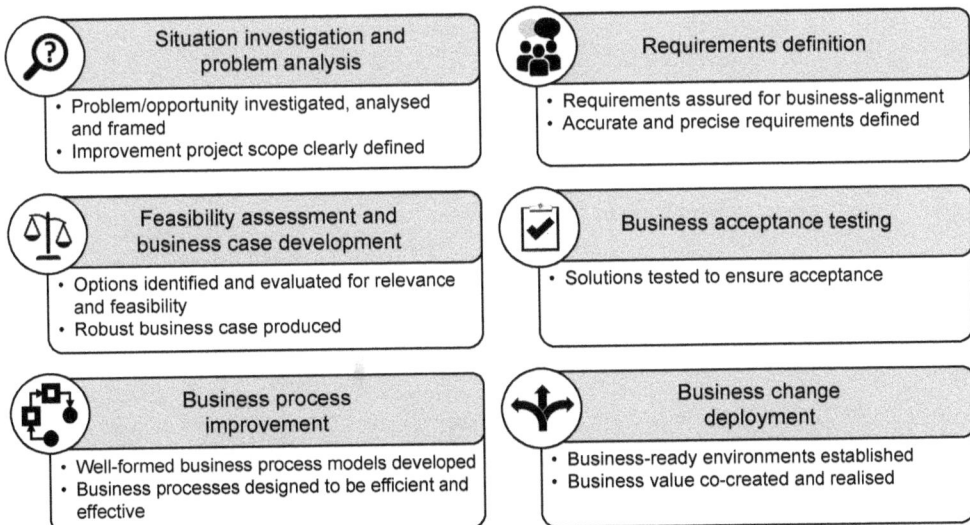

Situation investigation and problem analysis
- Problem/opportunity investigated, analysed and framed
- Improvement project scope clearly defined

Requirements definition
- Requirements assured for business-alignment
- Accurate and precise requirements defined

Feasibility assessment and business case development
- Options identified and evaluated for relevance and feasibility
- Robust business case produced

Business acceptance testing
- Solutions tested to ensure acceptance

Business process improvement
- Well-formed business process models developed
- Business processes designed to be efficient and effective

Business change deployment
- Business-ready environments established
- Business value co-created and realised

Stakeholder engagement is an auxiliary service.

Table 10.1 Business analysis service framework (Source: Adapted from Paul and Cadle, 2020)

Business analysis service	Service activities and value proposition
Situation investigation and problem analysis	**Service activities** Investigate business situations that are problematic or offer opportunities for improvement. Identify root causes of problems and distinguish them from the manifest symptoms. Analyse and frame the problem to be addressed. Define the scope of the desired solution. **Service value proposition** • The problem/opportunity is investigated, analysed and framed. • The improvement project scope is clearly defined.
Feasibility assessment and business case development	**Service activities** Identify and evaluate any proposed solutions from the business, financial and technical perspectives, taking into account the organisational capabilities. Develop a business case that explains the situation and the business needs to be addressed and explores the options available to the organisation in terms of the financial justification, affordability and risk and impact analysis. **Service value proposition** • The options are identified and evaluated for relevance and feasibility. • A robust business case is produced.
Business process improvement	**Service activities** Research, analyse and define current and proposed business processes. Conduct gap analysis to identify actions required to implement revised processes. **Service value proposition** • Well-formed business process models are developed. • Business processes are designed to be efficient and effective.
Requirements definition	**Service activities** Elicit, analyse and define requirements that are to be fulfilled by new or enhanced business or IT systems. **Service value proposition** • The requirements are assured for business alignment. • Accurate and precise requirements are defined to the relevant level of detail.

(Continued)

Table 10.1 (Continued)

Business analysis service	Service activities and value proposition
Business acceptance testing	**Service activities** Support business staff in testing business solutions. Raise awareness of the importance of testing, assisting with the creation of test scenarios and test cases, carrying out tests and documenting results. **Service value proposition** • Solutions are tested to ensure acceptance.
Business change deployment	**Service activities** Support the delivery and adoption of the business change and support subsequent realisation of business benefits. **Service value proposition** • Business-ready environments are established. • Business value is co-created and realised.

Dependencies and overlaps with business architecture services

The business analysis and business architecture service frameworks overlap as they both include the following services: situation investigation and problem analysis; feasibility assessment and business case development.

In some organisations, individuals or teams possess the knowledge, skill and experience required to conduct both business analysis and business architecture services. In these cases, the two overlapping services may be combined to incorporate the business analyst and business architect perspectives. Other organisations view these two roles as separate and distinct, so collaboration is needed to achieve the desired outcomes.

The other services within the business analysis portfolio may be required to support or enable business architecture services. For example, the following business architecture services may benefit from the insights and techniques offered by business analysts:

• Target Operating Model design;
• blueprint development and maintenance;
• strategic roadmap development.

Business analysis techniques that would offer a beneficial contribution to these services include business environment analysis, requirements definition and business process modelling.

Similarly, business architects may need to collaborate with business analysts on the following services: business process improvement; requirements definition.

For example, the business architecture views may help to clarify the context for requirements and process improvement and identify where capability reuse or leverage is possible. The business architects would be expected to take a high-level view, with the business analysts having responsibility for more detailed views.

Business architects are likely to have limited involvement in the delivery of business acceptance testing or business change deployment services. Similarly, business analysts would have limited involvement in the delivery of business architecture governance services.

To enhance value co-creation between business analysis and business architecture professionals, it is necessary to discuss and gain agreement on aspects of service delivery such as:

- the overall approach to be applied;
- the standards to be adopted;
- the roles and responsibilities of the actors;
- the policies that constrain the services;
- the measures to be achieved;
- the tools to be used;
- the required skills and knowledge.

Ensuring a firm basis for collaboration is likely to increase the potential for successful business outcomes.

BUSINESS ARCHITECTURE AND SERVICE DESIGN

The service design service framework shown in Figure 10.2 identifies the service portfolio offered by service designers. Each of the services shown within the service design service framework is described in Table 10.2.

Dependencies and overlaps with business architecture services

The overlap between the service design and business architecture service frameworks replicates the overlap between the business analysis and business architecture service frameworks. The overlapping services are situation investigation and problem analysis; and feasibility assessment and business case development.

This service overlap results from the overarching driver for the service designer, business analyst and business architect goals, which is to improve how organisations operate. Each of these roles is required to investigate problematic or opportunist situations to understand where problems originate and improvement opportunities lie. Individual roles bring distinct viewpoints and skills, so may generate particular insights. Some individuals may possess knowledge, skill and experience that is relevant to two or more of the business analyst, service designer and business architect roles. Where this is the case, an organisation may elect to combine the roles. This can enable greater

Figure 10.2 The service design service framework

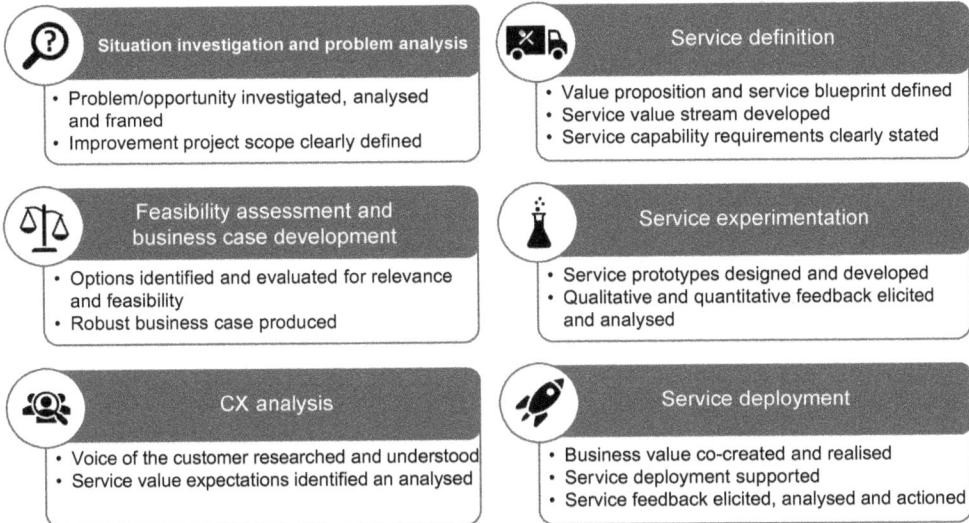

Situation investigation and problem analysis
• Problem/opportunity investigated, analysed and framed
• Improvement project scope clearly defined

Service definition
• Value proposition and service blueprint defined
• Service value stream developed
• Service capability requirements clearly stated

Feasibility assessment and business case development
• Options identified and evaluated for relevance and feasibility
• Robust business case produced

Service experimentation
• Service prototypes designed and developed
• Qualitative and quantitative feedback elicited and analysed

CX analysis
• Voice of the customer researched and understood
• Service value expectations identified an analysed

Service deployment
• Business value co-created and realised
• Service deployment supported
• Service feedback elicited, analysed and actioned

Stakeholder engagement is an auxiliary service.

Table 10.2 Service design service framework

Service design service	Service activities and value proposition
Situation investigation and problem analysis	**Service activities** Investigate business situations that are problematic or offer opportunities for improvement. Identify root causes of problems and distinguish them from the manifest symptoms. Analyse and frame the problem to be addressed. Define the scope of the desired solution. **Service value proposition** • The problem/opportunity is investigated, analysed and framed. • The improvement project scope is clearly defined.
Feasibility assessment and business case development	**Service activities** Identify and evaluate any proposed solutions from the business, financial and technical perspectives, taking into account the organisational capabilities. Develop a business case that explains the situation and the business needs to be addressed and explores the options available to the organisation in terms of the financial justification, affordability and risk and impact analysis.

(Continued)

Table 10.2 (Continued)

Service design service	Service activities and value proposition
	Service value proposition • The options are identified and evaluated for relevance and feasibility. • A robust business case is produced.
CX analysis	**Service activities** Research, analyse and define the voice of the customer and service value expectations. Investigate and analyse both stated and implied customer wants and needs. **Service value proposition** • The voice of the customer is researched and understood. • Service value expectations are identified and analysed.
Service definition	**Service activities** Research, analyse and define current and proposed business services. **Service value proposition** • The value proposition and service blueprint are defined. • The service value stream is developed. • The service capability requirements are clearly stated.
Service experimentation	**Service activities** Support the design and development of service prototypes. Elicit and analyse feedback against prototypes to enable iteration and continuous improvement. **Service value proposition** • The service prototypes are designed and developed. • Qualitative and quantitative feedback is elicited and analysed.
Service deployment	**Service activities** Support the deployment of enhanced business services. Elicit and analyse feedback against services to enable continuous improvement. **Service value proposition** • Business value is co-created and realised. • Service deployment is supported. • Service feedback is elicited, analysed and actioned.

collaboration whereby service designers either lead or support work associated with business architects, including:

- Target Operating Model design;
- strategic roadmap development;
- blueprint development and maintenance.

Service designers can offer techniques such as divergent and convergent thinking and service blueprint development, which may enhance the work to design a TOM or develop a strategic roadmap or business architecture blueprint.

Similarly, some business architects may lead or support work associated with the service definition service because they can apply techniques such as value stream modelling and business capability analysis.

Business architects are unlikely to have extensive involvement in the delivery of CX analysis, service experimentation or service deployment services. Similarly, service designers would offer limited contribution to the delivery of business architecture governance services.

Proactive discussion between service design and business architecture professionals to gain agreement on various aspects of service delivery helps to enable value co-creation. These aspects are listed earlier in this section when discussing the relationship between business architecture and business analysis.

BUSINESS ARCHITECTURE AND CHANGE MANAGEMENT

The change management service framework shown in Figure 10.3 identifies the service portfolio offered by change managers and the services shown within the framework are described in Table 10.3.

Dependencies and overlaps with business architecture services

The only overlap between the change management and business architecture service frameworks concerns the strategic roadmap development service. Collaboration between business architects and change managers in the delivery of this service can be beneficial in the enhancement of efficiency and the quality of outcomes for the organisation.

Outputs from the blueprint development and maintenance business architecture service are a useful input into change management services, including:

- business change governance and reporting – it may be mandatory for business architecture blueprints to be referred to as part of change governance and progress reporting;
- business change impact assessment – it may be mandatory for business architecture blueprints to be used within change impact assessments;
- business change engagement and communication – it may be useful for change managers to use business architecture blueprints as a basis from which to identify impacted stakeholders and decide on how to communicate with them when implementing business change initiatives.

Figure 10.3 The change management service framework

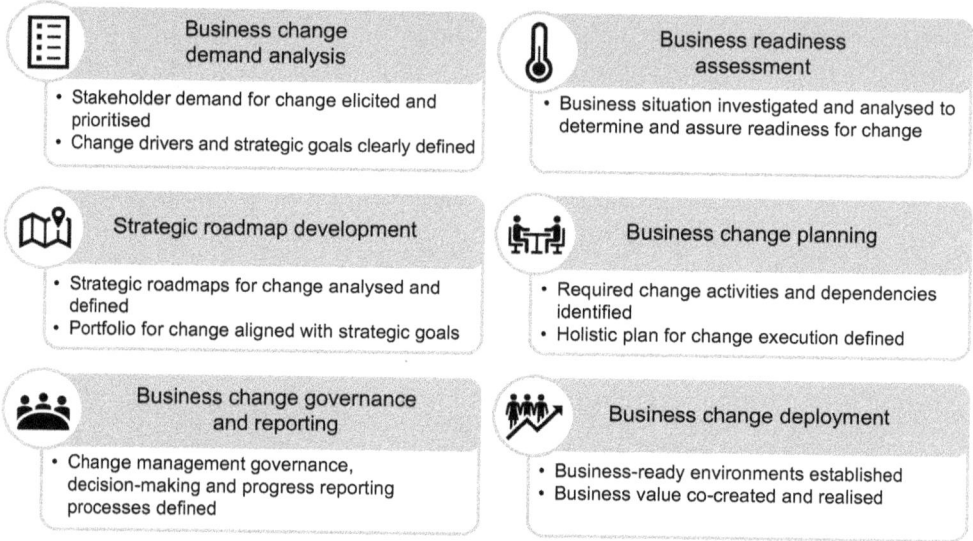

Business change demand analysis
- Stakeholder demand for change elicited and prioritised
- Change drivers and strategic goals clearly defined

Business readiness assessment
- Business situation investigated and analysed to determine and assure readiness for change

Strategic roadmap development
- Strategic roadmaps for change analysed and defined
- Portfolio for change aligned with strategic goals

Business change planning
- Required change activities and dependencies identified
- Holistic plan for change execution defined

Business change governance and reporting
- Change management governance, decision-making and progress reporting processes defined

Business change deployment
- Business-ready environments established
- Business value co-created and realised

Stakeholder engagement is an auxiliary service.

Table 10.3 Change management service framework

Change management service	Service activities and value proposition
Business change demand analysis	**Service activities** Investigate, analyse and prioritise individual stakeholder change demand requests relative to strategic goals and priorities. **Service value proposition** • Stakeholder demand for change is elicited and prioritised. • Change drivers and strategic goals are clearly defined.
Strategic roadmap development	**Service activities** Define and validate the organisation's strategic roadmap for change in alignment with: • organisational goals and strategic priorities; • internal and external environmental constraints and other factors; • organisational capacity and appetite for change. The roadmap for change should consider dependencies between proposed change initiatives, feasibility, risk and impact of delivery of the change portfolio.

(Continued)

Table 10.3 (Continued)

Change management service	Service activities and value proposition
	Service value proposition • Strategic roadmaps for change are analysed and defined. • The portfolio for change is aligned with strategic goals.
Business change governance and reporting	**Service activities** Define, communicate and execute change governance standards and processes. Change decision-making processes and progress reporting. **Service value proposition** • Change management governance, decision-making and progress reporting processes are defined.
Business readiness assessment	**Service activities** Investigate and analyse business readiness for change. **Service value proposition** • The business situation is investigated and analysed to determine and assure readiness for change.
Business change planning	**Service activities** Identify activities and dependencies required to enable effective and holistic change execution. **Service value proposition** • The required change activities and dependencies are identified. • A holistic plan for change execution is defined.
Business change deployment	**Service activities** Create business-ready environments. Elicit and analyse feedback against changes delivered as a basis for continuous improvement. **Service value proposition** • Business-ready environments are established. • Business value is co-created and realised.

In addition, blueprints are a useful input into strategic roadmap development and can also be used as a means from which to validate service outputs.

The situation investigation and problem analysis service offered by business architects may be an input into (or result from) a change manager undertaking the business change demand analysis service. In some instances, business architects may be undertaking this service concurrently with the business change demand analysis service. Where services are delivered in a co-ordinated and aligned fashion, this can be beneficial for both stakeholders and organisational outcomes. In contrast, a lack of alignment between the delivery of these services can be problematic.

Where stakeholders are contacted on multiple occasions by different individuals performing different roles about a particular change initiative, they may feel that this is highly inefficient, time-consuming and frustrating. Alignment between the delivery of these services across relevant roles represents an opportunity for both sharing knowledge and increasing efficiency. Co-ordinating activities that require stakeholder involvement is likely to improve stakeholder perceptions and increase their engagement.

Business architects (and business analysts) working on either feasibility assessment and business case development or TOM design services may provide input into strategic roadmap development. In addition, the work conducted by change managers in the delivery of business change impact and risk assessment may provide input into feasibility assessment and business case development services and vice versa.

Alignment between the processes and standards used by change managers in business change governance and reporting services and business architects delivering business architecture governance services can help to ensure consistency during change initiatives.

Some individuals may have experience and skill in delivering both change management and business architecture services. In some organisations, the change teams may contain business architects and change managers, which supports collaboration during the execution of change. This may be particularly helpful during strategic change execution that is likely to involve the business change engagement and communication and business change deployment services.

Proactive discussion between change management and business architecture professionals to gain agreement on various aspects of service delivery helps to enable value co-creation. These aspects are listed earlier in this section when discussing the relationship between business architecture and business analysis.

BUSINESS ARCHITECTURE AND PROJECT MANAGEMENT

The project management service framework shown in Figure 10.4 identifies the service portfolio offered by project managers and each of the services shown within the framework is described in Table 10.4.

Figure 10.4 The project management service framework

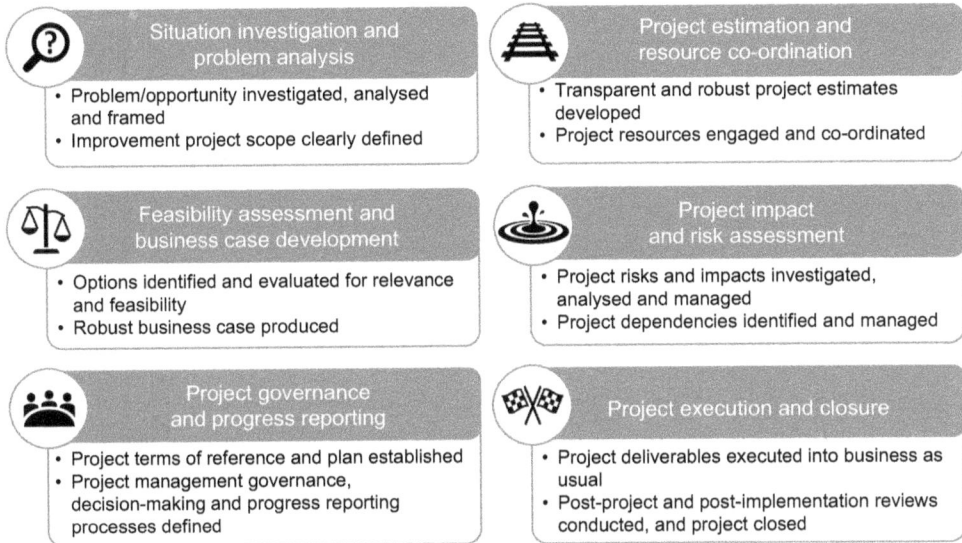

Situation investigation and problem analysis	Project estimation and resource co-ordination
• Problem/opportunity investigated, analysed and framed • Improvement project scope clearly defined	• Transparent and robust project estimates developed • Project resources engaged and co-ordinated
Feasibility assessment and business case development	Project impact and risk assessment
• Options identified and evaluated for relevance and feasibility • Robust business case produced	• Project risks and impacts investigated, analysed and managed • Project dependencies identified and managed
Project governance and progress reporting	Project execution and closure
• Project terms of reference and plan established • Project management governance, decision-making and progress reporting processes defined	• Project deliverables executed into business as usual • Post-project and post-implementation reviews conducted, and project closed

Stakeholder engagement is an auxiliary service.

Table 10.4 Project management service framework

Project management service	Service activities and value proposition
Situation investigation and problem analysis	**Service activities** Investigate business situations that are problematic or offer opportunities for improvement. Identify root causes of problems and distinguish them from the manifest symptoms. Analyse and frame the problem to be addressed. Define the scope of the desired solution. **Service value proposition** • The problem/opportunity is investigated, analysed and framed. • The improvement project scope is clearly defined.

(Continued)

Table 10.4 (Continued)

Project management service	Service activities and value proposition
Feasibility assessment and business case development	**Service activities** Identify and evaluate any proposed solutions from the business, financial and technical perspectives, taking into account the organisational capabilities. Develop a business case that explains the situation and the business needs to be addressed, and explores the options available to the organisation in terms of the financial justification, affordability, and risk and impact analysis. **Service value proposition** • The options are identified and evaluated for relevance and feasibility. • A robust business case is produced.
Project governance and progress reporting	**Service activities** Define, communicate and execute project governance standards and processes, including relevant project decision-making processes and progress reporting. **Service value proposition** • Project terms of reference and a plan are established. • Project management governance, decision-making and progress reporting processes are defined.
Project estimation and resource co-ordination	**Service activities** Identify and estimate the tasks required to deliver against the project scope. Identify, engage and co-ordinate the resources required to deliver against the project scope. **Service value proposition** • Transparent and robust project estimates are developed. • Project resources are engaged and co-ordinated.
Project impact and risk assessment	**Service activities** Identify, analyse and manage project impacts, risks and dependencies. **Service value proposition** • Project risks and impacts are investigated, analysed and managed. • Project dependencies are identified and managed.

(Continued)

Table 10.4 (Continued)

Project management service	Service activities and value proposition
Project execution and closure	**Service activities** Complete all tasks required to deliver against project scope. Task completion leads to project deliverables being ready for the transfer of ownership to business as usual. Implement support provision and closure of the project. **Service value proposition** • Project deliverables are executed into business as usual. • Post-project and post-implementation reviews are conducted, and the project is closed.

Dependencies and overlaps with business architecture services

As with business analysis, there is an overlap between the project management services and those offered by business architects. Each provide the following services: situation investigation and problem analysis; feasibility assessment and business case development.

As with previous roles, collaboration between individuals in different roles offering these services is desirable, if not essential, to achieve the required business outcomes.

There is overlap between the project governance and progress reporting and the business architecture governance service from the business architecture service framework. Alignment between the processes and standards used by change and project managers and those applied by business architects delivering governance-related services is often essential to achieve successful project and business change delivery. Where governance processes are not aligned, there may be discrepancies and conflicts within decisions. Where governance is aligned, there is an increased chance of alignment between decisions and the speed of decision-making.

The relationship between the services of project managers and business architects for other services can also be significant. For example, the project management service of project estimation and resource co-ordination may be instigated as a result of business architects or change managers delivering the strategic roadmap development service.

The project management service of project impact and risk assessment may be instigated and influenced by the work aligned with the feasibility assessment and business case development service. Business architecture blueprints offer a useful input into the project management service of project impact and risk assessment.

The project execution and closure service is likely to cause the business architecture blueprints to be updated, requiring close collaboration between business architects and project managers.

BUSINESS ARCHITECTURE CASE STUDIES

Case study 1: Claire Caulfield, British Library

Introduction

The British Library is the national library of the United Kingdom and is one of six legal deposit libraries in the United Kingdom and Ireland. It holds one of largest collections of printed material in the world, containing over 170 million items and featuring almost every known language. The collection also includes archives, manuscripts, audio, maps and newspapers.

The Business Analysis and Architecture teams at the British Library embarked on a mission to redefine the internal view of operational capabilities. The work was initiated by the creation of the 'Library on a Page Model' and the 'Business Capability Model' aimed at supporting the development of library services and bringing collective understanding and vocabulary across the organisation.

The challenges for the teams have been:

- understanding and developing the link between the two models;
- finding projects that took the models from theory into practice, and difficulty in retrofitting projects already in flight;
- achieving full organisational buy-in of the value of business architecture due to the initial lack of real-life use cases, data and awareness;
- moving from theory to practice – internal reputational risk and exposure before feeling 'ready'.

Original objectives

- Document the development and refinement of our business models.
- Highlight the practical applications and benefits of these models in real-life scenarios.

Cyber incident

In October 2023 the British Library experienced a major technology outage as a result of a cyber-attack. The outage affected the website, online systems and services, as well as some onsite services. The attack caused substantial damage that has been complex and challenging to repair. This resulted in an additional objective to the original set: showcase the collaborative efforts and their impact on our contribution to the recovery and rebuild process.

Methodology

Prior to the cyber incident the two strands of work were being developed independently, covering specific needs – the Business Capability Model was originally only looking at core library capabilities and the Library on a Page Model was developed to present a high-level view across the organisation and had a service-based view. The next stage was to begin to bring both models together, initially expanding the Business Capability Model to include enabling and direction-setting capabilities.

Immediately following the cyber incident, the teams were presented with a clear use case that involved interrogation of the models to support recovery from an architecture and design perspective.

The focus on restoring key services, such as access to the collections, provided the teams with the need to interrogate those models to provide a translation between those priorities and the systems and infrastructure that needed to be restored to support key services. This was set within the context of the complexity of analysing the legacy estate in the aftermath of the cyber incident and creating as-was views of the organisation. In turn, the repository was updated to reflect the newly emerging architecture complete with secure supported systems.

The approach involved:

- pre-cyber incident:
  - development of the high-level conceptual models to align with the organisational vision and business priorities;
  - engagement in collaborative efforts to refine the models by completing the missing capabilities and agreeing on a glossary of terms;
  - creation of cross-model relationships to support internal discussion;
- post-cyber incident:
  - utilisation of the models to support recovery initiatives, which included initial information gathering by business analysts in the immediate aftermath to reduce the risk of gaps in knowledge;
  - development of a single repository and integrating ArchiMate and business process model notation (BPMN) models.

Development of a single repository and integrating ArchiMate and BPMN models
This approach has naturally facilitated the involvement of the organisation on the co-creation of both interim and strategic long-term solutions, which reduces the risk of imposing changes to the way people work on a group of business users through technology alone.

What went well?

- Enhanced collaboration and buy-in from colleagues was achieved once practical application of the models was beginning to be used and shared.

- Successful engagement with external consultants and communities was achieved, which provided some early introduction to business architecture, enriched the approach and supported the learning process.

- Refinement of the models and their application in post-attack recovery projects was achieved.

- Increased content in the repository and the development of a longer-term strategy for ongoing use was achieved.

- Improved levels of confidence in the creation and use of the models was achieved.

What are the lessons learned?

During the early days of the development of the models there was some reluctance to demonstrate the work to colleagues due to a lack of confidence and supporting evidence. Any showcase of the work was done carefully to gain support gradually and refine the models once sponsors were identified.

As this was a new approach within the organisation, there was an understandable hesitancy in opening up the work to colleagues, bringing about a sense of nervousness about the exposure, but the benefit in doing so has been enriching to the models and the approach and created an increase in confidence in using a business architecture led approach.

As the work developed, what became clear from engagement and collaboration was:

- the importance of a clear service offering;
- the need to move from an academic exercise to real-life adoption;
- the necessity to answer specific business challenges;
- the effectiveness of using models to drive analysis and identify knowledge gaps.

Progress continues

Now that the teams have adopted this approach into their daily work, a new repository has been established with a structure that will accommodate the models from both an architecture and a business analysis perspective for identified British Library Live services. The existing Business Capability Model has been migrated into this new repository space, and each new project is being linked to the Library on a Page Model and to the business capabilities. Each service will be represented, and new projects will have dedicated spaces created.

The longer-term objectives of being able to use this approach to support strategic decision-making, track and report information using data attributes and feed into future projects with an accurate as-is view, will begin to realise even more benefits.

Case study 2: Michael Greenhalgh, Places for People

The context – where we started with business architecture

Places for People (PfP) is a large and complex social enterprise with more than 245,000 homes across all tenures, over 100 leisure centres, almost a million customers across the UK and more than 20 complementary companies. The organisation focuses on creating and supporting thriving communities by building new homes, investing in homelessness prevention, supporting customers with their finances and welcoming millions of visitors to leisure centres across the country.

The director of transformation formally introduced business architecture to support strategy execution and enhance the speed of change while embedding business architecture principles and applying methods collaboratively across the business.

The first tasks were to build stakeholder understanding of what business architecture is, why partners should collaborate and what to expect. This led to an agreement to start with an area of the business that covered a significant part of the value chain and, through practical application, provide examples of how business architecture and the artefacts produced could add clarity, insight and value to strategic analysis.

The impact on stakeholder time was reduced by using existing information such as service lists, organisation charts and strategic one-page summaries – an end-to-end customer-driven perspective was also added.

Early on, it was identified that a baseline business architecture, including business capability models and value streams, would provide a good starting point. Focus was applied to something that was important to PfP executive stakeholders, and subject matter experts were ready to work in partnership and co-create artefacts.

Reference models from the Business Architecture Guild provided some helpful inspiration, but needed to be adapted for the context and language stakeholders recognised and understood.

What went well?
A supportive senior leadership team recognised and actively championed the value of business architecture at PfP. Being part of the PfP Transformation Office and aligned to the director of strategy was extremely beneficial due to the significant complementary aspects.

Aligning business architecture with other domains requires consistency of approach and clear standards. Early agreements with business analysts, to align to BPMN, and business architects, to apply ArchiMate standards, were consolidated in a business architecture framework document. The framework outlined the PfP business architecture standards, defined the artefacts produced and the roles and responsibilities of those involved. Listening to feedback and adapting the framework aided adoption by clarifying what business architects needed and what would be provided and why.

Working closely with user experience (UX) and CX teams provided useful insights and established ongoing commitment to achieving better understanding of these complementary capabilities, aligning PfP's approach to strategy execution and ensuring customer engagement and operational excellence. This resulted in a holistic focus that proved highly effective.

Some excellent early opportunities to contribute to change initiatives and merger and integration work demonstrated the value of business architecture bringing clarity, and at the same time helped to build and validate the business capability model.

Working with multiple, unconnected formats of independent pieces of information quickly becomes unmanageable, and can lead to poor communication, errors and a lack of clarity and control. It was decided that an EA tool would enable a small core team of PfP business architects to operate at scale and help to address challenges with the assignment of ownership and maintenance of artefacts. Bizzdesign was selected as the designated EA tool for a four-month proof of concept exercise, and this helped to demonstrate potential value with a combination of newly created, imported and example artefacts.

PfP examples of business architecture artefacts, including a business capability model, value streams and an organisation map, were created and connected to metadata relevant for stakeholders across multiple business units and support functions.

Anticipated benefits of an EA tool were greater efficiency in modelling, enhanced knowledge retention and reuse. The proof of concept revealed additional benefits of collaboration, increased visibility, control and enhanced standardisation. Having access to simple, consistent models was valuable to stakeholders; inexperienced users demonstrated quicker understanding of artefacts and methods through in-tool guidance. As clarity improved, business and process analysts benefited from the layered approach to modelling.

Additional stakeholders saw value in the enhanced operational transparency the architecture tool brought, including greater visibility of risks and controls.

What did not go well?

Building a business architecture capability requires stakeholders to engage in an exercise that needs a team effort to ensure completeness and accuracy. It was challenging to secure time with partners across the business, given their competing business priorities. Given the complexity of the organisation, common vocabulary and cross-organisational views take time and effort to establish.

Cross-mapping business architecture artefacts with application(s), data and technology architecture to ensure coherence across the enterprise landscape has not been possible to date, as enterprise architecture is maturing. Plans are in place to build cross-mapping of relationships, between applications and stakeholders, business units, value streams and business capabilities.

It is not a one size fits all, and business architecture is complex and new to many PfP stakeholders. The communication is complex and trying to rush and communicate too much too soon has sometimes caused setbacks.

What are the lessons learned?

Business architecture literature, peers and consultants have repeatedly advised to start small and build over time, as doing too much too quickly is a common pitfall.

Reference models have helped to accelerate model population, but it has been important to set expectations and keep track of what is validated content and what is reference data. For example, the PfP business capability model originated from subject matter expert workshop outputs, captured alongside value streams, and Business Architecture Guild reference models adapted for PfP, which kept alignment to the language of stakeholders.

Starting by modelling the business unit ready for support, ensured business buy-in and gave something to expand on. These early adopters and advocates were needed to show the value and gain the support of others.

The PfP business architecture team had to be prepared to deal with imperfect circumstances, information and engagement. The team also needed to be creative and to iterate models. A combination of Visio, Excel, PowerPoint and whiteboards quickly became unmanageable and affected usefulness and accuracy of models, so it was important to be organised. An EA tool can help, but sufficient time for the analysis, selection, preparation, setup, training and implementation must be allowed when planning for this.

Given the multiple approaches and frameworks to take inspiration from, it is important to pick an approach and document it, so it is clear to others and can be put into practice and improved. The context of PfP, existing partners' frameworks and maturity were key considerations. To ensure outputs were meaningful and useful for stakeholders, the PfP business architecture framework had to evolve based on feedback.

While PfP are still in the early stages of the business architecture journey, conducting an extended proof of concept before adopting an EA tool was valuable. This gave a wide group of stakeholders confidence that the approach would be flexible enough for their needs and could capture and connect artefacts. Without this evidence it would be very difficult to align and engage with the wider EA community.

Case study 3: Marius Pelser, Royal London

Introduction
Since its inception in 2017, the business architecture practice at Royal London Group has evolved from a small team focusing on specific projects to a strategic, enabling function. The adoption of business capability modelling, as part of this growth, has been slower than anticipated, partly due to a lack of effective communication regarding the value this approach can bring. Previously, business capability modelling was being used in a limited way, not looking at outcomes or value.

This case study describes recent work conducted with the Royal London Ireland executive team and is focused on the business capabilities of Royal London Ireland. The primary aim of the work was to identify and assess the maturity of the capabilities. Maturity assessments were based on aggregated scores of people performing tasks, supporting processes and technologies that enable each individual capability. The desired result was a clear view of change delivery needed to realise business needs and strategic intent.

At the beginning of this work, outcomes to measure the value of the exercise were established. The outcomes were:

- to have an updated business capability model specific to Royal London Group (RLG);
- to have assigned stakeholder ownership by business function for each capability;
- for business capabilities to be used as a common language across RLG.

Actions taken
The first step was to gain business buy-in and to identify the business capabilities important to this specific part of the organisation. Royal London Ireland uses a blended

business model where some business services are sourced from the overarching group entity and some are specific to local activities. The culmination of comprehensive analysis resulted in the development of a current state maturity model that provided valuable insights to the management of business operations at the capability level.

Insights drawn from the exercise included:

- areas with lower people or process scores highlighted opportunities for potential low-cost improvements such as process enhancements/redesign or simplification and colleague upskilling or training;

- areas scoring low from a technology perspective were discussed with the Technology Architecture team, and potential improvements to solutions mapped to the technology roadmap;

- results required discussions with RLG's strategy team, which paved the way for the identification of strategic improvements due to enhanced understanding of business needs;

- target maturity scores that were captured during the analysis helped to ascertain those capabilities that may require additional funding – where relevant, these would be considered when planning the business change roadmap over the coming years.

Adapt or adopt

During the preparation for this exercise, there was a need to conduct a full review of the existing business capability model. The business architecture team recognised that, even though an industry model had been adopted previously, there was a need to adapt the model to ensure it fitted the language used within RLG and aligned with the RLG business model. Consequently, a rewrite of large parts of the model and associated definitions was undertaken. This helped to ensure that the model was written in a way that could be easily understood by the consumers of the model.

What went well?

The exercise raised the profile of business architecture practices across a wide section of stakeholders within RLG. The business capabilities are now seen as the cornerstone for the data policies, with data owners and data stewards being aligned to this model. Some parts of RLG are either developing a more detailed process taxonomy or have done so already in line with the capability model. This approach is helping to create a multidimensional blueprint of the business.

What are the lessons learned?

Democratisation of data was key to avoiding the creation of an 'architecture ivory tower'. This was achieved by developing a set of capability data views in the enterprise architecture repository and utilising PowerBI to display information pertinent to each business function. This allowed business users to view, interrogate and derive value from the information available.

The exercise highlighted that data is required to conduct certain activities effectively, but must be presented in a way that is informative and meets stakeholder needs.

Have we achieved our outcomes?

When reviewing the completed work, it has been generally accepted that the outcomes set out at the start have been achieved, while acknowledging that further developments will be required as the model is embedded.

RLG now has an updated business capability model tailored to the group that uses language familiar to key stakeholders. Stakeholder understanding of business capabilities has increased and other parts of RLG have begun to adopt the model.

The original intention of assessing only one business function has expanded to additional functions being assessed. These assessments were not initiated by the business architecture team, but were requested by interested parties who saw value in conducting this work.

The use of business capabilities as a common language across RLG has been further supported by the business capability model being explicitly referenced within recently updated data policies. This will help to ensure continual review and management of capability ownership and maturity assessments for the future. Further to this, the inclusion of the business capability model within the data policies also supports its continued embedding. Other areas of development include ensuring that future business planning is informed by business capability maturity assessments and other insights derived from the model.

Conclusion

This case study demonstrates how the business capability model has been used as a strategic tool to align business functions, data policies, processes and maturity assessments in RLG. The model can be used to facilitate cross-functional collaboration, provide insights into the current and desired state of the business and support decision-making and planning activities.

The RLG capability model is not static, but rather a living artefact that evolves with the business and its needs. Hopefully the RLG experience and lessons learned can inspire other organisations to adopt or adapt a similar approach and leverage the benefits of business capability modelling and maturity assessment.

CONCLUSION

Value co-creation requires collaboration between business architects and other related roles within the business change ecosystem. The key roles of business analyst, service designer, change manager and project manager have been discussed in this chapter and a service framework for each role has been proposed. Each of these service frameworks is intended to be a basis for discussion and requires customisation so that it is relevant to the particular context.

When executing strategic business change, various roles, each with their own skillset and toolkit, need to gain agreement on the following aspects of service delivery:

- What services will be offered?
- What is the value proposition of services offered?

- What approach will be used in the delivery of services?
- What policies and standards will be used in the delivery of services?
- Who will be responsible for which aspects of service delivery?
- What tools, skills and knowledge will be applied during the delivery of services?

A mindset that embraces continuous improvement and recognises the different service offerings provided by fellow professionals ensures a basis for successful business improvement. Business architects are at the heart of this work, so need to ensure that they adopt this mindset and recognise where collaboration with other actors in the ecosystem can help to deliver beneficial outcomes.

BIBLIOGRAPHY

Allee, V. (2002) *The Future of Knowledge: Increasing Prosperity Through Value*. London: Routledge.

Anthony, R.N. (1965) *Planning and Control: A Framework for Analysis*. Cambridge MA: Harvard University Press.

Biddle, B.J. (1986) 'Recent developments in role theory'. *Annual Review of Sociology*, 12, 67–92.

Bitner, M.J., Zeithaml, V.A. and Gremler, D.D. (2010) 'Technology's impact on the gaps model of service quality'. In: Maglio, P.P., Kieliszewski, C.A. and Spohrer, J.C. (eds). *Handbook of Service Science, Service Science:* Research and Innovations in the Service Economy series. New York: Springer.

Box, G.E. (1979) 'All models are wrong, but some are useful'. *Robustness in Statistics*, 202, 549.

Broderick, A.J. (1998) 'Role theory, role management and service performance'. *Journal of Services Marketing*, 12(5), 348–361.

Business Architecture Guild (2024) *A Guide to the Business Architecture Body of Knowledge®*, V8.5 [BIZBOK® Guide].

Cadle, J., Paul, D., Hunsley, J., Reed, A., Beckham, D. and Turner, P. (2021) *Business Analysis Techniques: 123 Essential Tools for Success*. Swindon: BCS Learning and Development.

Checkland, P. (1999) *Systems Thinking, Systems Practice*. Chichester: John Wiley & Sons Ltd.

Collins, J.C. and Porras, J.I. (2000) *Built to Last: Successful Habits of Visionary Companies*. London: Random House Books.

Donofrio, N., Sanchez, C. and Spohrer, J. (2010) 'Collaborative innovation and service systems: implications for institutions and disciplines'. In: Grasso, D. and Burkins, M.B. (eds). *Holistic Engineering Education: Beyond Technology*. New York: Springer.

Engel, F.K. (1999) 'The introduction of the magnetophon'. In: Daniel, E.D., Mee, C.D. and Clark, M.H. (eds). *Magnetic Recording: The First 100 Years*. Piscataway, NJ: IEEE Press.

Foote, B. and Yoder, J. (1997) 'Big ball of mud'. *Pattern Languages of Program Design*, 4, 654–692.

Geracie, G. and Eppinger, S. (2013) *The Guide to the Product Management and Marketing Body of Knowledge® (ProdBOK®)*. Reno, NV: Association of International Product Marketing and Management.

Girvan, L. and Paul, D. (2024) *Agile and Business Analysis: Practical Guidance for IT Professionals* (second edition). Swindon: BCS Learning and Development.

Hall, E.T. (1976) *Beyond Culture*. New York: Anchor Books.

Hammer, M. and Champy, J. (1993) *Reengineering the Corporation: A Manifesto for Business Revolution*. New York: Harper Business.

Handy, C. (1993) *Understanding Organizations* (fourth edition). London: Penguin.

Henderson, L.S., Stackman, R.W. and Lindekilde, R. (2016) 'The centrality of communication norm alignment, role clarity, and trust in global project teams'. *International Journal of Project Management*, 34, 1717–1730.

Hermans, P., (2015) 'The Zachman Framework for architecture revisited. On conceiving the informational enterprise'. Zachman International Enterprise Architecture. https://zachman-feac.com/resources/ea-articles-reference/159-the-zachman-framework-for-architecture-revisited-by-paul-hermans

Ho, J.K.-K. (2015) 'A review of frameworks for classification of information systems, notably on the Anthony's Triangle'. *European Academic Research*, 3(1, April), www.euacademic.org

Hofstede, G., Hofstede, G.J. and Minkov, M. (2010) *Cultures and Organizations: Software of the Mind* (third edition). New York and London: McGraw Hill.

Hofstede, G. and Minkov, M. (2010) 'Long- versus short-term orientation: New perspectives'. *Asia Pacific Business Review*, 16(4), 493–504.

Homann, U. (2006) 'A business-oriented foundation for service orientation'. Microsoft. www.businessarchitectureguild.org/general/custom.asp?page=002&DGPCrPg=1&DGPCrSrt=7A

Hunsley, J. (2023) 'How to transition into service design'. Assist Knowledge Development. www.assistkd.com/learning-zone/ba-manager-forum-search/how-transition-service-design

Kaplan, D. and Norton, R. (1996) *The Balanced Scorecard: Translating Strategy into Action*. Boston, MA: Harvard Business School Press.

Lemon, K.N. and Verhoef, P.C. (2016) 'Understanding customer experience throughout the customer journey'. *Journal of Marketing*, 80(6), 69–96.

Martin, J. (1995) *Great Transition: Using the Seven Disciplines of Enterprise Engineering to Align People, Technology and Strategy*. London: Amacom.

Meyer, E. (2016) *The Culture Map: Decoding How People Think, Lead and Get Things Done Across Cultures*. New York: Public Affairs.

Moore. G. (1965) 'Cramming more components onto integrated circuits'. *Electronics*, 38(8), 114–117.

Osterwalder, A. and Pigneur, Y. (2010) *Business Model Generation: A Handbook for Visionaries, Game Changers, and Challengers*. Chichester: John Wiley & Sons.

Osterwalder, A., Pigneur, Y., Bernarda, G. and Smith, A. (2014) *Value Proposition Design: How to Create Products and Services Customers Want*. Chichester: John Wiley & Sons.

Parasuraman, A., Zeithaml, V.A. and Berry, L.L. (1985) 'A conceptual model of service quality and its implications for future research'. *Journal of Marketing*, 49(4), 41–50.

Paul, D.E. (2018) *Defining the Role of the Business Analyst*, published doctoral thesis. Henley-on-Thames: Henley Business School.

Paul, D. and Cadle, J. (2020) *Business Analysis* (fourth edition). Swindon: BCS Learning and Development.

Paul, D. and Lovelock, C. (2019) *Delivering Business Analysis: The BA Service Handbook*. Swindon: BCS Learning and Development.

Porter, M.E. (1998) *Competitive Advantage: Creating and Sustaining Superior Performance*. New York: Free Press.

Quinn, J.B. (1980) *Strategies for Change: Logical Incrementalism*. New York: Richard D. Irwin, Inc.

Robertson, S. and Robertson, J. (2013) *Mastering the Requirements Process: Getting Requirements Right*. New York and London: Pearson Education.

Ross, J., Weill, P. and Robertson, D. (2006) *Enterprise Architecture as Strategy*. Cambridge, MA: Harvard Business School Publishing Corporation.

Schein, E.H. (2004) *Organization Culture and Leadership* (third edition), The Jossey-Bass Business & Management Series. Cambridge, MA: Sloan School of Management, MIT.

Schneier, B. (2016) *Data and Goliath: The Hidden Battles to Collect Your Data and Control Your World*. New York and London: W. W. Norton & Co.

Sinek, S. (2009) *Start with Why: How Great Leaders Inspire Everyone to Take Action*. London: Penguin Random House Group.

Spohrer, J.C. and Maglio, P.P. (2010) 'Toward a science of service systems: value and symbols'. In: Maglio, P.P., Kieliszewski, C.A. and Spohrer, J.C. (eds). *Handbook of Service Science*, Service Science: Research and Innovations in the Service Economy series. New York: Springer.

Sutton, J. (2012) *Competing in Capabilities: The Globalization Process*. Oxford: Oxford University Press.

Teece, D.J. (2007) Explicating dynamic capabilities: the nature and microfoundations of (sustainable) enterprise performance. *Strategic Management Journal*, 28(13), 1319–1350.

The Open Group (2022) *The TOGAF Standard, 10th Edition – Business Architecture*. Hertogenbosch, NL: Van Haren Publishing.

Van't Wout, J., Waage, M., Hartman, H., Stahlecker, M. and Hofman, A. (2010) *The Integrated Architecture Framework Explained: Why, What, How*. Berlin: Springer Science & Business Media.

Vargo, S.L. and Akaka, M.A. (2009) 'Service-dominant logic as a foundation for service science: clarifications'. *Service Science*, 1, 32–41.

Vargo, S.L. and Lusch, R.F. (2008) 'Service-dominant logic: continuing the evolution'. *Journal of the Academy of Marketing Science*, 36, 1–10.

Vargo, S.L. and Lusch, R.F. (2016) 'Institutions and axioms: an extension and update of service-dominant logic'. *Journal of the Academy of Marketing Science*, 44(1), 5–23.

Walsh, J.P. and Ungson, G.R. (1991) 'Organizational memory'. *Academy of Management Review*, 16, 57–91.

Whittington, R., Angwin, D., Regner, P., Johnson, G. and Scholes, K. (2023) *Exploring Strategy: Text & Cases* (thirteenth edition). Harlow: Pearson Education Ltd.

Wieland, H., Polese, F., Vargo, S.L. and Lusch, R.F. (2012) 'Toward a service (eco) systems perspective on value creation'. *International Journal of Service Science, Management, Engineering, and Technology*, 3(3), 12–25.

Zachman, J.A. (1987) 'A framework for information systems architecture'. *IBM Systems Journal*, 26(3), 276–292.

Zachman International (2015) 'A Historical Look at Enterprise Architecture with John Zachman: An Interview with The Open Group', https://zachman-feac.com/resources/ea-articles-reference/164-a-historical-look-at-enterprise-architecture-with-john-zachman-an-interview-with-the-open-group

ONLINE RESOURCES

Accenture, 'What is Customer Experience?' 'Why is great customer experience important?', https://accenture.com/us-en/insights/song/customer-experience-index

Chartered Institute of Personnel and Development, https://cipd.org/uk

DAMA International, DMBOK, https://dama.org/cpages/body-of-knowledge

ISO/IEC/IEEE 42010:2022, Software, systems and enterprise — Architecture description, https://iso.org/standard/74393.html

Object Management Group, Business Motivation Model Standard 1.3, http://omg.org/

The Open Group, Business Layer: ArchiMate 3.2 specification, https://pubs.opengroup.org/architecture/archimate3-doc/ch-Business-Layer.html

The Open Group (2011) TOGAF 9.1, https://pubs.opengroup.org/architecture/togaf91-doc/arch/index.html

The Open Group (2018) TOGAF 9.2, https://pubs.opengroup.org/architecture/togaf9-doc/arch/chap03.html

The SFIA Foundation, SFIA 9, 2024, https://sfia-online.org/en

Zachman International, The Zachman Framework, https://zachman-feac.com/zachman/about-the-zachman-framework

GLOSSARY

Activity diagram: A form of flowchart defined in the **Unified Modeling Language (UML)** that is used to represent diagrammatically a process and the differing paths through it. Can be used as a visual alternative to text to describe the **Tasks** in a **Swimlane diagram** in more detail.

Actor: An individual, group of individuals or business system that carries out a business system's work activities.

Affinity analysis: A technique that seeks to identify and analyse connections and patterns between different items or activities.

Agile: An approach to software development based upon the Agile Manifesto and using evolutionary development and incremental delivery approaches.

Applications architecture: The portfolio of applications used within an organisation and their alignment with the **Business architecture**.

ArchiMate: A standard published by The Open Group that provides a modelling language used to describe, analyse and represent an enterprise architecture.

Artificial intelligence: A term used to define intelligence offered by automated machines and technology.

'As is' business process model: A representation of a business process within an organisation as it is currently performed.

Balanced Scorecard: A tool that supports a strategic management system by capturing both financial and non-financial measures of performance. There are usually four quadrants: Financial, Customer, Internal Business Process, Learning and Growth. The Balanced Scorecard was developed by Robert S. Kaplan and David P. Norton.

BAU: See **Business as usual**.

BCS, The Chartered Institute for IT: The international professional body for the IT industry. BCS is responsible for setting standards for the IT profession and advises and informs industry and government on the use of technology across society and business.

Benefit: A positive gain to an organisation expected to follow from carrying out a business change **Programme** or **Project**.

Benefits dependency network: A visual representation of the actions needed to secure the benefits from a proposed change initiative.

Benefits map: See **Benefits dependency network**.

Benefits realisation: A process that is concerned with the delivery of the predicted business benefits defined in a **Business case**. This process includes managing projects so that they are able to deliver the predicted benefits and, after the project has been implemented, checking progress on the achievement of these benefits and taking any actions required to enable their delivery.

Benefits realisation report: The deliverable from carrying out a **Benefits review**.

Benefits review: A formal examination of the benefits expected to flow from a business change initiative and identification of any further actions that are needed to harvest those benefits.

BIZBOK: The Business Architecture Body of Knowledge – developed by the Business Architecture Guild.

Blueprint: A diagram or model that represents a view of the organisation; sometimes referred to as an artefact.

Blueprint development and maintenance: A **Service** within the **Business architecture service framework** that is concerned with the development of the blueprints that make up a **Business architecture**.

Brainstorming: A technique used during meetings and workshops whereby participants suggest ideas relating to a problem or issue. Brainstorming is based on the principles that an idea from one person will generate suggestions from others and that more suggestions will be generated if judgement is suspended initially.

Brainwriting: A technique used during meetings and workshops whereby participants are invited to write down ideas relating to a problem or issue. Brainwriting is based on the principles that an idea from one person will generate suggestions from others and that more suggestions will be generated if judgement is suspended initially.

Breakeven calculation: See **Payback calculation**.

British Computer Society: See BCS, The Chartered Institute for IT.

Business acceptance testing: A service within the **Business analysis service framework** that is concerned with supporting business staff in testing new business and IT changes to ensure their acceptability.

Business actor: Someone who has an interest in a project, either because they have commissioned it, they work within the business system being studied or they will be the user of a proposed new IT system. See **Stakeholder**.

Business analysis: A specialist service that co-creates value for organisations through delivering the services defined within the **Business analysis service framework**.

Business analysis service: An internal service function that provides **Business analysis** capabilities to its organisation.

Business analysis service framework: A framework that identifies a standard portfolio of services that may be offered by an internal **Business analysis service**. The standard services are: **Situation investigation and problem analysis; Feasibility assessment and business case development; Business process improvement; Requirements definition; Business acceptance testing; Business change deployment**. These services may be subject to adaptation and customisation in order to meet the needs of a particular organisation.

Business analyst: A person who performs **Business analysis**. Most people in a business analyst role are employed by organisations, but others work for consultancy companies, IT services firms and as freelance contractors. The scope of the business analyst role varies between organisations and includes: business BA or enterprise BA; technical BA or business systems analyst; digital business analyst; project business analyst; and proxy product owner.

Business analyst role: An advisory role that carries out some or all of the services within the **Business analysis service framework** in order to ensure the effective deployment of business changes and use of technology in line with the needs of an organisation.

Business architect: A person who carries out **Business architecture** work and develops business architecture blueprints.

Business architecture: A discipline focused on building shared understanding of the organising logic for an organisation. The discipline encourages a holistic approach that enables informed and aligned strategic and tactical decision-making.

Business architecture governance: A service within the **Business architecture service framework** that is concerned with effective definition, communication and maintenance of the principles and standards that underlie and govern the **Business architecture**. These principles and standards clarify the content of a business architecture and how it is applied to support organisational business decision-making.

Business Architecture Guild: A professional body for business architects that publishes and develops the **BIZBOK**.

Business architecture principles: The foundational guidelines for undertaking **Business architecture** work.

Business architecture service: An internal service function that provides **Business architecture** services to its employing organisation.

Business architecture service framework: A framework that identifies a standard portfolio of services that may be offered by an internal **Business architecture service**. These services may be subject to adaptation and customisation in order to meet the needs of a particular organisation. The standard services are: **Situation investigation and problem analysis**; **Feasibility assessment and business case development**; **Business architecture governance**; **Blueprint development and maintenance**; **Target Operating Model (TOM) design**; **Strategic roadmap development**.

Business as usual (BAU): The normal, ongoing, day-to-day activities carried out by an organisation.

Business capability model: A model that provides an abstract and conceptual representation of what an organisation has the ability or motivation to do.

Business case: A document that describes the findings from a business analysis study and presents a recommended course of action for senior management to consider. A business case normally includes an introduction, management summary, description of the current situation, options considered, analysis of costs and benefits, impact assessment, risk assessment and recommendations, plus appendices that provide detailed supporting information.

Business change demand analysis: A service within the **Change management service framework** that is concerned with investigating, analysing and prioritising individual stakeholder change demand requests relative to strategic goals and priorities.

Business change deployment: A service within the **Business analysis service framework** and **Change management service framework**. This service is concerned with the creation of business ready environments that support successful change execution and subsequent realisation of business benefits.

Business change governance and reporting: A service within the **Change management service framework**. This service is concerned with defining, communicating and executing change governance standards and processes.

Business change lifecycle: A visual representation of the stages that an organisation carries out to identify, evaluate, specify and implement business change. The stages involved are Alignment, Definition, Design, Implementation and Realisation. Each stage is governed by and contributes to the development of the **Business case** for change.

Business change planning: A service within the **Change management service framework**. This service is concerned with identifying activities and dependencies required to enable effective and holistic change execution.

Business domain: A sector of the economy or an industry.

Business environment: See **External business environment**; **Internal business environment**.

Business event: An event that initiates a business process, which is an organisation's response to the occurrence of an event. There are three types of business event: external, internal and time-based.

Business feasibility: The degree to which a proposed course of action is compatible with the strategy, structure and culture of an organisation and the business domain within which it operates.

Business information model: A model that provides an overview of the sets of **Information** (or 'information concepts') used within an organisation; also known as an 'information concepts model' or 'enterprise data model'.

Business model analysis: An analysis of the core logic that determines how an organisation is designed to deliver products and/or services within the context of its **Ecosystem**.

Business Model Canvas: An overall, generic, model template for an organisation, developed by Osterwalder and Pigneur (2010).

Business motivation analysis: The analysis of the rationale that underlies how an organisation acts or behaves.

Business Motivation Model (BMM): A framework for completing **Business motivation analysis**, published by the Object Management Group.

Business perspective: See **Stakeholder perspective**.

Business process: A linked set of tasks performed by an organisation in response to a business event. The business process receives, manipulates and transfers information or physical items in order to produce an output or reach a conclusion. See **Business process model**.

Business process hierarchy: A structure used to decompose business processes into lower levels of detail. The levels of the hierarchy are enterprise, event–response (business process) and actor–task.

Business process improvement: A service within the **Business analysis service framework** that is concerned with researching, analysing and defining current and proposed business processes and applying gap analysis to identify actions required to implement the revised processes.

Business process model: A diagram showing the tasks that need to be carried out in response to a business event and in order to achieve a specific goal. See **Swimlane diagram**.

Business process reengineering: A holistic approach that is applied to redesign and optimise the efficiency of an organisation's processes.

Business readiness assessment: A service within the **Change management service framework** that is concerned with investigating and analysing business readiness for change.

Business role: A role represents the responsibility for performing specific behaviour to which an **Actor** can be assigned, or the part that an actor plays in a particular action or event.

Business rule: A structured, discreet and enforceable instruction or procedure that determines how an activity, process, task or step should be conducted. There are two main types of business rule: constraints that restrict how an activity may be performed; operational guidance that describes the procedures for performing activities.

Business staff: The individuals or groups who carry out the work of an organisation and who will implement and use new business processes and/or systems.

Business strategy: The long-term direction defined for an organisation in order to achieve the **Vision**, **Mission** and **Objectives**.

Business system: A set of business components working together in order to achieve a defined purpose. These components are defined in the **POPIT model**. See also **IT system**.

Business use case: A function or feature that an **Actor** wants a **Business system** to offer. This is a 'case of use' of the business system by a specific actor and defines the interaction between an actor and a business system.

Business use case description: A description of an individual **Business use case**.

Business use case diagram: A holistic and conceptual representation of a **Business system**.

Capability: A task or action that an organisation has the ability or motivation to perform.

Capability analysis and leverage model (CALM): A framework for assessing the organisation's **Current state** and **Target state** against the questions why, what and how.

Capability Maturity Model Integration (CMMI): A model developed by the Software Engineering Institute of Carnegie Mellon University that consists of five stages, showing increasing maturity of operation. It provides guidance for improving the quality of processes.

Capability model: See **Business capability model**.

Capacity: The volume or quantity of items that may be delivered or tasks that may be carried out.

CATWOE: A technique from the Soft Systems Methodology that provides a framework for defining and analysing business perspectives. The acronym stands for: C – customer, A – actor, T – transformation, W – worldview, O – owner, E – environment. See also **Stakeholder perspective**; **Soft systems methodology**.

Change management: A discipline focused on enabling organisations to move effectively and successfully from a current state to a desired target state, in alignment with strategic goals and priorities.

Change management service: An internal service function that provides **Change management** services to its organisation.

Change management service framework: A framework that identifies a standard portfolio of services that may be offered by an internal **Change management service**. These services may be subject to adaptation and customisation in order to meet the needs of a particular organisation. The standard services are: **Business change demand analysis**; **Strategic roadmap development**; **Business change governance and reporting**; **Business readiness assessment**; **Business change planning**; **Business change deployment**.

Change manager: A person who performs **Change management** work.

Class: A definition of the attributes and operations shared by a set of objects within a business system. Each object is an instance of a particular class. See also **Object**.

Class model: A technique from the **Unified Modeling Language (UML)**. A class model describes the classes in a system and their associations with each other.

Cloud computing: A general term for the delivery of hosted services over the internet.

Competence: A general level of ability. Competence and competences are broad concepts that tend not to be focused on the achievement of a particular task.

Competency: A specific area of skill at a required level of ability. Competency concerns a skill at the level of ability needed to perform a particular task. Organisational competency is typically aggregated from competencies held by a group of individuals.

Compliance architecture: A definition of the organising logic required to fulfil an organisation's compliance obligations.

Context diagram: An outline visual representation of a business or IT system, comprising a box or circle and the interactions the system has with external actors and systems.

Convergent thinking: A thought process focused on evaluating options and deciding ways forward.

Core purpose: An organisation's fundamental reason for being (adapted from Collins and Porras, 2000).

Core values: The handful of principles that guide how a company acts and operates. Core values may or may not be written down (adapted from Collins and Porras, 2000).

Cost–benefit analysis: A technique that involves identifying the initial and ongoing costs and benefits associated with a business change initiative. Costs and benefits are categorised as tangible or intangible and a financial value is calculated for those that are tangible. The financial values are analysed over a forward period in order to assess the potential financial return to the organisation. This analysis may be carried out using investment appraisal techniques. See also **Payback calculation**; **Discounted cash flow**; **Net present value**.

Critical success factors (CSFs): The areas in which an organisation must succeed in order to achieve positive organisational performance.

Culture: The shared values and beliefs that influence how those working within an organisation behave, think and feel.

Culture pyramid: A model that supports the analysis of an **Organisational culture**. The model consists of three dimensions: the worldview, formal dimension and informal dimension.

Current state: The current operating model in place within an organisation or business area.

Customer experience (CX) analysis: A service within the **Service design service framework** concerned with researching, analysing and defining the **Voice of the customer** and service value expectations.

Customer journey map: A model of the activities, experiences and emotions encountered by a customer **Persona** when accessing a service in pursuit of a particular goal or outcome.

Data: A specific piece of evidence or a fact.

Data architecture: A discipline focused on building shared understanding of the organising logic of the data recorded and used across an enterprise.

Data modelling: An approach used to analyse, structure and represent data items.

Design thinking: An approach to generating options and solutions that encourages the use of product and service design concepts and techniques, including prototyping, experimentation and **Divergent/convergent thinking**. Design thinking is focused on delivering outcomes, understanding customer views and meeting customer needs.

Digital: A general term used to describe technologies that generate, store and process data in consistent and interoperable formats.

Discounted cash flow (DCF): An investment appraisal technique that takes account of the time value of money. The annual net cash flow for each year following the implementation of the change is reduced (discounted) in line with the estimated reduction in the value of money. The discounted cash flows are then added to produce a **Net present value**.

Divergent thinking: A thought process that encourages thinking broadly and expansively about potential problems and options.

Document analysis: A requirements elicitation technique where samples of documents are examined in order to analyse the data recorded and the use made of that data.

Domain knowledge: A general understanding of the business drivers, issues, pressures, dynamics, finances and technologies of a business domain. See also **Subject matter expertise**.

Ecosystem: See **Internal service ecosystem** and **External service ecosystem**.

Enterprise architecture: 'The fundamental concepts or properties of a system in its environment embodied in its elements, relationships, and in the principles of its design and evolution' (ISO/IEC/IEEE 42010:2011).

Ethnographic study: A form of **Observation** concerned with spending an extended period of time within an organisation, community or society in order to obtain a detailed understanding of its culture and behaviours.

Explicit knowledge: The knowledge of procedures and data that is foremost in the business users' minds, and which they can easily articulate. See also **Tacit knowledge**.

External business environment: The environment that is external to an organisation and is the source of forces that may affect the organisation. Types of forces may include the introduction of new laws, social trends or competitor actions. See also **PESTLE**; **Porter's Five Forces**.

External service ecosystem: The network of service systems that are separate legal entities to the organisation. The external service systems interact and engage with the organisation to deliver products and services, typically within the context of a contractual arrangement.

Facilitation: An interpersonal **Competency** required of **Business architects** that allows them to prepare for and manage a meeting or workshop.

Feasibility: The degree to which a proposed course of action is viable given the business, technical and financial constraints imposed by the organisation and the environment in which it operates.

Feasibility assessment and business case development: A service within the **Business architecture service framework**, the **Business analysis service framework**, the **Service design service framework** and the **Project management service framework** that is concerned with evaluating the options to meet the business need and supporting the development of the business case for change.

Financial feasibility: The degree to which a proposed course of action is compatible with the financial constraints and objectives of an organisation.

Fishbone diagram: A visual technique developed by Dr Kaoru Ishikawa whereby a problem and its causes are represented as the skeleton of a fish. The head shows the problem and the spines radiating from the backbone represent the causes.

Five Forces model: See **Porter's Five Forces**.

Focus group: An interactive group meeting used to gather ideas and feedback about a specific product, service or issue.

Function: Logical groupings of processes or activities that are applied to conduct the work of the organisation. They provide an abstract means of structuring and understanding an organisation.

Gap analysis: The comparison of two views of a business system: the current situation and the desired future. The aim of gap analysis is to determine where the current situation has problems, or 'gaps', that need to be resolved. This leads to the identification of actions to improve the situation.

Holistic approach: The consideration of all aspects of a business system and their interactions. This encompasses the **POPIT** elements.

Impact analysis: The consideration of the effect a proposed change will have on a business system, including on the people working within it.

Information: A summarised view of both **Data** and **Metadata** and typically presents data in a form that is relevant to the business.

Information concepts model: See **Business information model**.

Infrastructure architecture: A discipline focused on building shared understanding of the organising logic regarding the infrastructure applied across an enterprise. The infrastructure includes the hardware, cloud services, operating systems and communication networks.

Intangible benefit: A benefit to be realised by a business change project for which a credible, usually monetary, value cannot be predicted. See also **Tangible benefit**.

Intangible cost: A cost incurred by a business change project for which a credible, usually monetary, value cannot be predicted. See also **Tangible cost**.

Internal business environment: The internal capability of the organisation that affects its ability to respond to external environment forces. Techniques such as **VMOST analysis** or the **Resource audit** may be used to analyse the capability of the internal business environment.

Internal service ecosystem: The network of service systems that are internal to an organisation. Internal service systems interact with each other, and with the external service systems where relevant, to carry out the organisation's work.

Interview: An investigation technique to elicit information from business users. An interview agenda is prepared prior to the interview and distributed to participants. The interview is carried out in an organised manner and a report of the interview is produced once the interview has been concluded.

Ishikawa diagram: See **Fishbone diagram**.

IT system: A set of automated components hosted on a computer that work together to provide services to the system users. See also **Business system**.

Key performance indicators (KPIs): Specific areas of performance that are monitored to assess the performance of an organisation. Key performance indicators are often identified in order to monitor progress of the **Critical success factors**. Measurable targets are set for KPIs.

Lean: An approach focused on the systematic enhancement of the work conducted by an organisation. Lean makes extensive use of principles such as continuous improvement, waste reduction, enhancing value for customers and enhancing flow and quality.

Lean thinking: A thinking approach that advocates the following five principles: Specify value; Identify the value stream; Flow; Pull; Perfection.

Management summary: A brief summary that provides an overview of the background, findings and recommendations of a document.

Metadata: Data that describes the characteristics of the **Data**.

Migration: The process of moving an organisation from an existing business process or IT system to a new one.

Mind map: A technique pioneered by Tony Buzan that represents an issue as a diagram with the name of the issue in the centre and aspects associated with it as radiating branches.

Mission: The definition of what the organisation does or will do to achieve the organisation's **Vision**.

MOST analysis: An analysis of an organisation's mission, objectives, strategy and tactics to identify any inherent strengths or weaknesses. See also **Internal business environment**; **VMOST**.

Motivation: A reason for acting or behaving in a particular way. See also **Business motivation analysis**.

Net present value (NPV): The amount an investment is worth once all of the net annual cash flows are adjusted to today's value of money and are aggregated. The NPV is calculated using the **Discounted cash flow** approach to investment appraisal.

Object: An instance of a class.

Objective: A defined, desired goal or outcome. An objective is used to guide and measure progress towards the completion of the **Vision** and **Mission**.

Object Management Group (OMG): A non-profit, open membership organisation that develops and maintains technology standards.

Observation: A technique used within requirements elicitation where an analyst observes work being performed with a view to identifying issues and/or requirements to improve a business situation.

Options: The alternative courses of action considered in a **Business case**.

Organisational culture: 'The basic assumptions and beliefs that are shared by members of an organisation, that operate unconsciously and define in a basic taken-for-granted fashion an organisation's view of itself and its environment' (Schein, 2004).

Organisational memory: 'Stored information from an organisation's history that can be brought to bear on present decisions' (Walsh and Ungson, 1991).

Organisation model: A model showing the place of an organisation within the wider world and in relation to the external business environment within which it operates. The external environment encompasses the organisation's competitors, suppliers and customers.

OSCAR: An acronym that helps to identify the areas to be addressed in a **Project initiation document (PID)** or **Terms of reference (TOR)** for a project. The OSCAR elements are objectives, scope, constraints, authority and resources.

Outsourcing: A process by which an organisation entrusts certain aspects of its operations to other organisations. Organisations outsource for various reasons, including to lower costs or to secure specialist expertise not available internally.

Payback calculation: An investment appraisal technique where a cash flow forecast for a project is produced using the current values of the incoming and outgoing cash flows; no attempt is made to adjust them for the declining value of money over time. See also **Discounted cash flow**.

Persona: An artefact associated with **User role analysis**. It provides a representation of a **User role**, aggregating users with common characteristics, behaviour, attitudes and needs.

PESTLE: A technique used to analyse the external business environment of an organisation. The technique involves the analysis of the political, economic, socio-cultural, technological, legal and environmental forces that may impact upon an organisation. See also **Business environment**.

POPIT model: A model that illustrates the elements that need to be considered by business analysts in order to provide a **Holistic approach** to a business situation. The elements are people, organisation, processes, information and technology. The POPIT model is also used to conduct **Gap analysis** and **Business readiness assessment**, and provides a basis for a **Target Operating Model (TOM)**.

Porter's Five Forces: A technique used to analyse the industry or business domain within which an organisation operates.

Portfolio: The suite of business change **Projects** or **Programmes** for an organisation.

Power/interest grid: A visual representation of the relative importance of a project's stakeholders. They are shown in the position that represents the power or influence they can wield over the project and the level of interest they have demonstrated regarding it. The grid position suggests suitable strategies for the management of each stakeholder.

Problem analysis: A systematic approach to uncovering the root causes of a business problem or issue and to developing workable and acceptable solutions.

Process: See **Business process**.

Process model: See **Business process model**.

Product: An item created by an organisation and delivered to customers.

Programme: A group of **Projects** that all contribute towards the achievement of a business objective and which, because of their interdependence, must be co-ordinated.

Programme manager: A role responsible for planning, directing and managing a **Programme**.

Project: A discrete piece of work that is required to achieve a defined objective and has a defined start and end date, an agreed budget and specified deliverables.

Project estimation and resource co-ordination: A service within the **Project management service framework** that is concerned with identifying, estimating, resourcing and scheduling tasks required to deliver the project deliverables and achieve the project objectives.

Project execution and closure: A service within the **Project management service framework** that is concerned with completing all the tasks required to achieve the project objectives.

Project governance and progress reporting: A service within the **Project management service framework** that is concerned with defining, communicating and executing project governance standards and processes.

Project impact and risk assessment: A service within the **Project management service framework** that is concerned with identifying, analysing and managing project impacts, risks and dependencies.

Project initiation document (PID): A document that defines the business context for a project and defines the objectives, scope, deliverables, timescale, budget, authority and available resources.

Project management: A discipline focused on organising individuals and work activities to achieve project objectives within the defined scope and constraints.

Project management service: An internal service function that provides **Project management** capabilities to its organisation.

Project management service framework: A framework that identifies a standard portfolio of services that may be offered by an internal **Project management service**. These services may be subject to adaptation and customisation in order to meet the needs of a particular organisation. The standard services are: **Situation investigation and problem analysis; Feasibility assessment and business case development; Project governance and progress reporting; Project estimation and resource co-ordination; Project impact and risk assessment; Project execution and closure**.

Project manager: A person who is responsible for delivering the objectives of a **Project** and carries out **Project management**.

Project sponsor: A senior manager within an organisation who is accountable for the success of a project as a business undertaking, and who is responsible for making major decisions about its scope and direction, and ensuring the required resources are available.

Prototyping: A technique where a model, representation or simulation of a product or service is created and used to test assumptions, experiment, validate and obtain feedback.

Questionnaire: See **Survey**.

RACI matrix: A matrix that identifies the nature of stakeholder responsibilities regarding tasks or deliverables. The types of responsibility are: Responsible; Accountable; Consulted; Informed. A RACI matrix (sometimes called a RACI chart) may be used to clarify project or business-as-usual responsibilities.

RAG: A means of classifying the state or progress of an individual task, output or **Capability** using the categories red, amber and green.

Requirement: A feature that the business staff want or need a new business or automated system to provide.

Requirements definition: A service within the **Business analysis service framework** concerned with the elicitation, analysis and definition of requirements for business and IT system change initiatives.

Requirements engineering: A framework for the elicitation, analysis, validation, documentation and management of requirements.

Requirements management: A stage of the **Requirements engineering** framework and a governance approach that aims to ensure that each requirement is tracked from inception to implementation (or withdrawal) through all the changes that have been applied to it.

Requirements validation: A stage of the **Requirements engineering** framework where the requirements are reviewed and approved by selected external stakeholders.

Resource audit: A technique to analyse the assets held by an organisation. The resource audit considers five areas of organisational resource: tangible resources – physical, financial and human; intangible resources – know-how and reputation.

Risk/risk analysis: A problem situation that may arise with regard to a project or business situation. Potential risks are identified for each option in a **Business case**, the probability of the risk occurring and the likely impact of the risk are assessed and suitable countermeasures are identified.

Role: See **Business role**.

Root cause/root cause analysis: The detailed examination of a perceived problem to identify the actual underlying causes.

Scenario: A conceptual exploration of the ways in which business actors may interact with an organisation, function or IT system. Each scenario is triggered by a business event that initiates a number of alternative sequences of actions. A sequence of actions may lead to the desired outcome or to an alternative, sometimes less positive, outcome.

Scenario analysis: A technique used to develop and examine future events and various possible sequences of actions that may occur.

Security architecture: A definition of the organising logic required for the protection of enterprise assets from harm, loss or misuse.

Service: The application and integration of resources to realise beneficial outcomes for both service providers and their customers.

Service definition: A service within the **Service design service framework** that is concerned with researching, analysing and defining current and proposed business services.

Service deployment: A service within the **Service design service framework** that is concerned with supporting the implementation of enhanced business services.

Service design gaps model: A model adapted from the Gaps Model of Service Quality (Parasuraman et al., 1985; Bitner et al., 2010). The service design gaps model identifies five areas where it is possible that gaps exist between different activities within a service development, design and delivery process.

Service design service: An internal service function that provides service design services to its employing organisation. See also **Design thinking**.

Service design service framework: A framework that identifies a standard portfolio of services that may be offered by an internal **Service design service**. These services may be subject to adaptation and customisation in order to meet the needs of a particular organisation. The standard services are: **Situation investigation and problem analysis**; **Feasibility assessment and business case development**; **Customer experience (CX) analysis**; **Service definition**; **Service experimentation**; **Service deployment**.

Service ecosystem: 'A relatively self-contained, self-adjusting system of resource-integrating actors connected by shared institutional arrangements and mutual value creation through service exchange' (Vargo and Lusch, 2016).

Service experimentation: A service within the **Service design service framework** that is concerned with supporting the design and development of service prototypes.

Service science: A research discipline that concerns the study and identification of the concepts, principles and activities related to service analysis and engineering. The term 'Service Science' is an abbreviation of 'Service Science, Management, Engineering and Design', sometimes further abbreviated to SSMED.

Service system: An **Actor** (or entity) engaged in the delivery of a product or service that supports or enables **Value co-creation** with other actors.

SFIA and SFIAplus: An extensive framework of skills and competency levels relevant to those working in the information systems industry. SFIAplus is the extended version provided by BCS, The Chartered Institute for IT.

Situation investigation and problem analysis: A service within the **Business architecture service framework**, the **Business analysis service framework**, the **Service design service framework** and the **Project management service framework** concerned with investigating the root causes of problems, identifying where a business need exists and shaping a project to address this need.

Six Sigma: An approach to identifying process improvements with a view to decreasing the variability and improving the consistency of a process execution. The stages of a Six Sigma project are: Define (the problem); Measure (the data); Analyse (the problem); Improve (the process); Control (the effectiveness of the solution).

Skill: An ability that is acquired by an individual, typically through a combination of learning and experience.

SMART: An acronym used to ensure that objectives are clearly defined in that they are specific, measurable, attainable, relevant, time bound.

Soft systems methodology: A methodology devised by Professor Peter Checkland and his team at Lancaster University that provides an approach to analysing business situations.

Solution architecture: The practice of defining and describing the architecture for a holistic business solution.

Stakeholder: An individual, group of individuals or organisation with an interest in the change. Categories of stakeholder include customers, employees, managers, partners, regulators, owners, suppliers and competitors.

Stakeholder analysis: The investigation and consideration of the stakeholders involved in a change initiative. Techniques such as the **Power/interest grid** and **RACI** may be used to carry out stakeholder analysis.

Stakeholder engagement: An auxiliary service associated with the **Business architecture service framework**, the **Business analysis service framework**, the **Service design service framework**, the **Change management service framework** and the **Project management service framework**. Stakeholder engagement is concerned with supporting the achievement of business change and IT project success through stakeholder collaboration and communication, and effective stakeholder relationship management.

Stakeholder management: The definition of the most appropriate means of ensuring effective engagement with distinct categories of stakeholder.

Stakeholder management plan: A formal document that defines the strategy to be adopted to manage a specific project **Stakeholder**.

Stakeholder perspective: A view of the business system held by a stakeholder. A business perspective is based upon the values, beliefs and priorities of the stakeholder, which are encapsulated in a defined worldview. There may be several divergent business perspectives for any given business situation. See also **CATWOE**.

Stakeholder perspective analysis: An activity focused on understanding the view of the business system held by a stakeholder or set of stakeholders. See also **CATWOE**.

Strata: A layer within a **Business capability model** that defines a particular set of capabilities. There are three possible strata: Strategic, Customer-facing and Support (non-customer facing).

Strategic analysis: The application of techniques in order to analyse the pressures within an organisation's **External business environment** and the level of internal organisational capability to respond to these pressures.

Strategic roadmap development: A service within the **Business architecture service framework** and **Change management service framework** that is concerned with the execution of strategic change.

Strategy: The direction and scope of an organisation over the longer term. The strategy is defined in order to achieve the organisation's **Vision**, **Mission** and **Objectives**.

Stress testing: A form of intense testing used to determine how an organisation will respond to potential adverse **Scenarios**.

SUAVE: A set of quality criteria used for defining business capabilities. The acronym stands for stable, unique, abstract, valuable and executive.

Subject matter expert: A person within a project who offers **Subject matter expertise**.

Subject matter expertise: A detailed understanding of the terminology, processes, constraints and technology of a specific business area, product line or service. See also **Domain knowledge**.

Sufficiency: The extent to which an organisation has **Competency** in a particular area, which is based in the main on the volume of employees who can provide the required level of **Skill**.

Survey: An approach used to obtain data during an investigation of a business situation. The data obtained is usually quantitative data, but it is also possible to obtain qualitative data using a survey. Surveys are useful to obtain information from a large or dispersed group of people.

Swimlane: A row on a business process diagram/model that indicates the **Actor** responsible for a particular task. Actors may be departments, teams, individuals or IT systems.

Swimlane diagram: A technique used to model business processes. A swimlane diagram models the business system response to a **Business event**. The model shows the triggering event, the business actors, the tasks they carry out, the flow between the tasks, the decisions and the business outcome. See also **Business process model**.

SWOT analysis: A technique used to summarise the external pressures facing an organisation and the internal capability the organisation has available to respond to those pressures. The acronym stands for strengths, weaknesses, opportunities and threats.

Tacit assumption: A belief on the part of an individual that information they hold is correct, without checking to ensure that this is the case. See also **Explicit knowledge**; **Tacit knowledge**.

Tacit knowledge: Information held about business procedures and operations that an individual does not articulate or explain. This may be due to a failure to recognise that the information is required or because there is an assumption that the information is already known to the analyst. See also **Explicit knowledge**; **Tacit assumption**.

Tactics: Describes the specific and detailed means by which a **Strategy** is executed.

Tangible benefit: A benefit to be realised by a business change project for which a credible, usually monetary, value can be predicted. See also **Intangible benefit**.

Tangible cost: A cost incurred by a business change project for which a credible, usually monetary, value can be predicted. See also **Intangible cost**.

Target Operating Model (TOM): A model that illustrates how an organisation must be constituted in order to support the execution of its **Strategy** and the achievement of its objectives.

Target Operating Model design: A service within the **Business architecture service framework** that is concerned with designing, defining, deploying and maintaining the **Target Operating Model (TOM)** for an organisation or business area.

Target state: The desired **Target Operating Model (TOM)** for an organisation.

Task: A work activity carried out by a single actor in one place at a specific moment in time. The OPOPOT acronym is used to support task identification (one person, one place, one time). Tasks are represented within swimlanes on a **Business process model** or **Swimlane diagram**.

Task analysis: A technique used to analyse the work conducted during a given task. The analysis considers the event that triggers the task, the input information, the task outputs, the steps required to complete the tasks, the decisions relevant to the task and the measures applied to the task.

Technical feasibility: The degree to which a proposed course of action is compatible with the technical constraints and the infrastructure available to an organisation.

Terms of reference (TOR): An alternative name for a **Project initiation document (PID)**, sometimes preferred for consultancy assignments such as a feasibility study. The OSCAR acronym may be used to develop a TOR.

TIMWOODS: A tool for the analysis of **Waste**. The TIMWOODS elements are: transport, inventory, motion, waiting, overproduction, overprocessing, defects, skills.

TOGAF: The Open Group Architecture Framework.

TOM: See **Target Operating Model**.

Trait: A distinguishing characteristic or quality that is inherent in an individual. There are some fundamental traits that a business architect needs to deliver the business architecture services. Traits can be honed and developed but may be possessed more naturally by some people.

T-shaped professional: A concept that represents the need for individuals to have deep skills in their own professional discipline and broad, generic skills that span other disciplines and enable them to interact effectively with anyone working in those disciplines.

Unified Modeling Language (UML): A suite of diagrammatic techniques that are used to model business and IT systems.

Unified process: A process model that underpins the **Unified Modeling Language (UML)**.

Use case: A feature that an actor wants a system to offer; it is a 'case of use' of a business or IT system by a specific actor.

Use case description: A definition of the interaction between an **Actor** and a **Use case**. A use case description may be formed using either text or a diagram, such as an **Activity diagram**.

Use case model: A technique from the **Unified Modeling Language (UML)**. A use case model is made up of a diagram showing the **Actors**, the boundary of the system, the **Use case** and the associations between them. It may be supported by a set of **Use case descriptions**.

User role: A generic title for a role taken by an individual or group of actors who require access to a particular set of features offered by a business or IT system.

User role analysis: A technique used to identify and understand the **User roles** that need to interact with a business or IT system.

Value: The beneficial outcome offered by an organisation and co-created with customers who use the features offered by a delivered **Product** or **Service**.

Value chain: A construct developed by Michael Porter to identify the primary and support activities deployed within organisations to deliver a **Value proposition** to their customers.

Value co-creation: The engagement and collaboration between **Service systems** to realise **Value** from delivered products and services.

Value network analysis: A technique devised by Verna Allee (2002) that is used to represent a 'network of relationships' between the various actors and other stakeholders within an organisation's ecosystem, as a series of exchanges of **Value**.

Value proposition: A clear statement of the **Value** that an organisation offers customers through the delivery of a **Product** or **Service**.

Value stream: A representation of the activities carried out by an organisation that collectively offer a **Product** or **Service** to internal or external **Stakeholders**.

View: A representation of a specific perspective of an organisation. Views are conceptual or abstract representations. They are not models of physical, real-world business systems.

Vision: The aspirational target state for an organisation without regard to how this will be achieved. The state should be realised through the accomplishment of the **Mission**.

VMOST: An extension of the **MOST analysis** technique for an organisation where **Vision** is added to the **Mission**, **Objectives**, **Strategy** and **Tactics**.

VMOST analysis: The investigation of an organisation's **Vision**, **Mission**, **Objectives**, **Strategy** and **Tactics** to determine how well it is defined, internally consistent, communicated within the organisation and used to generate direction and commitment among staff. See also **VMOST**.

Voice of the customer: The view of a situation, service or product from the customer perspective.

Waste: Several areas, defined in **Lean**, where possible process improvements may be identified. See also **TIMWOODS**.

Workshop: A meeting run by a facilitator and attended by a range of selected business **Actors** for the purpose of eliciting, analysing or validating information. An agenda is prepared prior to the workshop and distributed to participants. The actions and decisions are recorded by a scribe.

Zachman Framework: A taxonomy of the discrete elements that together represent the architecture of an organisation.

INDEX

Page numbers in italics refer to figures or tables.

Taylor, F W 5

teamwork 27, 28

TIMWOODS (transportation, inventory, motion, waiting, overproduction, overprocessing, defects, skills) 115

TOGAF Enterprise Architecture framework 38–40, 39

TOM (Target Operating Model) 28, 40, 175

    design *23*, 24, *167*, 174, *174*, 187, 190

touchpoints 121, 123, 124

transparency 2, 55, 134, 198

UML (Unified Modelling Language™) 175

validated persona 163

value chain 126, 197

    diagram 109, 112, 174

    example *107*

    model 51, 106, 108, 112

    Porter's 71, 105–8

value co-creation 11, 52, 87, 99, 101–2, *101*, 135, 184, 187, 190, 201

value concept 99–100

value network 49, 50, *125*

value network analysis 75, 124–6

value proposition 13, 24, 49, 52, 57, 66–8, 75, 102–5, 124, 146, 153, 176

    analysis 165–6

    concept 161–6

    delivery 106, 108, 145, 155

    dimensions *103*

    elements 166, *166*

    service 182–3, 185–6, 188–9, 191–3

    understanding customers 161–5

value stream 23, 24, 41, 43, *110*, *114*, *142*, *168*, 170, *172–5*

    activities 52, 113, 115, 127–9, 140–5, *144*, 148, 150, 167, 175, 179

    analysis 30, 98, 105–19, 121, 168

business events 112

delivery 153

diagrams 51, 79, 85, 101–2, 108–11, 137, 142, 143, 154, 160, 168

    elements 108

    example *110*

    Lean 115, *117*

    map/mapping 112–16, *117*

    modelling 30, 105, 112, 115

    Porter's value chain 105–8

VMOST (vision, mission, objectives, strategy and tactics) 26, 29, 31, 50, 58, 80, 94, 97, 119

    analysis 56, 57, 58, *59*, 60, 66, 168

    examples 57, 58

Walker, P Duane 'Dewey' 4, 5

worldviews 76, 78, 157, 158, 159

Zachman framework 4, 5, 34, 35–8, *36*, 45, 95

Zachman, John 5

231

www.ingramcontent.com/pod-product-compliance
Lightning Source LLC
Chambersburg PA
CBHW050039220326
41599CB00044B/7225